DESTINATION MOON

THE REMARKABLE AND
IMPROBABLE VOYAGE
OF APOLLO 11

DESTINATION
MOON

THE REMARKABLE AND
IMPROBABLE VOYAGE OF APOLLO 11

RICHARD MAURER

SQUARE
FISH

ROARING BROOK PRESS
New York

SQUARE
FISH

An imprint of Macmillan Publishing Group, LLC
120 Broadway, New York, NY 10271 • mackids.com

Square Fish and the Square Fish logo are trademarks of Macmillan and
are used by Roaring Brook Press under license from Macmillan.

Our books may be purchased in bulk for promotional, educational, or
business use. Please contact your local bookseller or the Macmillan Corporate
and Premium Sales Department at (800) 221-7945 ext. 5442 or
by email at MacmillanSpecialMarkets@macmillan.com.

Library of Congress Control Number: 2018955851

Originally published in the United States by Roaring Brook Press
First Square Fish edition, 2023
Book designed by Monique Sterling
Square Fish logo designed by Filomena Tuosto
Printed in the United States of America by Lakeside Book Company,
Harrisonburg, Virginia

ISBN 978-1-250-83011-1 (paperback)
1 3 5 7 9 10 8 6 4 2

LEXILE: 1150L

To Jessamyn and Hannah

CONTENTS

CAST OF CHARACTERS

(IN ORDER OF FIRST MAJOR APPEARANCE)

KEY FIGURES

Maxime "Max" Faget: Submarine officer during World War II. Later America's premier spacecraft designer and lead engineer for Apollo.

Thomas O. Paine: Submariner, engineer, visionary leader. Headed NASA from 1968 to 1970. A Clark Kent look-alike with a taste for risk.

Donald K. "Deke" Slayton: One of the Original Seven astronauts. Grounded for a health problem and put in charge of choosing the Moon crews.

Samuel C. Phillips: Career Air Force officer. A wizard at organizing complex projects, asked to manage the most difficult of them all— Apollo.

Wernher von Braun: Pioneer of spaceflight, acquaintance of Hitler, designer of the Moon rocket. A born showman and charming opportunist.

James E. Webb: Brilliant public servant who could get things done in Washington. Led NASA through the trailblazing era of early human spaceflight.

SUPPORTING CAST

Astronauts

Alan B. Shepard: First American in space.

Virgil I. "Gus" Grissom: Second American in space. Apollo 1 commander.

John H. Glenn: First American to orbit the Earth.

Neil Armstrong: Gemini 8 and Apollo 11 commander. A superb pilot, considered accident-prone by some.

Frank Borman: Apollo 8 commander. One of the top-ranked astronauts.

James Lovell: Apollo 8 crewmember and navigation specialist.

William Anders: Apollo 8 crewmember and science specialist.

Michael Collins: Apollo 11 command module pilot. Easygoing and coolly professional.

Edwin "Buzz" Aldrin: Apollo 11 lunar module pilot. An aggressive competitor with a doctorate in orbital mechanics.

Engineers

Charles Stark "Doc" Draper: Engineering professor and entrepreneur. Friend of James Webb.

John Houbolt: Advocate of the lunar-orbit rendezvous strategy for Apollo.

Managers

Hugh Dryden: Head of the NACA, then second-in-command of its successor organization, NASA, until his death in 1965.

T. Keith Glennan: First head of NASA, 1958 to 1961.

Robert R. Gilruth: Director of NASA's Manned Spacecraft Center in Houston.

Robert Seamans: Influential NASA manager. Succeeded Dryden as second-in-command.

Brainerd Holmes: First overall head of the Apollo project.

George Mueller: Succeeded Holmes as head of Apollo and all manned spaceflight.

Christopher C. Kraft: Chief of Mission Control in Houston.

George Low: Head of Apollo operations in Houston. Hatched the bold plan for Apollo 8.

Mission Control (during the Apollo 11 landing)

Eugene Kranz: Steely-calm flight director.

Charles Duke: Capcom, the astronaut who communicates with the crew.

Stephen Bales: Responsible for monitoring the spacecraft computer operations.

John Garman: Apollo Guidance Computer expert.

Robert Carlton: Responsible for control of the lunar module.

Edward Fendell: Head of communications.

U.S. Political Leaders

Franklin D. Roosevelt: U.S. president, 1933 to 1945. Led the country through the Great Depression and most of World War II.

Harry S. Truman: U.S. president, 1945 to 1953. Confronted the Soviet Union to start the Cold War.

Dwight D. Eisenhower: World War II general. Later U.S. president, 1953 to 1961.

John F. Kennedy: U.S. president, 1961 to 1963. Embarked on Project Apollo.

Lyndon B. Johnson: U.S. president, 1963 to 1969. Space enthusiast and president during Apollo's coming-of-age.

Russians

Joseph Stalin: Brutal dictator of the Soviet Union, 1922 to 1953.

Nikita Khrushchev: Leader of the Soviet Union, 1953 to 1964. First to grasp the propaganda value of space achievements.

Yuri Gagarin: First human in space.

Jules Verne's astronauts
blast off from a giant
cannon.

Moon map
contemporary with
Verne's novel

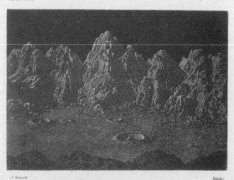

MAP OF THE MOON
with the names given by Riccioli in the 18th century
and others added by succeeding observers

Verne's astronauts approach
the Moon.

PLATE XXIII.

GROUP OF LUNAR MOUNTAINS. IDEAL LUNAR LANDSCAPE.

Artist's concept of rugged lunar landscape, 1874

BRIEFING:
The Ultimate Destination

In the 1860s, French science-fiction author Jules Verne started work on a new novel. It involved a giant engineering project and an impossibly distant goal. He set the plot in the United States—land of people who think big. His three explorers start out from Florida, travel a quarter of a million miles through space in a large capsule, view the Moon from close-up, and then return to Earth, splashing down in the Pacific Ocean. Along the way, they experience weightlessness and other strange phenomena. Realizing that he had an epic on his hands, Verne split his narrative into two parts. He called the first volume *From the Earth to the Moon*, and the second *A Trip Around the Moon*.

Of course, he made it all up. However, sometimes truth catches up with fiction, which it did . . . a hundred years later.

This book is the true story of Apollo 11, which in the 1960s achieved Verne's amazing vision—down to the country involved, the size of the crew, the launch location, the destination, the splashdown site, and the unearthly experiences. There is another eerie coincidence. In Verne's novel, the technology and expertise that allow his explorers to go to the Moon emerged from the recently ended American Civil War. Apollo, too, was built on the inventions, experiences, and attitudes developed in a catastrophic war.

And therein lies a tale. Do not be misled if the account that follows begins in a place as far from the Moon as one could possibly get, in circumstances that seem to have nothing to do with a lunar voyage . . . for they have everything to do with it.

PART 1
WAR

The war made us. It was and is our single greatest moment.
The memory of the war is a key to our characters.

—John F. Kennedy, U.S. senator and later president, 1954

Moonset from space

20¢

ASTOUNDING STORIES

A CLAYTON MAGAZINE

THE SARGASSO OF SPACE

Astronauts clash on the cover of *Astounding Science Fiction*, 1931.

1

ENSIGN FAGET'S CLOSE CALL

The vessel drifted silently through a limitless realm. Aboard, only row after row of lights and gauges told the crew that, so far, all was well. Out of contact with any other humans on Earth, they felt alone in a way that was primordial. They could have been on their way to another planet. But they knew something was about to happen, and the sweat was already starting to bead on their faces.

Then, *click . . . BANG!* The craft shook.

They all knew what it was.

Then another *click . . . BANG!* An anxious pause. *Click . . . BANG!*

As the junior officer, Ensign Max Faget, age twenty-three, was hyper-alert for any signs of trouble. He was probably too preoccupied to count the explosions. But others kept a tally.

"Three . . . four. They're getting closer."

Click . . . BANG! The hull groaned.

The *click* was the sound of an arriving pressure wave, like the lightning flash that precedes thunder. Then came the main blast of detonating high explosives—depth charges being dropped by Japanese warships trying to kill them, for they were aboard an American subma-rine and this was World War II.

It was February 20, 1945, the last year of the war, but no one knew that yet. As far as the men in the USS *Guavina* were concerned, it could be their last *minute* of the war.

Click . . . BANG!

"That's six," someone whispered.

●

Like practically every other American at the time, Maxime "Max" Faget (pronounced "fah-ZHAY") was involved in the war effort. The men of his generation were doing the fighting, but millions of others, men and women, were helping out in factories, offices, and hospitals, on farms, railroads, and docks. Those who weren't directly involved participated in other ways—by buying war bonds and, if nothing else, by paying high taxes to support the nation in the largest, most devastating, and most expensive conflict in world history.

It had all started across the sea. In 1937, Japan invaded China. Then in 1939, Nazi Germany, led by Adolf Hitler, invaded and quickly overran Poland. Britain and France came to Poland's defense by declaring war on Germany. Within a year, Germany had defeated France and was poised to invade Britain. Italy joined on Germany's side. In June 1941, the war took a surprising turn when Germany changed course and at-tacked the Soviet Union—previously its partner in a nonaggression pact.

Even more surprisingly, Japan attacked the American fleet at Pearl Harbor, Hawaii, on December 7, 1941. President Franklin Roosevelt branded it "a date which will live in infamy" and asked Congress to de-clare war on Japan, which it immediately did. Soon after, Hitler threw his support behind Japan by declaring war on the United States. A war

Max Faget before the war

that had started as a series of regional conflicts in Asia and Europe now encompassed the globe.

What was it all about? Germany wanted control of Europe, and Japan wanted an empire in Asia. American interests in both regions inevitably drew the U.S. into the fighting.

You might think that Germany, Italy, and Japan, known as the Axis powers, would have little chance when most of the rest of the world, known as the Allies, were lined up against them. The Allies included the United States, Great Britain, the Soviet Union, and China, plus the occupied countries and a host of smaller nations. But Germany and Japan had been vigorously preparing for war for years, and their overwhelming success at the outset showed it. By early 1942, they were on the verge of achieving their major war aims. All they had to do was hold on to their winnings.

Faget's small role was to help chip away at those gains.

●

And that's why *Guavina* was at the bottom of the South China Sea, just off the coast of Vietnam. A short time earlier, the submarine had sunk a Japanese tanker carrying badly needed crude oil from Japanese-occupied Indonesia to Japan's home islands. Thanks to American submarines, Japan was increasingly starved of resources. Unfortunately,

Max Faget stands at the depth gauge as *Guavina* dives past 90 feet, 1945.

one of those subs, *Guavina*, was now cornered by enemy ships determined to destroy it.

Click . . . BANG!

The depth charges continued to fall. *Guavina*'s captain, Ralph Lockwood, had ordered "silent running," meaning that all mechanical equipment was turned off—motors, fans, air-conditioning, anything that made noise that could be picked up by the enemy's sonar and betray their location. Most of the crew had nothing to do and waited silently. With the fans and air-conditioning off, the air became stale and hot, making breathing difficult. A thawing turkey in the galley started to smell. No one moved unless they had to. Eighty-five sailors and officers were as still as death.

During the next seven hours, a total of ninety-eight depth charges rocked *Guavina*. It was one of the most relentless anti-submarine actions of the war. "We experienced hell," Captain Lockwood later wrote in his official report.

"Words cannot express the feelings and emotions that surged through my mind while waiting helplessly," recalled one sailor. He saw that most of the men "had the look of fear on their faces. Everyone reacts differently in times of stress," he noted. "One man sat down on the floor and started to giggle, but soon brought it under control." Another, pouring with sweat, began bumping his head against the bulkhead until he was led away.

The closest explosions caused havoc on the boat. Lightbulbs shattered in their sockets. Cork insulation fell to the deck, where the pieces bounced with each new blast. A pipe broke, and seawater gushed into the mess hall; sailors immediately found a safety valve and stemmed the flood. No one could think of anything but the coming catastrophic crash that would break the hull apart and engulf them in a fatal blast of water.

But it didn't come.

Guavina belonged to a new class of submarines built with a strong hull for deep diving. The same high-tensile steel that could resist water pressure at a depth of up to 900 feet also protected the crew from all but the closest hit. During a lull in the action, when the sub chasers returned to a nearby port for more depth charges, *Guavina* surfaced, turned on its diesel engines, and headed back into the open ocean, taking stock of damage and giving sailors a desperately needed dose of fresh air.

For Ensign Faget, a Louisiana native making his first war patrol, there were many lessons. He was a recent graduate of Louisiana State University, where he had studied mechanical engineering, and he had just seen unforgettable proof of how a properly engineered craft can sustain humans under the most perilous conditions. Hull, radar,

USS *Guavina* ready for launching, 1943

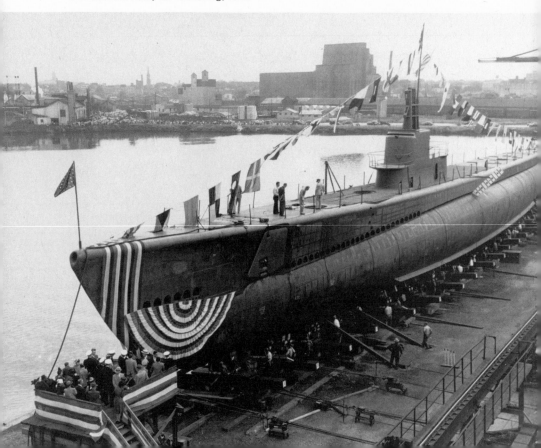

sonar, propulsion, control, communications, environmental systems, weaponry—all were perfectly matched to the task of sinking enemy ships and then escaping.

But an engineer with Faget's ceaselessly inquiring mind, who was also an avid reader of science fiction, might imagine using the same technology for another type of vessel, one that could sail a far vaster ocean. "A submarine is a very high-tech ship—very compact, and full of machinery," Faget reminisced much later, adding, "like a spacecraft."

World War II recruiting poster for the Submarine Service

2

PIRATES OF THE WESTERN PACIFIC

Oddly enough, a submarine during World War II was an ideal place for someone who loved the stars.

In the era before nuclear power allowed submarines to submerge almost indefinitely, a sub could stay underwater for no more than a day or two, powered by a bank of storage batteries. When the batteries ran out, the boat had to surface and switch on air-breathing diesel engines. These recharged the batteries and also provided propulsion, just as a gasoline engine keeps an automobile battery charged while simultaneously turning the wheels.

The usual strategy for a sub was to submerge during the day, when enemy planes and ships could easily spot it. At night, the boat would come up and cruise on diesel power beneath a canopy of stars, searching for prey. This was a good time to make celestial sightings with a sextant to confirm the sub's position.

When lookouts spotted a hostile ship, the boat would dive, taking less than a minute to get everyone inside, close the hatches and vents, flood the ballast tanks, and switch to electric power. The captain would

A Japanese destroyer sinks, viewed through the periscope of an American submarine, 1942.

inspect the target through a periscope, maneuver into range, and then fire a salvo of torpedoes. With luck, the underwater missiles would score another success against the Japanese navy or its merchant fleet, bringing the war a little closer to an end.

Lieutenant (junior grade) Thomas O. Paine loved this game. The same age as Faget, he had a more swashbuckling attitude, perhaps because his father was a Navy man and young Paine had grown up with sea yarns. "We were the last of the corsairs," he bragged about the submarine service. "The life of [a] pirate is given to few people. We were part of the tooth-and-claw simplicity of the sea." For Paine, the unpredictability of war gave the experience a strange clarity. You were always focused on the moment. The past and the future meant nothing, for they could be extinguished—along with your life—in an instant.

Paine had been through his share of close calls. On his fourth war patrol, scheduled to last the usual six to eight weeks, a torpedo aimed at a Japanese cargo ship had malfunctioned and circled back toward his sub, USS *Pompon*. Only hasty evasive action saved the situation. It was on this voyage that Paine volunteered for a diving emergency. A certified deep-sea diver, he went over the side at night off enemy shores to repair a broken valve in *Pompon*'s sewage system. He succeeded—to the relief of all—and was rewarded with a stiff drink and ten hours of uninterrupted sleep.

Known as the "silent service" for its tactic of striking without warning, the submarine corps appealed to independent-minded young mariners. What could "a mere ensign do" on the massive ships of the surface navy?—mused an officer on another boat. "But submarines," he marveled, "that was a different story. Submariners were younger men, and they were right there in the front lines delivering telling blows."

During Paine's fifth war patrol in January 1945, *Pompon* was diving just before dawn while stalking a convoy. As the last man to clear the deck pulled the hatch shut, it jammed and wouldn't close. Seawater immediately cascaded into the control room and began filling the vessel. The diving officer shouted, "Surface! Surface!" High-pressure air shot into the ballast tanks, which was the method for increasing the sub's buoyancy to bring it up. But the flooded compartments pulled the

boat down, and only the conning tower and bridge poked above the waves.

The situation was dire. There they were, bobbing low in the water 300 miles from Japan, with enemy ships nearby and the sun coming up, exposing them for all to see. The pumps and blowers were knocked out. So were the radar, sonar, and radio. All the

Tom Paine in his college yearbook, 1942

crew could do was organize a bucket brigade to bail out by hand, throwing water over the side, while also trying to fix the most vital equipment. Luckily, they weren't spotted. After seven hours, some of the machinery was working and they resubmerged to finish the repairs in the safety of the deep.

The radio was still out, which meant *Pompon* couldn't communicate with headquarters. And if headquarters didn't know where *Pompon* was, then it was an unidentified vessel, subject to attack by American planes and ships. Threatened by friend and foe alike, *Pompon* gingerly made its way across 3,000 miles of ocean to Midway Island, the only American base that was authorized to receive unscheduled submarines. They arrived on February 11, 1945.

A war-battered American submarine arrives at port.

Seven weeks later, *Pompon* was patched up and ready for another mission. Lieutenant Paine was back aboard, chalking up his sixth war patrol. Surviving that, he embarked in mid-June on his seventh.

Most submariners were transferred to shore duty after four to six patrols. Their nerves were usually shot by then, since submarines had the highest casualty rate of any branch of the U.S. Armed Forces. By the end of the war, nearly one-fifth of America's fighting subs had been destroyed: fifty-two boats. The vast majority were entombed with their crews at the ocean bottom, accounting for the deaths of over 3,500 men.

But the prospect of a watery grave didn't seem to bother Paine. He was having the time of his life. "I saw many strange and wonderful things," he later recalled. "Bali by moonlight, with the smell of the flowers and the spices drifting across the water. Even now I think I could navigate around the island as though it were the back of my hand. Standing watches at night, the heavens became enormously familiar. You could understand the beginnings of myths and legends. Schools of whales accompanied us, sometimes for weeks at a time."

A fan of the writer Joseph Conrad, who penned popular stories about the sea decades before World War II, Paine identified with Conrad's storm-tossed heroes.

"Youth and the sea. Glamour and the sea!" one character exclaims at the end of Conrad's story "Youth." "The good, strong sea, the salt, bitter sea, that could whisper to you and roar at you and knock your breath out of you."

Living at close quarters with men in the prime of life, sharing their dangers, roaming across the wide ocean, diving at a moment's notice, eluding the enemy, and then, at the chosen instant, destroying him in a fiery blast. Above all, playing a part in the greatest war in human history—what more could an adventure-seeking twenty-three-year-old ask?

B-25s return to base after a bombing mission in northern Italy, 1945.

3

LIEUTENANT SLAYTON FLIES
ANOTHER MISSION

If submarines were risky places, then bombers, depending on the mission, could be close to suicidal. World War II saw the birth of strategic bombing, designed to destroy the enemy's morale and its war-fighting industries—as opposed to tactical bombing, which focused on specific battlefield targets such as tanks and supply depots. The improved technology of airplanes made it possible, for the first time in history, to take the battle deep inside enemy territory—not just on a onetime raid but every day, day after day, with the goal of breaking the enemy's will and ability to carry on the conflict.

Since air crews had to be highly trained, the most efficient use of their skills was to keep the crewmembers flying until they were shot down, while having plenty of replacements in training. During World War I—fought between 1914 and 1918—the life span of pilots on combat duty was just a few weeks. And the planes in that war were simple compared to the complex machines being flown in World II, not to mention the sophisticated defenses that had been developed to shoot them down.

Following the fall of France in 1940, the German air force—called the

Luftwaffe—began an eight-month air offensive against Great Britain to soften its defenses for an invasion. Known as the Blitz, this aerial assault on dozens of British cities, carried out mostly at night, failed thanks to Britain's Royal Air Force (RAF), which exacted a heavy toll on Nazi aircraft. The invasion never came. After the Blitz, the British intensified their own bombing campaign against Germany. During July 1941, the RAF averaged over a hundred bombing sorties (attacks by individual aircraft) per day against targets on the European continent. Within two years, the United States had joined the air war, and over 1,000 Allied bombing sorties per day were the norm in Europe, with many more raids by smaller fighter aircraft.

Today it is common to look up in the sky and see an airplane or two. Imagine, though, seeing hundreds at one time. If you lived in eastern England, this was the sight almost every morning during the last two years of the war as Allied bombers headed east toward Germany, flying in tight formation. And every afternoon, you saw a somewhat smaller number returning from their dangerous missions.

Second Lieutenant Donald K. Slayton was a nineteen-year-old farm boy from Wisconsin fighting on the Mediterranean front of this war. He was assigned to the 340th Bombardment Group of the Twelfth Air Force, U.S. Army Air Forces. The group was stationed in southern Italy, flying bombing missions against bridges, airfields, railroads, and other targets. Just before Slayton arrived in the fall of 1943, Italy had surrendered to the Allies. But German troops immediately occupied the most important Italian defensive positions, and the war in southern Europe raged on.

Slayton was the copilot of a twin-engine B-25 medium bomber. A typical B-25 crew had a pilot, copilot, bombardier, and three gunners, with one gunner doubling as the radio operator. The lead plane in a formation always had a navigator, and the last plane had a photographer to record the bombing results.

Don Slayton, B-25 copilot

Every evening, Slayton and the other men in his squadron stopped by the operations tent to see if they were scheduled to fly the next day. Working with target orders from headquarters, the staff decided how many planes to send and which crews. The usual mission was a formation of eighteen planes: six from each of three squadrons, with the fourth squadron in the group getting a rest. The operations officer for each squadron determined who would fly from his unit, rotating the men so that everyone on flying status got two or three combat assignments per week, with training flights in between. That was the system.

Crews never stayed intact for long, since one man might be on leave, another might be promoted to a different job, yet another might be transferred out, and someone else would be sick, wounded, or just too rattled to keep flying. Of course, some men would die, get captured, or simply never return from a mission, their fate unknown.

Just as in the submarine service, no one could handle the stress of combat indefinitely, so headquarters set a limit on how many missions an airman had to fly before he was rotated back to the U.S. With a huge pilot-training program, America could afford to do this. Germany and Japan, which were stretched for resources, could not. They flew their crews until they were killed or captured. Eventually, America started feeling the weight of this problem as well, as too many planes were being shot down. The training program couldn't keep up, so the mission limits increased. For medium bombers in the Twelfth Air Force, the limit was originally twenty-five missions. Then it was raised to thirty-five. By the time Slayton arrived, it was fifty missions. Considering the loss rate in the group, fifty missions gave flyers about a 30 percent chance of getting shot down during their combat tour. In other words, one in three airmen either crashed (usually fatally) or bailed out (to be captured, die, or escape back to friendly territory) before reaching the mission limit.

Echoing the feelings of their German and Japanese counterparts, some American airmen chalked a slogan on their T-shirts: *Fly 'til I die.*

On November 16, 1943, the crews assigned for the next morning couldn't believe their bad luck. For the third day in a row they would be attacking Luftwaffe airfields around Athens, Greece. "Same time, same place, same direction!" Slayton later wrote. "We all thought it was kind of stupid going to the same place the same time, three days in a row. But nobody stepped up and said so."

In fact, it couldn't be helped, since a battle for a strategic Greek island was raging 160 miles east of Athens. The mission for Slayton's group and another unit was to keep as many German planes as possible out of that battle. The total air armada would be seventy-two B-25s,

The American P-38 fighter, nicknamed the "fork-tailed devil" by German adversaries, 1944

protected by several dozen P-38 fighters, which were agile single-seat aircraft designed to shoot down enemy planes.

At 10:10 a.m. on the assigned day, they took off. The flight to Athens took a little over two hours. Then "everything happened," according to one pilot.

First there was ack-ack—antiaircraft gunfire, also called flak. German spotters calculated the height of the attackers and then set shells to explode at that altitude. It didn't require a direct hit, since a nearby burst could lacerate an aircraft with jagged chunks of metal, maiming the crew and disabling the plane.

Next were enemy fighters. They "were on us before we hit the target," reported another pilot, "coming at us from the sun"—so they couldn't be seen. "Were we scared? Hell, yes. We continued on our run with the fighters on our tail and ack-ack all around us."

Over the target the bombardiers let go. The bombs hit perfectly, with explosions ripping the airfield from one end to the other. Meanwhile, dogfighting German and American fighters tangled overhead as the bombers zigged and zagged to avoid flak.

Don Slayton (right) leans against his A-26 bomber on a Pacific island, 1945.

On the way back German planes surprised the formation by releasing bombs from above. P-38s came to the rescue, breaking up the attack and downing three enemy aircraft. Miraculously, only one American plane was shot down. It was from Slayton's squadron. Four crewmen out of the six aboard were seen parachuting to enemy-held territory below.

Slayton's plane was safe, but he had experienced the closest of close shaves. When his ship got back to base, it had over 300 flak holes, the tires were blown out, the landing-gear hydraulics were dead, and the crew had to crank down the wheels by hand to land safely. But everyone was alive.

The following day the men learned that the fifty-mission limit was being raised. There were just not enough replacement crews. Slayton went on to fly fifty-six missions. By the time he rotated back to the States, he had been promoted to full lieutenant and first pilot. Since his ambition was to fly fighters like the P-38, he volunteered for more combat. But the Air Force had other ideas and trained him on the latest two-engine bomber. Then they sent him to drop bombs on the Japanese in the Pacific.

German technicians work on a V-2 rocket, the largest in the world, 1942.

4

CAPTAIN PHILLIPS BOMBS MAJOR VON BRAUN

Don Slayton wanted to be a fighter pilot because that was what the best pilots did. Lieutenant Samuel C. Phillips was a member of this elite group, flying missions over Germany from a base in England. Many years later, he was asked to name his most important experience as a fighter pilot during World War II. "Surviving," he said.

An electrical engineer from Wyoming, Lieutenant Phillips arrived in England in February 1944 with the 364th Fighter Group of the Eighth Air Force. Born the same year as Max Faget and Tom Paine, he was about to turn twenty-three. During the next fifteen months, until Germany surrendered, he saw his original squadron of twenty-eight pilots cut by half. Seven were killed in action, two died in training accidents, and five were shot down and captured. A common event at his and every other combat unit was the arrival of replacements.

Phillips started out in P-38s, the same fighter that Slayton dearly wanted to fly. In July 1944, his group switched to the even more impressive P-51 Mustang. Built by the firm North American Aviation in California, the Mustang had many of the latest advances in aircraft technology.

Sam Phillips in the cockpit of a P-51 Mustang

Other new airplanes did, too, but the Mustang combined qualities that made it the best all-around fighter of the war. Most important was its streamlined shape and powerful engine, which was British-designed. This gave it speed, maneuverability, and the range to accompany bombers from England to Berlin and back—something no other fighter could do.

One of the Mustang's most advanced features was its wing. A little-known U.S. government organization called the National Advisory Committee for Aeronautics (NACA) devoted years to studying the effectiveness of different airfoils. The airfoil is the wing's cross section, as if sliced like a loaf of bread. The shape of this cross section influences lift and also air resistance, or drag. In the late 1930s, NACA researchers discovered an airfoil with remarkably low drag, which translates into greater speed and fuel economy. The Mustang was the first fighter to exploit this discovery.

P-51's innovative airfoil

P-51 on a bomber escort mission, 1944

After the war, the head of Hitler's Luftwaffe, Hermann Göring, re-marked that the arrival of P-51s over Berlin was decisive. "The greatest surprise of the war to us," Göring explained, "was the long-range fighter bomber that could take off from England, attack Berlin, and re-turn to its home base." From then on, Nazi leaders despaired of stop-ping the Allied bombing offensive that was systematically destroying their cities.

But technological surprises work both ways, and the Germans had a big one for the Allies.

On August 25, 1944, having recently been promoted to captain, Phillips took off with his squadron of Mustangs to join an armada of 171 fighters and 376 heavy bombers. Their targets were military installations in and around a secret research facility on a secluded peninsula called Peene-münde, which jutted into the Baltic Sea on Germany's northern coast.

Aerial surveillance showed a new type of weapon being tested at the site. The mission was the third Allied attack on Peenemünde in six weeks and the fourth in a little over a year. The air crews knew the place was important, but they were in the dark about what exactly was going on there.

But Allied leaders knew well and were alarmed. Mounting clues pointed to a new weapon unlike any ever built. Hitler's plan was apparently to obliterate London with unstoppable, long-range, high-explosive projectiles, since evidence showed that his engineers were perfecting the world's most powerful rocket.

The Allied air armada that day hit the test site, a nearby propellant plant, and surrounding airfields. But it was too late. The leaders of the rocket project, including its brilliant technical director, SS Major Wernher von Braun, had moved production of the missiles elsewhere, and hundreds were poised to descend on England.

That summer, Wernher von Braun was thirty-two years old. More than a decade earlier, he had been a carefree engineering student in love with the dream of spaceflight.

Von Braun belonged to a club that had built liquid-propellant rockets, which are rockets that produce thrust by burning fuel and oxidizer in liquid rather than solid form. Liquid fuels such as alcohol and kerosene contain much more energy than a comparable quantity of solid chemicals such as gunpowder—the propellant used in fireworks. Although far more complex than solid rockets, liquid-propellant rockets generally go faster and farther; and maybe one day, von Braun and his friends hoped, to the Moon and planets. At the time, rockets were only going a few thousand feet in the air. To reach the edge of space, they would need to go more than a hundred times higher, to an altitude of at least sixty miles. And to reach the Moon, they would have to travel an unimaginably distant 240,000 miles. Obviously, it was crazy even to consider it!

Nonetheless, it was a hobby, and club members were on the lookout for other enthusiasts who might be willing to provide financial support to help move the technology forward. They never expected that the German army would offer to underwrite their experiments. Von Braun's friends were reluctant to submit to army control, but he jumped at the chance, and in 1932 he was made the civilian head of Germany's military rocket research program. The army had no interest in space, but they did see promise in rockets as explosive-carrying projectiles that could travel much farther than artillery shells.

Von Braun threw himself into the assignment. He recruited gifted engineers, including fellow space enthusiasts. On his advice, the army established a secret rocket test center at Peenemünde. Then World War II broke out, and Nazi officials started putting pressure on von Braun to produce results quickly, especially after Allied air attacks began destroying the effectiveness of the Luftwaffe. Feeling that his life was on the line, von Braun worked as he had never worked before.

He had good reason to fear for his safety, because the rocket project had been taken over by the most brutal arm of the Nazi regime—the SS, or special police force, which ran the concentration camps where millions of Jews and other victims of Nazi ideology were being murdered. Ominously, SS chief Heinrich Himmler made von Braun an officer in the terror organization. Von Braun seldom wore his SS uniform, but yearly promotions made it appear he was involved in their crimes, whether he was or not, and by 1944 he was a major.

The SS also kept him supplied with thousands of skilled workers drawn from concentration camps and prisoner-of-war camps. Suspicious of his loyalty, at one point Himmler had him arrested on charges of sabotage, supposedly for advocating spaceflight over military goals.

German generals visit Wernher von Braun (in dark suit) at his secret rocket base, 1941.

It took Hitler's intervention to get von Braun released. "It could have very easily led me to the firing squad," he recalled with a shudder in later years.

On September 8, 1944, two weeks after Captain Phillips flew on the Peenemünde raid, von Braun's rockets began falling on London. Two fell the first day, and an average of two or three more followed every day for the next six months. Other rockets struck elsewhere in England, as well as in Allied-held regions of France and Belgium. Most were launched from German-occupied Holland, about 200 miles from London. During their arcing, five-minute flights, the wonder weapons soared to the brink of space. No human-made object had ever flown so high or so fast. Since they were traveling faster than sound, the rockets arrived without warning, detonating their payloads of high explosives with enough force to demolish a large building.

Von Braun was ordered to target London because of Britain's role in the bombing campaign against Germany, but also because his missiles were not yet advanced enough to reach the U.S. The Germans called the rocket "Vengeance Weapon 2," or V-2. (The V-1 was a less sophisticated, jet-propelled bomb.) During the six months of rocket attack, over 3,000 V-2s took off. More than 1,100 struck England and about 500 hit London. Altogether, they were responsible for some 5,000 deaths—not including the estimated 10,000 forced laborers who died from starvation and maltreatment while building them.

●

As formidable as the V-2 was, it was a failure as a weapon. It took as much labor to build one as to construct a heavy bomber, yet it was only good for a single mission, and it was barely accurate enough to target an entire city, much less a specific building. It never came close to achieving Hitler's goal of wiping out the British capital, and the V-2 project may actually have hastened Germany's defeat because of the resources it drained from more effective weapons.

Von Braun survived repeated bombing raids on Peenemünde, where most of those killed were Russian prison workers. The bigger risk to him, by far, was the SS. "Once they felt they could do without you, and you were in their way, they'd . . . destroy you," he told an American audience after the war. Defending his work for the Nazis and the SS, von Braun implored listeners to put themselves in his shoes: "The man living under dictatorship adjusts himself to business as usual, whether he likes it or not, because he must, in order to survive."

Soldiers and equipment pour ashore in France a few days after the D-Day invasion, 1944.

5

MAJOR WEBB FACES THE BIG ONE

When Lieutenant Phillips arrived in Britain with his fighter squadron in the winter of 1944, he ran into American troops everywhere. There were a million on the island, plus an even greater number of British, Canadian, French, Polish, and other Allied soldiers, all preparing for the largest seaborne invasion in history. Up to this point in the war, the major land battles in Europe had mostly taken place in eastern Europe, where Soviet troops were fighting toward Germany's eastern border, retaking territory they had lost in the early part of the conflict. The invasion from England would establish a western front, putting further pressure on Nazi forces. Called D-Day, this massive attack took place in the Normandy region of France on June 6, 1944. Some 156,000 troops landed on the first day, and by the end of the month 875,000 Allied soldiers were ashore, fighting stiff German resistance. Pushed back simultaneously from the east and the west, Germany managed to hold out for a little less than a year before finally surrendering unconditionally on May 8, 1945.

But the Pacific war raged on. In the summer of 1945, a year after

D-Day, another mammoth invasion was in the works. Set for November 1 and code-named Operation Olympic, this assault involved an even larger force than D-Day and would target the southernmost of the main Japanese islands, landing Allied troops on Japanese soil for the first time. Then on March 1, 1946, an even bigger invasion, called Operation Coronet, was due to attack the Tokyo area on Japan's central island with the goal of bringing World War II to its apocalyptic end.

Military planners predicted Japan's defeat by 1947, but American soldiers and sailors in the Pacific were not so sure. They had a saying, "Golden Gate in '48," meaning they didn't expect to be returning home beneath San Francisco's Golden Gate Bridge until 1948—if they survived. In fact, Japan's defense of its occupied territories had been so fierce and American casualties so high that it seemed foolhardy to believe *any* prediction about the final end of World War II.

◗

Among the quarter of a million troops assembling for Operation Olympic was Major James E. Webb. Thirty-eight years old and hailing from North Carolina, he had a small but vital role in the coming action. Though he was a veteran aviator in the U.S. Marine Corps Reserve, his flying days were behind him, and he now commanded the First Marine Air Warning Group—2,000 officers and men assigned to wade ashore on invasion day and set up early-warning radar to guard against enemy air attack, particularly at night when radar would provide the only alert. Radar was one of the wonder weapons of the war, and the portable radar units Webb was helping to create seemed almost miraculous.

So important was Webb's assignment that he was temporarily given control over all Marine air transportation in the United States so he could gather radar components from factories around the country for

Jim Webb, put in charge of portable radar units for the planned invasion of Japan

final assembly and testing at his group's headquarters in North Carolina. In early August 1945, he, his men, and their equipment prepared to ship to a staging area in the Far East. Olympic was only three months away.

Like Max Faget and Tom Paine, Webb had a profession outside of the military. Faget and Paine were both engineers, while Webb was a lawyer with a talent for managing complex projects and a taste for trying ambitious new ventures.

When he was in his twenties and struggling to launch a career during the Great Depression, he had taken advantage of a Marine Corps program to train college graduates to be military pilots. The Marines taught him to fly the open-cockpit biplanes of the day. He served on active duty for two years and then went on reserve status. By the time World War II started almost a decade later, the corps had plenty of aggressive young flyers but needed experienced managers, which was what Webb had become. Weighing his own talents, he judged: "My forte was putting things together and getting a team that can play the ball game."

When the war came, Webb was serving as a vice president at the Sperry Gyroscope Company, headquartered in Brooklyn, New York. He had helped build it from 800 employees into a major defense contractor with 33,000 workers. After Pearl Harbor, his first thought was to enlist, especially when his younger brother was captured in Japan's assault on the U.S. base at Wake Island at the end of 1941. But the government preferred him to stay at Sperry, which was flooded with war orders.

"War is a hurly-burly kind of thing," Webb recalled. "We were hiring lots of people every day, training new people, getting rid of people who couldn't make the grade. Worrying about the security problems, finding espionage agents sent over by Germany in our plant. We had to get rid of them. Just a million things to be done . . ."

Many of Sperry's products were based on the gyroscope, a freely spinning disk that holds its position in space no matter how its housing frame is rotated. A gyroscope makes a remarkably reliable reference point for anything that needs to be directed to a precise location, such as an airplane, a submarine, a torpedo, or for that matter von Braun's V-2, which used gyroscopes in its guidance system (its targeting problems were for other reasons).

Educated as a lawyer and not an engineer, Webb still had to know enough about technology to negotiate multimillion-dollar contracts for delivery of devices that had never been built before. He recruited experts to do research and development, while he kept close tabs on their progress to ensure that the products were finished on time. One

The "kamikaze killer" gunsight, developed under Jim Webb's guidance

As Operation Olympic approached, the Japanese put up fierce resistance. Here, two kamikazes have just struck an American aircraft carrier, 1945.

consultant he trusted completely was Charles Stark "Doc" Draper, an eccentric engineering professor at the Massachusetts Institute of Technology (MIT) in Cambridge, Massachusetts. Draper's lab was hired by Sperry for a variety of projects, such as creating a gyroscopic gunsight for the U.S. Navy. This device allowed sailors to target airplanes closing in at 300 miles per hour. Teamed with a powerful antiaircraft gun, the gunsight became known as the "kamikaze killer" for its ability to shoot down Japanese suicide planes targeting ships. More than 85,000 were built, saving countless American lives.

In the third year of the war, Sperry was running so smoothly that Webb was finally allowed to enlist. The Marines gave him a crash course on radar. Then they put him in charge of the First Marine Air Warning Group with orders to produce something that didn't exist yet: portable radar units. To Webb, it was a familiar assignment: do something that had never been done.

"The contractors said it would take us six, maybe eight months," he recalled. "We wanted them yesterday." He didn't get them quite that fast, but as the deadline for Olympic approached, Webb and his men had the radar sets stockpiled and knew how to use them.

They were ready.

This defense worker, known as Rosie the Riveter, displays the attitude that won the war.

"WE NEED IT YESTERDAY!"

The news came on the day that Max Faget's submarine, *Guavina*, was cruising out of San Francisco Bay bound for Pearl Harbor and yet another war patrol. That same day, Tom Paine was on Guam where his boat, *Pompon*, was being refitted for more combat. Some 1,400 miles northwest of Guam, Don Slayton was with his new bomb group on Okinawa, the site of a recently concluded ferocious battle with the Japanese that was a grim preview of Olympic. For Slayton, Olympic had already started, since his sorties were targeting defenses around the landing beaches, an hour and a half away by air.

On the other side of the world, Sam Phillips was in Germany with the American occupation forces. Wernher von Braun was also in Germany, under house arrest by the U.S. Army, being questioned almost daily along with other members of his rocket team. And in the United States, Jim Webb was barely a week away from his departure for the Olympic staging area. After almost four years of war, its privations and tragedies, the American people were exhausted, but resigned to more months, even years, of conflict.

But then the news flash came. The date was August 6, 1945. The bulletin said that a Japanese city called Hiroshima had been obliterated by a single, powerful new bomb. "We didn't think that much about it," remembered Slayton. "Nobody was telling us the war was over. Two days later I was on another raid."

But the most destructive war of all time was about to end. In three days' time, another superbomb was dropped, on the city of Nagasaki. The short interval was intended to convince the Japanese that there was an arsenal full of these doomsday weapons, called atomic bombs. In fact, there were very few. Also on August 9, the Soviet Union, which until now had been neutral in the war with Japan, attacked Japanese forces in China with an army of well over a million soldiers. China was where World War II had started eight years earlier.

This devastating series of blows convinced the Japanese emperor to order his government to surrender.

The war was over.

●

World War I had seen new technology exploited for lethal ends: airplanes, rudimentary submarines, tanks, poison gas, high explosives, and machine guns. But none of these could be called a superweapon. By contrast, World War II produced superweapons of almost unimaginable sophistication: heavy bombers, long-range fighters, deep-diving submarines, guided missiles, mammoth battleships and aircraft carriers, and the superweapon to end them all: the atomic bomb—and then the even more cataclysmic hydrogen bomb that followed a few years later.

The Manhattan Project, which created the atomic bomb, was the prime example of a secret, technically challenging crash program with a no-holds-barred budget. But it was hardly unique; it was only one such effort among many during World War II. The operations that broke the Nazi and Japanese codes on an almost daily basis were no less secret, and the airplane that dropped the atomic bomb, the B-29 Superfortress, came out of a more expensive program of comparable technical difficulty. Radar may have been more crucial to winning the

The atomic bomb—the ultimate superweapon of World War II

war than the bomb. And the lowly Jeep and two-and-a-half-ton truck, built in the hundreds of thousands and the backbone of Allied land armies, were also hurry-up projects that cut corners to get into production and yet delivered outstanding results. Britain made key contributions to some of these projects, but America excelled at them. Through astute management, industrial power, innovation, and healthy budgets, the United States had discovered how to work technological miracles.

One of the secrets of success was a sense of urgency. Workers, managers, and engineers in defense plants everywhere believed that their project, whatever it was, was the most important of all, and they knew only one deadline: "We need it yesterday!" Anyone inclined to business as usual faced getting replaced by someone with a more can-do spirit. A famous story tells how as the war loomed, U.S. Army Chief of Staff General George C. Marshall asked for 150 updated field manuals to train troops in the latest military doctrine. He gave the general in charge a deadline of three months.

"It will take eighteen months," he was told.

"I need them in three," Marshall insisted.

"It can't be done," was the reply.

"I'm sorry, then you are relieved." Marshall sent the general into retirement and found someone who was up to the challenge.

Marshall was known for firing generals who didn't excel at their jobs, and he was a master at spotting new talent. He detected extraordinary ability in a lieutenant colonel named Dwight D. Eisenhower. The relatively young officer was promoted rapidly through the ranks, eventually becoming supreme commander of the Allied forces in Europe—the general in charge of D-Day. Eisenhower was later elected president of the United States.

Another secret of success was that companies figured out how to tackle giant projects of bewildering complexity. The B-29 Superfortress, which dwarfed Slayton's B-25, was the brainchild of General Henry H. "Hap" Arnold, the head of the Army Air Force. In 1939, he had asked Boeing Company executives if they could design a warplane with more than double the range and bomb load of the heaviest bomber then in the U.S. arsenal. But not only that—General Arnold demanded that this plane fly higher and faster, have powerful defensive armament, and be pressurized to allow the crew to fly in comfort at high altitude, without oxygen masks and arctic clothing. The goal was a bomber that could deliver a punishing blow to the enemy across thousands of miles.

It sounded like something in a science-fiction magazine, but the Boeing team got out their slide rules and started calculating. Officially given the job the following year, Boeing broke with aircraft industry tradition by attacking all of the airplane's intricate systems at the same time, assigning thousands of engineers to the effort. Everything about the ship—its airframe, electronics, armament, and other features—had to function in perfect synchrony. This required unprecedented coordination among many separate groups. Boeing also had to work with thousands of suppliers, including the manufacturer of the engines, a crucial component that was as complicated as the rest of the airplane put together.

One manager warned there was no room for error in such a high-performance machine. Success, he said, "depends upon everything working as planned."

For the longest time, it didn't. The worst day was February 18, 1943, when the ninth frustrating test flight of prototype number two started well enough. But after a few minutes in the air, an engine on the left side caught fire. The fire suppression system quickly extinguished it, and the pilot—Eddie Allen, one of the most experienced test pilots of the day—banked the giant B-29 to return to Boeing Field. On the way in, his left wing burst into flames and began disintegrating. Allen lost control and crashed into a meatpacking plant. All eleven crewmen died, along with twenty on the ground.

The most sophisticated aircraft of its day, the B-29 challenged engineers to solve seemingly impossible problems.

The engines were blamed, and there was pressure from Congress to pull the plug on the B-29. Critics argued that the Superfortress was a complex monstrosity destined to fail. But the plane's engineers and managers redoubled their efforts to get things right. A review board ordered changes in the engines. Meanwhile, problems were fixed in the remote-controlled gun turrets, the bomb bay doors, wing de-icers, propellers, and other systems. The government and military tightened their oversight of production, which was behind schedule. They decided to gear up assembly lines before all the kinks were worked out, which was a giant risk. But within fourteen months, the B-29 was flying in combat, and by 1945, it had changed the course of the war. Unlike Germany, Japan had not yet suffered significant attacks on its homeland. Now formations of B-29s, often hundreds at a time, began systematically destroying the cities and factories of the island nation, ultimately dropping two atomic bombs.

For better or worse, the B-29 proved its mettle. With this superweapon, no less than with the atomic bomb, industry and government had found a system for tackling a seemingly impossible task.

●

But that was war, and now peace had come. Faget, Paine, Slayton, Phillips, von Braun, Webb, and millions of others could thank their lucky stars that they had survived and look to the future. What would that hold?

The Wright brothers' first flight, 1903

Aviation pioneers (including Orville Wright) meet at a 1934 NACA conference.

A captured Japanese Zero in U.S. Army markings, 1943

The rocket-powered X-1, the first aircraft to fly faster than sound, 1947

BRIEFING:
The NACA

Wilbur and Orville Wright made history with the world's first airplane flight in 1903. Success came only after a methodical research program run out of their bicycle shop in Dayton, Ohio, and their flight-test camp in Kitty Hawk, North Carolina. The brothers spent the next few years improving their invention and making it practical. In 1915, the United States government established the NACA—the National Advisory Committee on Aeronautics—to continue the brothers' work. The new agency helped enhance practically every aspect of airplanes: wings, propellers, engines, streamlining, stability, control. Wilbur Wright died in 1912, but Orville served on the NACA advisory board until his death in 1948, only a few months after the first supersonic flight—another NACA project.

The NACA played a key role in making American planes among the top-performing fighters and bombers in World War II. NACA experts focused not just on U.S. aircraft but on the enemy's. During the war, a captured Japanese Zero—the fighter plane that had bombed Pearl Harbor and given American pilots so much trouble in dogfights—was sent to a NACA facility to have its flight characteristics analyzed, so that U.S. planes could counter it more effectively.

In 1958, the NACA became the nucleus for NASA—the National Aeronautics and Space Administration—and many of its aeronautical engineers turned their attention to spaceflight, among them Abe Silverstein, who had directed the Zero study, and Bob Gilruth, an expert on aircraft flying qualities. They and other creative problem solvers approached their new task with the same passion for imaginative thinking and rigorous testing that they had brought to aviation—guaranteeing that the spirit of the Wright brothers lives on in the space age.

PART 2
DREAMS

To place a man in a multi-stage rocket and project him into the controlling gravitational field of the moon, where the passenger can make scientific observations, perhaps land alive, and then return to earth—all that constitutes a wild dream worthy of Jules Verne. I am bold enough to say that such a man-made moon voyage will never occur regardless of all future advances.

—Lee de Forest, electronics pioneer, 1957

The full Moon, seen through a telescope on Earth

20¢

AUGUST
1950

SCIENCE and MECHANICS

The Magazine That Shows You How

Raymond Loewy's
Car of the Future

The car of the future in 1950 symbolizes the new "rocket age."

7

AMERICA LANDS ON ITS FEET

The fatalistic slogan of Pacific troops was "Golden Gate in '48," and the flippant answer was "Bread Line in '49." The implication was that the booming war economy would grind to a halt after the enemy surrendered. Factories would close and returning veterans wouldn't be able to find work. This was exactly what had happened after World War I ended in 1918. Everyone expected the same after the Axis surrendered in 1945.

Surprisingly, the economy kept booming. Several factors seem to have been responsible. For one thing, there was a huge pent-up demand for consumer goods—everything from bicycles to radios to shoes— that dated to the start of the Great Depression in 1929. The Depression was a decade-long economic crisis, during which up to a quarter of the workforce in the United States couldn't find jobs. The Depression was ended by World War II, when practically everyone who wanted a job could get one, but there was very little to spend money on during the war. With the arrival of peace, factories converted from producing armaments to consumer products, which people now had the savings to purchase.

For another thing, the United States was the only great power to emerge unscathed from the war. Its cities were not bombed, its infrastructure was not destroyed, and the country was not deeply in debt to other nations for food, oil, and weapons (as some of the Allies were to the U.S.). Practically anything the world needed, America could supply. Furthermore, American foreign aid helped rebuild Western Europe under the Marshall Plan, named for its champion, General George C. Marshall, who became the U.S. Secretary of State after the war. The Marshall Plan was a wise investment for many reasons, not least because it created a market for American exports.

Yet another wise investment was the G.I. Bill, which provided education, housing, and business start-up benefits to war veterans, allowing them to land on their feet when they disembarked from troop ships. Instead of a breadline, they could get into a college enrollment line or a line at a bank for a low-interest loan that they could use to buy a house or open a business. With the war over, the energy that had gone into winning battles now went into starting families, getting ahead, and enjoying life.

There was also a more fundamental change going on. For many decades, the quality of life in much of the world had been advancing at a remarkable pace, particularly in the United States. In 1945, an American who had been born in 1900 had seen astonishing changes. When that person was an infant, life expectancy was just forty-seven years—which is today considered the prime of one's working life. By 1945, a newborn could expect to live almost two decades longer, thanks to improved public health, better doctor training, and radical new medical treatments. In 1900, only a third of homes had running water, and just half of those were equipped with flush toilets. Electrical lighting, telephones, and central heating were almost unknown. Affordable automobiles, washing machines, and mechanical refrigerators hadn't been invented yet, nor had radios or airplanes. By 1945, all of these dramatic improvements had spread widely.

And they were still spreading after World War II. By itself, this wholesale transformation of society gave an enormous boost to the American economy. It would last until what are now considered the necessities of life—running water, electricity, appliances, telephones, and automobiles—were nearly universal in the United States. For people living in the middle of this revolution, it was easy to think that the dramatic changes would keep coming without limit, as one new invention after another transformed their lives. The technological miracles of World War II reinforced this impression. Atomic energy, radar, electronic computers, and jet planes were straight out of the pages of the pulp magazines that Max Faget read, yet now they existed and had helped win the war. Furthermore, they held the promise that *anything* was possible.

●)

At the end of 1949, a random sample of Americans were asked to look half a century into the future—to the year 2000—and predict progress in three areas. The person-in-the-street's confidence in technology was almost boundless.

"Do you think that fifty years from now trains and airplanes will be run by atomic power?" Yes, said 63 percent. (In fact, no such vehicles have ever been built.)

"Do you think that a cure for cancer will be found within the next fifty years?" A hefty 88 percent responded yes. (Unfortunately, cancer

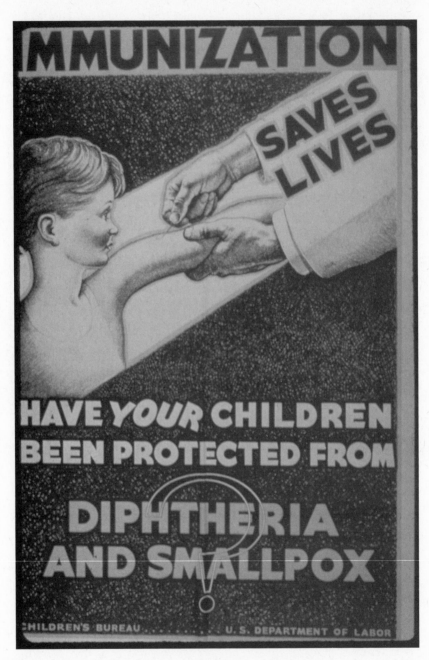

Immunization and other medical advances transformed society in the twentieth century, inspiring almost limitless optimism about the future.

still rivals heart disease as the leading cause of death in the United States.)

But starry-eyed optimism failed with the last question: "Do you think that men in rockets will be able to reach the Moon within the next fifty years?" This was a technological leap too far for 70 percent, who resoundingly answered no. Another 15 percent had no opinion. Only the remaining 15 percent thought that humans would actually fly to the Moon by 2000, fifty years in the future.

Who would have believed that people would make the trip far sooner than that?

Wernher von Braun holds a model of his V-2 rocket in the early 1950s.

VON BRAUN LANDS IN AMERICA

"That guy upstairs wants to go to the Moon." Glancing at the ceiling, Major James P. Hamill was hinting to a reporter that the civilian employee on the next floor was slightly mad. The major added: "That's his passion—space travel. Whether it will be war or peace on Earth comes after that for him."

"That guy upstairs," at the U.S. Army's Redstone Arsenal outside Huntsville, Alabama, in October 1950, was the most sought-after genius from Hitler's Germany: Wernher von Braun. As futile as von Braun's rockets had been during the war, the V-2 still attracted intense interest from the Allies. None of them had a missile nearly as powerful, and all reasoned that if it could be made more powerful still—and accurate— then it might be a decisive weapon in the next war.

Before Germany surrendered, von Braun knew that the Soviets advancing from the east and the Americans and British approaching from the west would be eager to capture him and his rocket team. He guessed that the Soviets would be none too pleased by Germany's treatment of Russian prisoners of war at Peenemünde, and the British might hold a grudge about the V-2 bombardment of London. Therefore, he gambled that the Americans would be the most welcoming.

He had never been to the United States, but his older brother, Sigismund, had studied law in Ohio for a year before the war. Impressed with America's vitality and openness to new ideas, Sigismund told Wernher, "America is the place for you to build your Moon rockets."

That settled the matter. As Hitler's empire collapsed around him, von Braun and several hundred of his staff risked execution for treason by the SS and made their way across Germany to the American lines. In early May 1945, a few days before the surrender, the rocket men turned themselves over to U.S. forces. Eventually they found themselves under the charge of Major Hamill.

●

The Army's first priority was to seize a large number of unused V-2s to ship back to the United States for testing. Army intelligence officers interrogated von Braun and his team, confirming that these men were indeed the talent behind the V-2 and probably had a lot to teach American rocket engineers. If nothing else, they would be essential for assembling and launching V-2s in the U.S.

The Germans were not shy about discussing their interest in space, but none of the Americans took this seriously. In fact, it seemed to exonerate the rocket men from complicity in Nazi war crimes, including the abuse and execution of prison laborers at the V-2 factories. Their sincere, wildly impractical visions of spaceflight made them look like dreamers who had been exploited by the Nazis, not enthusiastic collaborators in an evil regime. Probably, they were a mix of both. No one was as obsessed with spaceflight as von Braun, yet he had still done his best to win the war for Hitler. Even after the war he didn't seem to grasp what victory for Germany would have meant.

"If Germany had won the war," he mused lightheartedly in 1950, "der Führer would probably have lost interest in rockets. His enthusiasm would have shifted to a huge reconstruction project in the Ukraine or some such. I just know it."

The horror that von Braun glossed over was that Hitler's plan was to remake Ukraine as a German colony, exterminating or expelling most of its inhabitants. The Nazis succeeded to the extent of killing virtually all of Ukraine's Jews plus millions of others in the region—this on top of the additional millions who died at their hands in the rest of Europe.

The U.S. Army brought von Braun and more than a hundred of his best engineers and technicians to Fort Bliss, Texas, where they were to live under Army supervision. Their work would be at the nearby missile proving ground at White Sands, New Mexico, where the first atomic bomb had been tested. The rocket team came voluntarily under a one-year contract that paid them a small amount and guaranteed their families back in Germany housing and a degree of security in the postwar chaos of their devastated homeland.

The German rocket team in Texas, 1946. Von Braun is in the front row, right of center, with a white handkerchief in his breast pocket.

At White Sands, the visitors taught their hosts how to fire V-2s, advised them on improvements to the missile, briefed visiting scientists and engineers on the mechanics of the rocket, and assisted with the V-2's new mission of high-altitude research, for it was now launching scientific instruments instead of warheads.

When one year was up, the Army asked the Germans to stay, raising their pay and promising to bring their families over from Germany. The rocket men had proved so efficient that the Army wanted them indefinitely for other missile projects. They were even offered eventual U.S. citizenship. On the one hand, von Braun and most of his team were willing. On the other hand, they were deeply discouraged that they had been given no ambitious new rockets to work on, especially none that could venture higher than the hundred miles or so achieved by the V-2.

Also, the U.S. Congress was less than pleased about their presence. With the war over, legislators had little interest in expensive new weapons, particularly unreliable long-range rockets. The Army tried to make the case that rockets would be as important in future wars as aircraft carriers, submarines, and heavy bombers had been in the last one. But the Army was competing for funds with the other military branches, notably the Air Force, which had become a separate service in 1947. Airpower had strong support in Congress, in part because innovations in warplanes often made their way into civilian aircraft. For rockets, there were no such civilian uses. Certainly, no one in the Army was arguing that rockets could one day carry explorers to the Moon!

Meanwhile, von Braun and some of his colleagues were considering shifting to private industry or returning to Germany. "At Peenemünde, we'd been coddled. Here they were counting pennies," he complained. America was not the paradise for building Moon rockets that he had pictured. Plus, the Germans were beginning to feel unwelcome.

A V-2 rocket topped by a slender second stage takes off, 1950. This series of tests reached a record altitude of nearly 250 miles and a record speed of more than 5,000 miles per hour.

The Army had tried to be discreet about importing German technical advisers, not just in rocketry but in other fields with military applications. Eventually, word got out that hundreds of "former pets of Hitler" were now influential consultants to the U.S. military and might even become U.S. citizens. The Council Against Intolerance in America sent a telegram to President Harry Truman, who had become commander in chief upon the death of Franklin Roosevelt in April 1945. "We hold these individuals to be potentially dangerous carriers of racial and religious hatred," the council objected. The signers included the world's most famous physicist, Albert Einstein, along with Rabbi Stephen S. Wise, a prominent American Jewish leader. Asked their opinion in a national poll, a majority of Americans agreed that harboring Nazi scientists was a bad idea.

The protests might easily have grown until the government felt pressured to send Hitler's engineers back home. But America was starting to forget its old enemies and focus on a new one. In due time, Congress would be sufficiently alarmed to approve funds for a bold new project for the German rocket team.

They would be staying after all.

An American atomic bomb test in the Pacific, 1946

9

THE COLD WAR

In 1947, both Max Faget and Sam Phillips were working at the same U.S. government compound, although they didn't know each other at the time. Faget was a newly hired aeronautical engineer at the Langley Memorial Aeronautical Laboratory—the NACA facility that had developed the airfoil for the P-51 Mustang. Next door at Langley Field, former P-51 pilot Phillips was now Major Phillips with a job in air traffic control. Neither was thinking that another war might be imminent. Little did they suspect they were in the calm before the storm—a very long and chilly storm, for America was about to enter a decades-long conflict with the Soviet Union called the Cold War.

●

The Soviet Union had been America's ally during World War II, but the relationship was complicated. For one thing, the Soviets had been Hitler's ally at first—until 1941, when the Nazi dictator double-crossed the Russians and invaded their country. If any world leader could be compared to Hitler in bloodthirstiness, it was the Soviet dictator Joseph Stalin, who was responsible for the deaths of millions of his own citizens by execution, starvation, and imprisonment under brutal conditions. On the principle that "the enemy of our enemy is our friend," the United States and Great Britain cooperated with Stalin in the war against Germany, despite what was then known about Stalin's brutality. The U.S. and Britain even shipped millions of tons of military equipment to the Soviet Union, providing a vital lifeline that the Soviet government largely hid from its own people so that they wouldn't feel friendly toward the West. This was one of the many ways that Stalin controlled Soviet public opinion. An additional grievance for the U.S. and Britain was that Stalin did nothing to assist them in their fight against Japan until the last days of the war. And when American B-29s made emergency landings on Russian soil, the planes were impounded and taken apart piece by piece so that the Soviets could see how they were made, and so that they, too, could manufacture this wonder weapon. In short, as an ally Stalin was less than trustworthy.

Then there was ideology. Stalin was only the second ruler of his young nation, which had been established in the Communist Revolution of 1917. Its full name was the Union of Soviet Socialist Republics, or the U.S.S.R. for short. It was often called simply Russia, because that was the largest republic in the union. The United States had been at odds with the Soviets since the beginning, due to the Soviets' promotion of worldwide revolution. Soviet leaders appealed to workers everywhere to organize themselves and seize control of their governments, just as they had done, with all private property to be used for the common good. In practice, this meant total state control of all land, housing, services, factories, and personal freedoms. In 1945, the Soviet Union was the only major country to have taken this drastic step, but the country's leaders were determined to see the system spread around the globe.

They started with their neighbors. No sooner had the war against Germany ended than Stalin began setting up puppet communist regimes in the countries bordering his. Stalin's guarantee that he would allow free elections in these nations—which included Poland, Czechoslovakia, Hungary, and Romania—meant nothing. War-weary, the Americans and British objected but did little to stop the dictator. One outcome was that Germany stayed divided for decades between the eastern part of the country, which Soviet troops had overrun, and the western part of the country, which had been occupied by American, British, and French forces. Divided Germany became a symbol of a world increasingly split between communist and capitalist forms of government, especially after Stalin's successor, Nikita Khrushchev, ordered the construction of the Berlin Wall, a physical barrier preventing communist East Berliners from escaping to the greater prosperity and personal freedom of the American, British, or French zones of the city.

On the one hand, Stalin's policy of installing compliant governments along his borders was easy to understand, since Russia had suffered terribly from attacks by neighbors in wars going back for many centuries. On the other hand, his promotion of universal revolution was a new development in international affairs and threatened the world order that the United States felt obliged to safeguard. World War II had been fought to free the world from tyranny, but now a new tyrant loomed—one that posed a real danger, since the Soviet Union maintained the largest active army in the world. In 1945 President Truman had assured Americans that "we have emerged from this war the most powerful nation in the world—the most powerful nation, perhaps, in all history." The United States was truly a superpower, but the Soviet Union was determined to surpass it.

Joseph Stalin (front row, left) stands next to Harry Truman at their only meeting, July 1945.

Still, the Soviets didn't have the atomic bomb, which was the first weapon to exploit the incomprehensible power of nuclear energy. Invented by the U.S., atomic bombs were at first an American monopoly. Most Americans realized, however, that it was only a matter of time before the Soviet Union broke this monopoly. The man in charge of the Manhattan Project, General Leslie Groves, knew better than anyone what it took to build an atomic bomb, and he assured government officials that twenty years was a good estimate for how long it would take the Russians to catch up. Therefore, it was a profound shock when the Soviets set off their first nuclear explosion in 1949, just four years after the U.S.'s first atomic bomb test.

"The calmer the American people take this, the better," counseled the chairman of the Joint Chiefs of Staff when the news broke. But few took it calmly. One reaction was to believe that the Soviets had stolen the plans. In fact, they *had* stolen the plans, thanks to their spies. But there is far more to building a nuclear weapon than just having the plans. Their achievement hinted at a technical sophistication that was troubling. Moreover, American intelligence officials suspected the Russians were interested in rockets and were being advised by V-2 engineers who had stayed behind at Peenemünde, which was now in the Soviet occupation zone.

Adding to the unease, Chinese communists proclaimed a new Soviet-style government in China just a few days after the Russian atomic bomb surprise. Many Americans felt their backs were to the wall. "Better get out your old uniform," former soldiers told each other.

Emboldened by his ability to challenge American power, Stalin gave the okay to the communist government in North Korea to invade democratic South Korea in 1950. He expected the U.S. to stay out of this conflict, but he was wrong. Determined to block Soviet aggression so it wouldn't spread, President Truman sent in hundreds of thousands of U.S. troops under the auspices of the newly established United Nations, an international organization of countries, including the U.S., with the mission to promote peace. The Korean War raged for three years, ending in a stalemate in 1953, with the border between North and South Korea scarcely changed, despite the deaths of tens of thousands of American soldiers, as well as millions of Koreans on both sides, including civilians. The Soviets were also involved—but only to the extent of providing weapons and medical aid to their North Korean allies. They were careful not to come into direct conflict with American forces—except in one area.

In some aerial dogfights, American pilots suspected they were facing Russian airmen flying North Korea's Soviet-built fighters. This was the first war that saw the widespread use of jets, which flew faster and higher than propeller-powered aircraft like the Mustang. Surprisingly, Russia's jets turned out to be better than America's. Apparently, Russian flight instructors would lead their North Korean pupils into combat in squadrons of these superb flying machines. Communist China also fought on North Korea's side, with ground troops as well as pilots. Therefore, American pilots could be facing either North Korean, Russian, or Chinese adversaries.

The thousands of Americans involved in the air war included a naval aviator named Neil A. Armstrong and an Air Force pilot, Edwin E. "Buzz" Aldrin Jr. The two young men didn't know each other—yet. In the course of scores of sorties, both had their close calls. Flying a flak-riddled jet on one mission, with the wing partially sheared off, Armstrong nursed his ship into friendly territory before ejecting to safety. During the ordeal, he had a remarkably calm discussion with a fellow pilot about the best solution to this life-or-death emergency. For his part, Aldrin's adventures included shooting down two enemy jets, one after a grueling dogfight. Years later, the two coolheaded airmen would join forces for a very different adventure.

The Korean War was the first in a series of wars in which the United States and Soviet Union supported opposite sides—and sometimes sent in substantial numbers of troops—while avoiding, as much as possible, fighting each other. Such a direct conflict could easily have escalated into a nuclear war, with apocalyptic consequences. Throughout the 1950s, '60s, and beyond, armed struggles raged in places such as Korea, Cuba, Vietnam, Chile, and Angola, with the United States backing the democratic, capitalist side, and the Soviet Union sponsoring the totalitarian, communist side. Despite the bloodshed, these were considered engagements in the Cold War. Always, there was the risk that the Cold

Ensign Neil Armstrong (left) and Lieutenant Buzz Aldrin (right) during the Korean War. Aldrin has just returned from shooting down an enemy jet.

War could become "hot"—that it would spiral out of control into a full-scale clash between the two superpowers. Despite the risk, American and Soviet leaders persisted in jockeying for advantage, determined to see their nation's values and interests prevail around the world.

Like World War II, the Cold War drew on the resources of the entire nation. When World War II ended, Americans assumed that the declared state of national emergency would lift and defense expenditures would plummet, which is what happened for a few short years. But by 1950 the military budget had climbed back to about half of what was spent during the peak year of World War II. Many who had expected to enter a peaceful profession found themselves either still in the military or working on military projects.

Although the NACA was a civilian agency, its defense work boomed. Faget belonged to a special group called the Pilotless Aircraft Research Division (PARD), headed by a savvy engineer named Robert R. Gilruth. PARD's work focused on rocketry, particularly experimental rocket planes designed to fly faster than the speed of sound, which is roughly 700 miles per hour at jet altitudes. This research was put to use on missiles and advanced fighters and bombers.

Meanwhile, Major Phillips was sent to the University of Michigan to get an advanced degree in electronics. Then he landed in Ohio,

American F-86 jets patrol the skies over Korea, 1953.

managing weapons programs such as the one that developed the B-52 bomber—a jet-powered behemoth that surpassed the B-29 Super-fortress by as much as the B-29 had dwarfed Slayton's two-engine B-25. The B-52 could fly faster, higher, and farther than the B-29, and carry a much heavier payload. The intended payload was nuclear weapons, and the intended target, should hostilities break out, was the Soviet Union.

For his part, Don Slayton was now a captain with the new nickname Deke, concocted from his initials, DK, to distinguish him from another Don in his unit. He was finally flying fighters as a test pilot for the Air Force's latest supersonic jets at Edwards Air Force Base in California.

Elsewhere, Faget's fellow submariner Tom Paine was leading re-search in high technology for the General Electric Company, much of it having military applications. Former Marine major Jim Webb was President Truman's budget director before taking the number two job at the State Department during the early stage of the Korean War. Later he joined an energy company as a troubleshooting executive. And almost no one was questioning the presence of Wernher von Braun and his German rocket team in the United States. They were now America's rocket team in the contest with the Soviet Union.

Collier's

OCTOBER 18, 1952 • FIFTEEN CENTS

MAN ON THE MOON

Scientists Tell How We Can Land There In Our Lifetime

Astronauts land on the Moon in a realistic space journey recounted in *Collier's* magazine, October 18, 1952.

10

DISNEY TO THE RESCUE

The Moon orbits Earth at a distance of 240,000 miles, taking a little less than a month to make one complete circuit of our planet. There's no reason the Moon couldn't orbit closer, say at 100,000 miles, where it would complete an orbit in about a week. Or closer still, at 10,000 miles, where it would take less than half a day to go once around. Actually, you wouldn't want the Moon to get *that* close, since Earth's tidal force would cause it to disintegrate into a ring of debris, like Saturn's. However, smaller objects—say, a spy camera, a television relay, or a spaceship with a human aboard—can orbit the Earth as little as 100 miles overhead. Any lower, and the tiny amount of air at the edge of space slows an object, causing it to plunge to Earth's surface in a matter of hours or days.

Objects at this 100-mile distance circle Earth in 88 minutes at a blistering 17,500 miles per hour. Von Braun knew that if he could launch a rocket at least this high and get it going at least this fast, while it traveled horizontal to Earth's surface, then its motor could switch off and it would keep circling. The higher the orbit, the longer it would stay up, possibly for many years. It would be an Earth satellite, just as the Moon is. Moreover, it would be the first step on the long journey to the Moon.

These matters were on his mind one day in the early 1950s, when he excitedly told a colleague, "With the Redstone, we could do it!"

"Do what?"

"Launch a satellite, of course!"

In 1950, von Braun and his rocket team moved into a vacant Army facility called the Redstone Arsenal, near Huntsville, Alabama. It was their first real home in America, and they had a well-funded rocket project to go with it: an advanced version of the V-2 named, appropriately, Redstone. The Army's intended use for Redstone was to loft a nuclear warhead across several hundred miles. The missiles would be stationed in West Germany as a deterrent against a Soviet invasion of noncommunist Europe, which was a growing worry.

But von Braun had other plans. If instead of a heavy nuclear bomb, Redstone carried a payload of smaller rockets, stacked on top of one another like scoops of ice cream on a cone, then the rockets could be fired in stages. The first stage—the Redstone missile itself—would exhaust its propellant at a very high altitude and speed, and then drop away. Then the second stage would ignite, boosting the remaining stages even higher and faster. Then the second stage would drop off, the third stage would ignite, and so on. Von Braun figured that four stages would be enough to launch a payload weighing a few pounds into orbit.

Here's another way to think about it. Suppose you want to climb Mount Everest, the tallest mountain in the world. To make it to the top, you require a lot of supplies, such as food, water, cooking fuel, and bottled oxygen (to breathe because of the high altitude). In fact, you need more than you can possibly carry by yourself. So you hire three help-ers. After the first day's climb, the four of you make camp and have din-ner, consuming some of the supplies (you've already been breathing the oxygen). The next day, two of the helpers head back down the mountain, while you and the remaining helper resume the climb, fully replenished with supplies thanks to what the others left behind. The same thing happens at the next camp, leaving you by yourself on the third day. Thanks to the "boost" given by your helpers on stages 1 and 2 of your climb, you can make the final ascent to the top by yourself with all the supplies you need. The principle is much the same with

Two-stage
research rocket,
1951

multi-stage rockets. The bottom stages make it possible for the top stage to reach orbit.

The German rocketeer knew that in a few years' time, after Redstone was designed, built, and working properly, it would be a relatively simple matter to convert one into a satellite launcher. His big problem was to convince his bosses to let him do it.

◖

Collier's magazine was one of the most popular periodicals in America in the first half of the twentieth century, and its March 22, 1952, issue arrived like a trumpet blast from the future. The cover art showed a winged spaceship shedding a lower stage as it rocketed into Earth orbit. The headline proclaimed: "Man Will Conquer Space *Soon.* Top Scientists Tell How in 15 Startling Pages." Turning to the special section

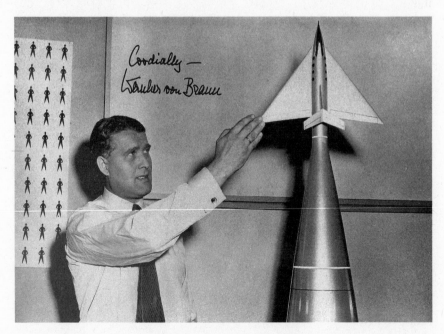

In an autographed photo, von Braun shows a model based on his *Collier's* spaceship.

inside, readers were told, "What you will read here is not science fiction. It is serious fact."

Von Braun was one of the contributors, and his article described in realistic detail the steps for leaving Earth, orbiting the planet, assembling a space station, constructing a deep-space exploration vehicle, and then heading out to the Moon. Just as in science fiction, he pictured humans as a necessary part of the mission. Automated and remote-control devices had advanced greatly since World War II, but most people, including von Braun, assumed that humans would be indispensable on any ambitious space project, since they would be needed to operate the complicated equipment.

A few months earlier, von Braun had met a member of the *Collier's* staff at a small conference on space medicine. Initially skeptical, the editor fell in love with the idea that rocket ships and Moon missions could really happen, and he asked von Braun to write an article about it, sticking to what could actually be done. Von Braun welcomed the opportunity and discovered he had a knack for communicating his enthusiasm to ordinary people. Plus, he had an excellent editor to correct his still-uneven English. The issue was so successful that *Collier's* continued the series with seven more parts, including "Man on the Moon: Scientists Tell How We Can Land There In Our Lifetime." Von Braun was the main contributor, and his enthusiastic readers ventured with him as far as Mars by the close of the series in 1954.

It's hard to recapture the tremendous impact of the *Collier's* articles. It would be almost as if in the early twenty-first century a group of scientists announced that time travel was really possible, and outlined plans for a time machine trip to ancient Egypt. The initial reaction would be that they had lost their minds! Space travel was in a similar boat in the early 1950s. However, the door had opened a crack. Newsreels, which were short news programs preceding the main feature in movie theaters, showed V-2s impressively taking off in New Mexico.

This paved the way in the public's mind for more ambitious achievements in rocketry. In terms of the time-travel analogy, it would be as if scientists already had a machine that could go back an hour or two—in which case, the idea of going back thousands of years might still seem far-fetched, but perhaps not impossible.

Opening the *Collier's* eight-part space series, in the spring of 1952, was an ominous warning from the editors: "The U.S. must immediately embark on a long-range development program to secure for the West 'space superiority.' If we do not, somebody else will. That somebody else would very probably be the Soviet Union."

●

Collier's made von Braun a national celebrity. He was interviewed on the brand-new medium of television, where he was so captivating, even with his strong German accent, that Walt Disney booked him for three episodes of his *Disneyland* series, broadcast on the ABC television network on Wednesday evenings.

Addressing Disney's audience of children and their parents, von Braun made spaceflight seem as if it were just around the corner. He spelled out the details of rocket stages, propellant weights, cutoff velocities, and other facts with such offhand assurance that he became the classic rocket scientist in the public mind.

"Disney's immediate achievement," wrote a reporter after the first episode aired in March 1955, "is the suggestion that space travel no longer is a wild dream; that it is so near that we can practically feel the Earth tremble under the rocket blast from Dr. von Braun's spaceship." The reporter made a prediction: "Half of the voting population of the U.S.A. has probably reached two impressive conclusions: 'It CAN be done!' and 'Let's get on with it!'"

Among the millions tuning in was U.S. president Dwight Eisenhower.

Walt Disney and
Wernher von
Braun, 1954

He was so intrigued that he called Disney and asked to borrow a copy of episode 1, "Man in Space," to show at the Pentagon. According to Disney's director, the president "made all the generals sit down and look at what was almost a childish primer on how we were going to go into space someday, because the brass had no idea of how this was all done."

A few weeks later, on July 29, 1955, Eisenhower's press secretary announced that the United States would launch an Earth satellite sometime during an upcoming international scientific effort, extending from the second half of 1957 through 1958. Of course, the administration had much more than a children's TV program to go on. Several technical reports recommending a satellite launch had been issued in the preceding years, including one by von Braun involving the Redstone. But whatever the inspiration, America was going into space.

America's Vanguard rocket explodes, December 6, 1957.

11

THE EMPIRE STRIKES BACK

President Eisenhower may have been enthusiastic about launching an Earth satellite, but his predecessor, former president Truman, called it "a lot of hooey!"—using one of his favorite expressions. Truman was no doubt thinking of the foolery about space he had read in *Collier's*.

But Eisenhower was an ex-military man and understood the tremendous promise that satellites had for reconnaissance, communications, and other defense needs. The president was also a strategic thinker, and he recognized the public relations value of a civilian, as opposed to a military, satellite project. The Soviets loved to paint the U.S. as a belligerent capitalist power trying to dominate the world. They would waste no time interpreting a satellite launch as a hostile act, particularly if the U.S. Army's Redstone Arsenal was involved.

Eisenhower agreed with his advisers that the first satellite should be launched on a research rocket, not a military missile, and that it should carry a scientific payload with instruments to measure the properties of outer space. The only problem was, there were no sufficiently powerful rockets available. The launch vehicle his advisers had in mind, called Vanguard, was still on the drawing board. And America's most experienced missile man, Wernher von Braun, had nothing to do with it.

●

The situation was driving von Braun crazy. He knew his Redstone could launch a satellite on short notice and do it at far less cost than Vanguard, which was a low-priority program being run by the scientific research arm of the U.S. Navy. By mid-1955, development work on the Redstone was nearly complete, and it was about to go into production. The following year, von Braun convinced the Army to let him produce an elongated, four-stage version of the Redstone to test missile components for even larger rockets. This souped-up Redstone was tantalizingly close to being able to launch a satellite, but the U.S. government wouldn't let von Braun do it. That was Vanguard's job.

In November 1956, when a scientist connected with Vanguard visited Huntsville, von Braun took him aside and told him that top secret information revealed that the Russians would soon be capable of their own satellite launch. So far, there had been no urgency in getting Vanguard or indeed any American satellite aloft. Von Braun felt like a gold miner in the Old West who was about to see his claim stolen—by the Russians. He implored the man to take a message back to the head of the Vanguard project: "I want you to tell him that if he wants to, he can paint 'Vanguard' right up the side of my rocket. He can do anything he wants to, but he is to use my rocket, not his, because my rocket will work and his won't."

The German rocketeer wasn't finished. He told the scientist he knew exactly what the project director would reply: that it made no difference who launched the first satellite, since what mattered was science. "Will you say to him," von Braun implored, "if that's what he really thinks, will he for Christ's sake get out of the way of the people who think it makes a hell of a lot of difference!"

Less than a year later, on October 4, 1957, von Braun was in his office in Huntsville when he got the bad news: The Soviets had done it. The world's first artificial satellite was now orbiting Earth. Bitterly disappointed but hardly surprised, he reacted with an expression he had picked up in Texas.

"I'll be damned!"

Von Braun was not shocked, but the rest of the U.S. plunged into a nervous breakdown. Russia's success with an atomic bomb in 1949 had been bad enough, but Russia had come in second in that contest. With their satellite, Sputnik (Russian for "traveling companion"), they had achieved a stunning first-place finish. It was all the worse because the entire world could hear and see Sputnik, which periodically passed over practically every inhabited region of the planet. Those below could tune into its radio signal—a steady *beep, beep, beep.* And, if its passage coincided with the time around dusk or dawn, they could see its dim starlike form moving steadily across the sky. More visible still was the giant rocket stage that had boosted Sputnik into orbit. It, too, was circling Earth—a menacing reminder of the Soviet Union's technological prowess.

Politicians wasted no time sounding the alarm. Senator Lyndon B. Johnson from Texas opened a series of hearings by declaring that Sputnik was "a disaster . . . comparable to Pearl Harbor." His fellow Democratic senator Henry M. Jackson of Washington called the Soviet achievement "a devastating blow to the prestige of the United States as the leader of the free world."

Eisenhower, a Republican, tried to play down the significance of the

The Detroit News

Suburban, City High School Grid Highlights

WEATHER Fair; not quite so cool. (Details on Page 2)

SATURDAY FINAL

SATURDAY, OCTOBER 5, 1957, VOL. 85, NO. 44 — THE HOME NEWSPAPER—ESTABLISHED 1873 — 22 PAGES — SEVEN CENTS

RED 'MOON' PASSES OVER DETROIT TODAY

Arkansas Peace Formula Given to Ike, Faubus

By ROBERT S. BALL
Staff Correspondent, The Detroit News

LITTLE ROCK, Ark., Oct. 5.—The White House has been given a new formula for ending the Little Rock school integration crisis, Rep. Harris (D-Ark.) disclosed to The Detroit News today.

Harris said he has submitted his proposal to Gov. Orval E. Faubus and to ranking members of President Eisenhower's staff, and that he has reason to believe Faubus will accept the formula. No word has yet been received from the White House.

Second Riot Is Smashed in Warsaw

WARSAW, Oct. 5.—Angry students and other Poles hurling police and militia in Warsaw's streets last night in the second violent anti-government demonstration in two days.

Speeds 18,000 MPH
560 Miles Over Earth

From AP and Reuters Dispatches

WASHINGTON, Oct. 5.—The earth's first man-made satellite launched by the Russians yesterday, is making at least six trips over the United States today, American scientists said today.

(The "moon" will pass over Detroit between 6 and 7 p.m., according to Detroit experts, but Moscow puts the time much later.)

AROUND THE WORLD IN 95 MINUTES—Global projection illustrates the orbit of the satellite launched by the Russians. Traveling in a north-south direction, it takes an hour and 35 minutes to encircle the earth.

Look at Satellite Here Is in Doubt

Fear Soviet Has Jump on U.S. in Moon Rocket

WASHINGTON, Oct. 5.—U.S. satellite chief John P. Hagen said today the rocket that blasted the Soviet satellite skyward may have been "close to" an intercontinental ballistic missile (ICBM).

Questions, Answers on Earth Satellite

Cool, Clear for Football

Saturday Specials

INDEX

'Ham' Records Satellite's Signals

By ROBERT POPA

Sputnik's launch on October 4, 1957, shocked America. (Soviets were known as "Reds" after the color of their flag.)

event, but Senators Johnson and Jackson had raised two issues that deeply worried the American public: that Sputnik gave the Russians a powerful military advantage; and that other countries would be tempted to ally themselves with Russia, which now appeared to be the most technologically advanced nation in the world.

A month after Sputnik was launched, the Soviets succeeded again, with Sputnik 2. Weighing more than half a ton, it was six times heavier than its predecessor and carried a passenger: a dog named Laika. The heavy payload implied that if the satellite launcher was used as a military missile, it could loft nuclear warheads partway around the planet to the United States—a range far in excess of Redstone's. And the living passenger (who sadly died after a few hours) was surely a sign that the Soviets were preparing to send human spacefarers. It was beginning to dawn on Americans that they were in a space race and losing badly.

Soviet leader Nikita Khrushchev, who had seized power after Stalin's death in 1953, enjoyed taunting his capitalist rivals. He would later boast that his intercontinental rockets were coming off the assembly line "like sausages" and that the Soviet system "has triumphed not only fully, but irreversibly."

All was not lost, for America was about to stake its own claim to space with Vanguard. True, Vanguard's satellite weighed just over three pounds, and even with the rocket's maximum payload of roughly twenty pounds, it would need more than fifty launches to put into orbit as much cargo as a single Sputnik rocket. But U.S. officials stressed that Vanguard was aiming for a higher orbit. If all went well, its tiny moon would circle the planet for centuries instead of a few months, as with the Sputniks.

Furthermore, Russia had launched its satellites in secret, but

Vanguard's preparations were taking place in the open—though not yet on television. When the rocket was ready for launch from Cape Canaveral, Florida, on December 6, 1957, a large audience from all walks of life watched from several miles away, searching for clues of the impending takeoff. Peering through binoculars, they saw the rocket servicing platform roll back, a red warning signal appear, and observation planes starting to circle overhead. Meanwhile, in the firing room, the nerve-racking countdown was progressing toward zero.

Reporting to his boss in Washington over a long-distance phone line, the deputy director of the project, J. Paul Walsh, described the climactic moment:

"Zero . . . fire . . . ignition . . ."

With a blast of flame, Vanguard lifted a few feet into the air. It hesitated, as if changing its mind, then fell back toward the pad.

"Explosion!"

According to one reporter, the unfolding cataclysm "bore a remarkable resemblance to atomic-bomb detonations . . . It took the shape of a fiery stem topped by an expanding mushroom-shaped cloud of flame." The newsman continued in a poetic vein: "This configuration lasted for only a few seconds, and was replaced by a pillar of greasy black smoke which gradually dissipated as it was carried inland by offshore breezes." All that was left were smoldering pieces of Vanguard—America's answer to Sputnik—littered across the launch site. Fortunately, no one was hurt.

Around this time, movie theaters across the world were screening a Russian short animated film called *After Sputnik—the Moon?* Looking like a mini-episode of Disney's TV series on space, it showed a rocket taking off from Earth, performing orbital maneuvers, and then heading out to the Moon, where it deposited a robotic explorer.

Produced for audiences in the Soviet Union, this charming educational cartoon was picked up for distribution by a British newsreel company, whose announcer asked pointedly at the end: "Propaganda? Wishful thinking? Sober prophecy? We'll have to wait and see!"

Von Braun (right) helps raise a full-scale model of the Explorer 1 satellite at a press conference on February 1, 1958. Scientists William Pickering (left) and James Van Allen (center) were responsible for the satellite, von Braun for the launch vehicle.

12

EXPLORER

A month before the Vanguard disaster, the U.S. Department of Defense gave von Braun the green light to prepare a modified Redstone for a satellite launch. It was an insurance policy against Vanguard's possible failure, a prospect that was starting to worry government officials, including the president. Von Braun insisted that sixty days was all he needed. His boss at the Redstone Arsenal, General John Medaris, asked for ninety days just to be sure. This gave the rocket team until early February 1958.

Von Braun's souped-up, four-stage version of Redstone was called Juno I. It had a longer rocket body than Redstone, which would allow it to hold more propellant. It also required a different type of fuel, since the alcohol and liquid oxygen combination for Redstone didn't produce quite enough thrust to loft a spacecraft into orbit. To avoid costly changes to the rocket, the new fuel had to work in the existing engine and plumbing, which posed a difficult challenge. A chemist named Mary Sherman Morgan formulated an entirely new compound called hydyne, which, when burned with liquid oxygen, gave exactly the right performance. Morgan was one of the many talented women who played a largely unsung role in the early space program. Coincidentally, the launch vehicle propelled by her new fuel was named after a woman, the Roman goddess Juno. It was a rare distinction in a pantheon of American rockets with masculine monikers like Jupiter, Thor, Atlas, and, eventually, the mighty Saturn.

In late January, von Braun's team completed preparations for a launch attempt at Cape Canaveral. Their target date was Wednesday, January 29, barely a week before their ninety-day deadline. A series of delays due to high winds in the upper atmosphere pushed the date to Friday, January 31, 1958—probably their last chance. After that, it was Vanguard's turn, since its problems from the December catastrophe had been fixed—although new ones kept cropping up. As commanding officer at the Redstone Arsenal, General Medaris was responsible for the Juno launch decision. Meanwhile, von Braun was in Washington, ready for a high-profile press conference in case of success.

Watching the unruly winds that day was the same Army forecaster who had helped ensure the success of D-Day in 1944. Don Yates, together with his British counterpart, James Stagg, had advised General Eisenhower that a break in bad weather would allow the invasion of Normandy to go ahead. Now Yates was aiding an operation in the Cold War. The battle of winds, his team reported, seemed to be turning in Juno's favor. Measurements showed that airflow in the stratosphere was down to about 100 miles per hour, which Medaris found tolerable. He gave the go-ahead. Juno was to take off at night, so the high-altitude firing of the upper stages could be observed against the black sky.

The countdown went like clockwork. At 10:48 p.m., the firing command was given. Juno slowly came to life. The strange, tublike device atop the missile, which held the upper stages, had already started spinning at 550 revolutions per minute. This would ensure the stability of the second, third, and fourth stages when they eventually fired. Inside the first stage, vents automatically closed, and the propellant tanks began to pressurize. A steam generator started up, which drove a turbine that powered pumps, forcing high-pressure hydyne and liquid oxygen into the combustion chamber. There, an igniter set them ablaze. This all took fourteen seconds.

Then a "tremendous jet burst from the base of the rocket, tearing an incandescent hole in the night," wrote a *New York Times* reporter. For one and three-quarter seconds the rocket stayed Earthbound, as it built up thrust and automatic checks showed that everything was in order.

Only then did the rocket begin to rise—with "incredible slowness," wrote the *Times* man. Few people had ever seen such a giant rocket take off, and reporters outdid each other describing the spectacle. One called it "a flame-footed monster." Another was overcome by the noise of the engine, calling it "terrific" and noting that "observers had to shout at each other, and even then could not make themselves understood." Upward Juno went with ever-increasing speed.

Waiting nervously in Washington, von Braun saw none of this, since there was no live television broadcast. Instead, he listened to a radio reporter in Florida, who was observing the event through binoculars. "Slow rise, faster, faster!" came the excited voice over the speaker. Soon the newsman could only see a bright light against the dark sky—and then he could see nothing. "It is out of sight, but it *must be successful!*" he proclaimed.

Juno takes off with Explorer 1 (the pencil-like top stage), January 31, 1958.

And then, seven minutes after launch, the vehicle was in orbit. Or so everyone hoped. General Medaris pestered the technician who was busy calculating the craft's trajectory by hand. Half an hour after launch the mathematician reported "with 95 percent confidence" that there was a 60 percent probability the satellite was in orbit.

"Don't give me that crap," growled the general. "Is it up?"

"It's up."

But definite word had to await reception of the satellite's radio signal in California, as the fourth stage with its radiation and micrometeorite detectors came around Earth near the end of its first orbit. The team waited anxiously. The predicted time for the signal came and went.

Eight long minutes passed before four stations on the West Coast picked up the transmission. "Those moments were the most exciting eight minutes of my life!" von Braun later recalled. The delay meant the payload—now officially a satellite called Explorer 1—had reached a slightly higher orbit than planned, circling Earth every 113 minutes.

Before the launch, von Braun was a TV celebrity with a funny accent. Now he was a national hero. And in his eyes, it was only the beginning. He had often talked about the next step. A few years earlier, at a late-night discussion with friends, he laid it out: "Once the first satellite is in orbit, others will follow. Also, there will be probes to the Moon." Then von Braun envisioned human flights on rockets, first on suborbital flights that would soar briefly into space and back, followed by Earth-orbiting missions. After that, a permanent space station made the most sense.

"We will then begin to make plans for a manned expedition to the Moon," he predicted. "Really, I couldn't think of a serious technical problem that would prevent us from traveling to the Moon."

Von Braun had said similar things countless times—before civic groups, national TV audiences, and congressional committees. The usual response was always, "Amazing! But will it really happen?"

After Explorer 1, people were starting to think it might.

A modern version of the Russian R-7 takes off on a pillar of fire.

With an arsenal of engines, the R-7 packs a powerful punch.

Carrying a Mercury capsule, the Redstone soars aloft on a single jet of exhaust.

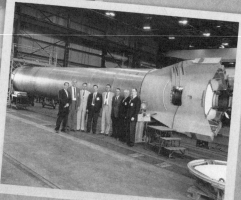

The back end of the Redstone—less than a tenth as powerful as the R-7

BRIEFING:
Russia's Rocket

These photos show the back ends of two rockets: Russia's R-7 and America's Redstone. The R-7, which launched Sputnik, produced more than ten times the thrust of Redstone, which was modified into Juno for launching Explorer 1. Why was Russia's rocket so much more powerful than America's?

The reason traces to a meeting Joseph Stalin had with his generals and rocket engineers in April 1947. World War II had been over for a year and a half, and the Cold War was just starting. Russian scientists were hard at work on an atomic bomb, but unlike America, Russia did not have a system of long-range bombers and international air bases for delivering nuclear weapons. As Stalin explained at the meeting, a nuclear-armed intercontinental missile was the perfect device for threatening the United States.

Referring to then president Harry Truman, who years before had run a clothing store, Stalin exhorted, "Do you realize the tremendous strategic importance of machines of this sort? They could be an effective straitjacket for that noisy shopkeeper Harry Truman. We must go ahead with it, comrades. The problem of the creation of transatlantic rockets is of extreme importance to us."

Soviet engineers went ahead and ultimately designed a rocket that could loft Russia's heavy nuclear bombs halfway around the planet. Meanwhile, America had developed lightweight nuclear weapons and relied on its bomber fleet, as well as on medium-range missiles such as Redstone that could be launched from allied countries near the Soviet Union.

When Russia's rocket, the R-7, was finally ready in 1957, it could easily put a satellite into space, which the new leader, Nikita Khrushchev, decided to do for propaganda purposes. America's most powerful rocket at that time, the Redstone, had to be "souped up" to launch a satellite weighing a fraction as much.

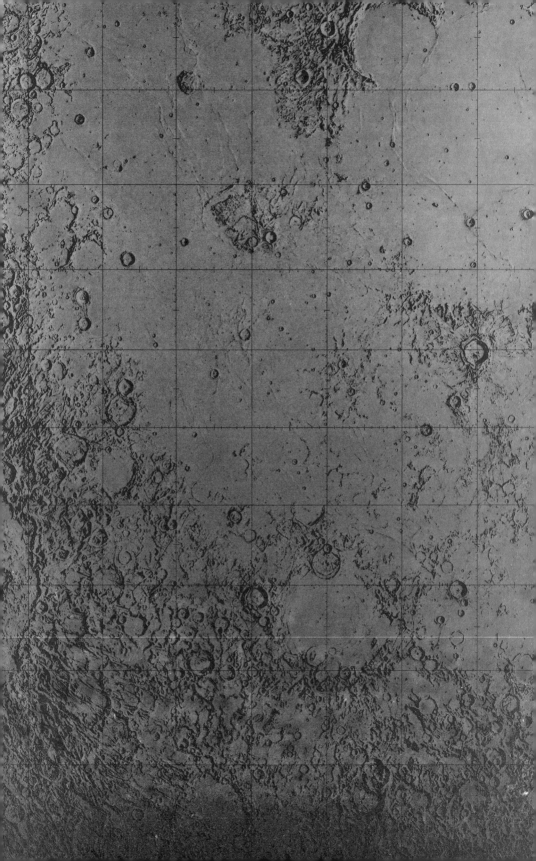

PART 3
SPACEMEN

Your plan will provide the most expensive funeral man has ever seen.

—George Kistiakowsky, presidential science adviser, reacting to the plan to launch a human into space, 1958

Map of the Moon's near side

An unconventional shape for a spacecraft—a blunt cone—is tested in a giant wind tunnel, 1959.

13

MAX MAKES HIS PITCH

Since boyhood, Max Faget had been a fan of science
fiction, so he was probably familiar with the skepticism about human
spaceflight shown by the editor of one of the most popular sci-fi magazines, *Amazing Stories*. This publication's motto was "Extravagant fiction today . . . cold fact tomorrow," but managing editor T. O'Conor
Sloane firmly believed that human trips into space would simply never
be "cold fact."

Sloane, a scientist himself, spelled out his objection in a 1929 editorial: "If voyages were to be made from the Earth to any of the planets, or
even to the Moon, the distances are so great that starting from rest as
the travelers would do, they would have to attain a high velocity in a
very short space of time . . . sufficient to kill the person."

In other words, no one could survive the rapid acceleration of
launch. Rising slowly wouldn't do, since it would take an unlimited
amount of propellant to fight Earth's gravity all the way into space. Any
space launch would have to happen relatively quickly. Sloane believed

that the force exerted on the human body would be like hitting the ground after falling "from the Washington Monument."

There were other concerns, too. According to experts who had pondered the unknown environment beyond Earth's atmosphere, spaceflight was dangerous in lots of ways. Some had expressed alarm about the potential effects of weightlessness. Once in Earth orbit or on a trajectory beyond Earth, the spacecraft would drift in a state of "free fall"—falling around Earth or on whatever path the ship was following. By contrast with the trip into space, during which travelers would weigh more than their normal weight due to the rocket's acceleration, once the motor was shut off they would appear to weigh nothing at all. If they let go of something, it would float as if suspended in water—and so would everything not bolted or strapped down. The feeling would be like falling without ever hitting the ground. Heinz Haber, a space medicine specialist who appeared on Disney's von Braun program, believed "it will take iron nerves waiting for the impact that never comes." Others speculated that the disorienting feeling of weightlessness would drive people crazy and render them helpless.

Furthermore, there is no air in space, which means a spaceship must have an elaborate life-support system. It's similar to the situation aboard a submarine, except a submarine can get air through a snorkel; in space, there is no such option. Plus, the temperature of an object in space can range from broiling hot in full sun to subarctic cold in shadow, putting extreme stress on the ship and its equipment. Another hazard is that harmful radiation from the Sun and interstellar space rains down on everything—as do meteors, which are mostly dust-grain size but traveling so fast that particles as large as a pebble can puncture the wall of a spacecraft. Earth's atmosphere and magnetic field shield anything close to the ground from most of these hazards, but there is no such protection in space.

Then there is the sheer danger of traveling by rocket, which is both the world's riskiest form of transportation and the only practical way to get into space. All rockets are prone to exploding catastrophically from minor malfunctions, such as a stuck valve or excessive vibration. Returning to Earth is also high-risk, since few materials can withstand the extreme temperature of reentry into the atmosphere, as air friction does the work of slowing a vehicle from 17,500 miles per hour or faster to a safe landing speed.

To an engineer like Faget, these were simply problems to solve. For example, Sloane's worry about high acceleration during takeoff was answered by tests showing that a human can survive acceleration equal to all but the fastest rocket launches—as long as the occupant is positioned like the driver of a car, facing in the direction of travel. In this position, the acceleration pushes the body evenly into a supporting seat. Experts also realized that during reentry, rapid deceleration (slowing down) can exert even more force on the body than the acceleration of launch. Since deceleration pushes the opposite direction from acceleration, a returning space traveler is safest if facing *backward* from the direction of travel, which, again, causes the body to be pushed against the seat.

As for the other problems, Faget subscribed to the optimistic outlook of automobile pioneer Henry Ford, who wrote in 1922: "I refuse to recognize that there are impossibilities. I cannot discover that anyone knows enough about anything on this Earth definitely to say what is and what is not possible."

In mid-October 1957, shortly after the launch of the first Sputnik, Faget attended a secret conference devoted to the future of high-speed flight. The meeting was sponsored by his organization, the NACA, which was involved in rocket plane research that in 1947 had pushed human flight beyond the speed of sound (known as Mach 1); past Mach 2 (twice the speed of sound) in 1953; and even to Mach 3 in 1956. Unfortunately, the Mach 3 flight killed the pilot when his aircraft spun out of control. Now Faget and his colleagues were discussing flights in excess of Mach 17, more than *five* times faster than anyone had ever flown. Eventually, the goal was Mach 25, the speed needed to go into orbit around Earth. No one was seriously considering manned flight in the neighborhood of Mach 35—the speed needed to reach the Moon.

A rocket-powered X-2 drops from its mother ship, 1955. The following year, the X-2 would crash during the first flight to achieve Mach 3.

Most of the engineers at the conference assumed that Mach 25 ships destined for Earth orbit would be upgrades of the rocket planes already built. That is, they would be winged vehicles that pilots could fly like an aircraft during the atmospheric portion of the trip, particularly during reentry. Even von Braun, the world's authority on spaceflight, thought this was the obvious approach—as shown by his proposed spaceship in the *Collier's* and Disney presentations, which had wings on its top stage.

But Faget had his doubts. Alarmed by the surprise launch of Sputnik, he realized that the race was now on to send a human into space. There wasn't time to perfect the sleek, aerodynamic shape of a space plane, heavily clad in an exotic metal alloy that could withstand the searing heat of reentry. Something simpler and cheaper was needed that could be built quickly.

Looking for answers, Faget turned to his NACA colleagues Harvey Allen and Alfred Eggers. They had discovered that the ideal shape for an object capable of surviving the meteor-like plunge through the atmosphere was less like a jet plane and more like a cannonball. The blunt profile would create a shock wave that dissipated heat far more readily than a streamlined shape. And just like a real cannonball, this space "capsule" (for it would be little more than a manned container) would follow a fixed trajectory. Instead of being piloted to a pinpoint landing like a plane, it would come hurtling back and use a parachute in the last few minutes to touch down in a large landing area. This was an unglamorous way for a space pilot to return to Earth, but Faget considered its simplicity a great advantage.

Faget soon discovered that a cone, not a cannonball, was the most effective shape for such a capsule. Sitting atop a rocket, with the cone's pointed end up, it would penetrate the atmosphere with minimal drag during launch. Then the blunt end would be aimed in the direction of travel on the way down, behaving just like a cannonball. The blunt end would be covered with a heat shield to absorb the heat of reentry and protect the occupant inside. On a simple shape like a cone, this vital component could be much smaller and lighter than the extensive shield required for a winged vehicle.

Also ideal, Faget realized, was the pilot's position. Inside the cabin,

$$Q = \left(\frac{C_p S}{C_D A}\right)\left(\frac{1}{2} m V_E^2\right)$$

$$\left(\frac{dH_s}{dt}\right)_{max} = 6.8 \times 10^{-6} \sqrt{\frac{\beta m \sin\theta_E}{3 e C_D \sigma A} V_E^3}$$

at

$$y = \frac{1}{\beta} \ln\left(\frac{3 C_D \rho_o A}{\beta m \sin\theta_E}\right)$$

Bow Shock

Harvey Allen explains his blunt-body concept, 1956. The idea inspired Max Faget to propose a blunt-cone shape for a spacecraft.

the pilot would recline against the blunt end of the ship. During takeoff, the force of acceleration would push him into the seat as the vehicle headed skyward. During reentry, the force of deceleration would also push him into the seat, as the capsule plunged backward toward Earth.

Working with two other colleagues, Faget fleshed out the details and formally presented this brainstorm when the high-speed-flight conference reconvened five months later. The reception was less than enthusiastic.

One member of the audience was Korean War veteran Neil Armstrong, who was now a rocket plane pilot for the NACA. Armstrong looked forward to flying space planes, yet he had just heard a very impassioned and convincing argument that this was not the best approach in the present competition with the Soviets. A trained engineer, Armstrong saw that Faget's analysis made sense, but like practically everyone else in the audience, he had a natural suspicion of unconventional ideas, and this was *very* unconventional. "Max made his pitch," Armstrong later recalled, noting that the zealous engineer appeared "frustrated that everyone could not immediately seem to see the logic of his proposal."

Undaunted, Faget was determined to move ahead. America had lost round one of the space race to Sputnik. He did not want to lose round two.

Neil Armstrong after a flight in the X-15. In 1962 he flew the rocket plane to over Mach 5. For true spaceflight, Mach 25 or faster is needed.

Zazel, the first human cannonball performer, 1887

14

"LET'S GET ON WITH IT"

Hugh Dryden, head of the NACA, was getting testy under questioning by a congressional committee. A month after Faget's presentation at the high-speed conference, Dryden was being pressed to comment on an Army proposal very much like Faget's: loft a human into space inside a capsule atop a Redstone rocket. It was von Braun's idea, and the German rocketeer was pushing it vigorously.

Dryden wanted to keep human spaceflight out of the hands of the military. Like practically all aeronautical engineers, he thought of space travel in terms of winged vehicles, and this was the NACA's turf. He bluntly told the legislators: "Tossing a man up in the air and letting him come back . . . is about the same technical value as the circus stunt of shooting a young lady from a cannon." He had surely heard of Faget's proposal, but he apparently didn't think much of it. He also had a point, since launching a man into space on a rocket just so you could say you'd done it first was beneath the dignity of a serious engineer. To Dryden, it was a trick designed to attract attention.

Meanwhile, thanks to the national panic over Sputnik, the NACA was being transformed right under Dryden's feet. A few months after his testimony, the NACA was reorganized as a new government agency called NASA: the National Aeronautics and Space Administration. NASA kept all of the previous agency's functions in flight research with the added responsibility for space, especially human spaceflight. The new agency also inherited government research centers such as the Jet Propulsion Laboratory, which had created the upper stages of Explorer 1. Within a year, von Braun and his Army rocket team were also transferred to NASA, much to von Braun's dismay, since he had little hope for visionary leadership from the NACA crowd, especially after the harsh words from the man who was now his boss, Dryden. Still, von Braun's new job was to create rockets larger than any ever built, and the new agency's budget would grow sharply, too. The old hands quipped that NA¢A had become NA$A.

Dryden was the logical person to head NASA. However, his "circus stunt" comment had rubbed Congress the wrong way, since a stunt was exactly what Congress and the American people wanted. They wanted to upstage the Russians. They wanted to lead the world in the space race. Dryden was demoted to the number two spot, and T. Keith Glennan, president of Case Institute of Technology, a prestigious engineering school in Cleveland, Ohio, became NASA's first administrator.

Meanwhile, von Braun's Army proposal was practically dead, and Faget's plan was gaining momentum. As stripped down as it was, the plan was more versatile than von Braun's, which was little more than a passenger pod for a test subject, who would be hurled briefly into space before plunging back to Earth—much like a V-2 during the war except with a parachute. Von Braun's defense was that his program was designed to get a human into space at the earliest possible moment—nothing more.

Faget also envisioned such suborbital flights, but only at the start of his program, which was much more ambitious. After the conical capsule proved itself and humans showed they could endure short bouts of weightlessness, he was confident that orbital flights would follow. A rocket like the Redstone would be sufficient for the suborbital tests. But orbital missions would need a more powerful launch vehicle, and the earliest one available would be an intercontinental missile called Atlas being developed for the Air Force. Von Braun had nothing to do with the Atlas, and this may have been the reason he was unenthusiastic about Faget's plan. But the deeper reason was that both men were brilliant and stubborn. They each came up with dazzling proposals that would work and then pushed them relentlessly.

For all its simplicity, Faget's capsule was a true spaceship. It could keep its occupant alive for many hours, point itself in any direction, perform a variety of missions, and exit its hostile environment at a moment's notice. Faget even included a periscope to allow observations outside the ship. In many ways, it was like a submarine.

NASA opened for business on October 1, 1958. The following week, Faget's boss, Bob Gilruth, presented Faget's man-in-space proposal to Glennan, who had little taste for stunts or crash programs. On the other hand, the country wanted dramatic action. After hearing the pitch, the new NASA chief wasted no time: "All right. Let's get on with it."

Surprised by the suddenness of the decision, Gilruth tried to start a discussion about how to proceed. Glennan cut him short: "Just get on with it!"

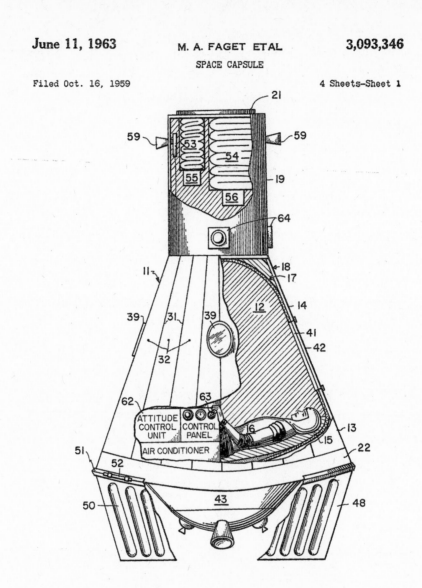

Max Faget's patent for the Mercury spacecraft, approved in 1963

Just like that, America was committed to putting a man in space. The order had all the informality of the command that had set D-Day in motion in 1944. General Eisenhower had listened to the weather report forecasting a break in the storms that were battering the landing areas.

After thinking it over, he said simply, "Okay, we'll go." Now, fourteen years later, President Eisenhower's appointee was being just as terse and decisive. He was setting in motion an invasion that would eventually spread to worlds beyond our own—although no one knew that yet.

Heeding Glennan's order, Gilruth sat down with Faget and two other top engineers, and they started putting together a team. Drawing mostly on talent at the Langley Research Center in Virginia, where Gilruth's PARD rocket division was headquartered, they picked a total of forty-five engineers and other staff, including themselves. The outfit would be called the Space Task Group.

Gilruth also began searching for brave souls to ride the capsule into space. These men would be called *astronauts*, based on the ancient Greek words for "star sailor." The volunteers were to be drawn from jet pilots, balloonists, submarine officers, Arctic explorers, parachute jumpers, combat veterans, and others with a taste for adventure. But when President Eisenhower heard the qualifications, he put his foot down. Only military test pilots would be considered, he ordered. He may have been adamant that manned spaceflight would be a civilian program, but as a practical matter, military test pilots were highly skilled, already on the government payroll, and accustomed to following orders.

"It was one of the best decisions he ever made," Gilruth later admitted. "It ruled out the matadors, mountain climbers, scuba divers, and race drivers, and gave us stable guys who had already been screened for security."

The pieces of America's man-in-space program were falling into place. One loose end was a name for the project. NASA manager Abe Silverstein had a passion for mythology and suggested Project Mercury.

Max Faget wears a pressure suit to test the tight fit inside the Mercury capsule (at left).

It stuck. Mercury was the speedy messenger god with winged sandals. It fit because the astronauts would travel faster than any humans before them. However, if you looked deeper into Roman mythology, you might have noticed that Mercury had another role: he was the god who conveyed the dead to the underworld. That, too, was a distinct possibility with Project Mercury.

The Mercury astronauts in their military flight suits. Left to right: Carpenter, Cooper, Glenn, Grissom, Schirra, Shepard, and Slayton.

15

THE ORIGINAL SEVEN

Driving around Edwards Air Force Base in the California desert, Deke Slayton passed through entire neighborhoods where the streets were named, one after another, for dead test pilots. Even the base itself was named after Captain Glen Edwards, an acclaimed Air Force test pilot who died on the job. It was easy to imagine a new subdivision where Deke himself would be similarly memorialized should his luck run out.

For this reason, Slayton didn't think he was risking much by applying for the job of astronaut. The newsreels were full of images of missiles blowing up, including the Atlas rocket that he expected to fly into orbit if he was accepted. But how dangerous could it be compared to the Air Force, where a few years earlier sixty-two fighter pilots had died during thirty-six weeks of training? And test pilots lived far riskier lives than fighter pilots! Slayton's chances had probably been better flying bombing missions during the war than flying unproven planes at Edwards.

NASA added a few extra criteria to Eisenhower's test pilot rule. Age, height, weight, and other factors narrowed the pool down to 110 qualified candidates, including Slayton. Gilruth expected only a fraction of that number to be interested. He was surprised and pleased when the vast majority were eager to compete for the half dozen or so slots.

Only men would be considered. At the time, there were no female military test pilots, although some women had thousands of hours of flight time and met the medical requirements for the astronaut corps. Since they were generally shorter and lighter than males, females would have made excellent space travelers in the cramped, weight-restricted Mercury capsule. However, it was not to be. In those days, only men were trained for the extreme dangers that faced astronauts riding rockets. If nothing else, the likelihood of a fatal accident kept women out of the program. NASA administrator Glennan had said that "one tragedy would not stop this project," implying that an astronaut might very well die. That was entirely acceptable if it was a man, but the death of a female astronaut would have been a public relations catastrophe in the family-oriented climate of the 1950s, with stay-at-home mothers and working fathers.

The seven pilots who were finally chosen had remarkable backgrounds. The best known was Marine Lieutenant Colonel John H. Glenn Jr., who two years earlier had made the first supersonic transcontinental flight, jetting from California to New York at bullet-like speed. He had also flown 149 combat missions in World War II and Korea. And of course, like the others, he had risen to the pinnacle of the flying profession as a test pilot.

The others had less publicized records. Navy Lieutenant Commander Alan B. Shepard had served in World War II aboard a destroyer and then entered flight training to become one of the Navy's top aircraft carrier pilots. Air Force Captain Virgil "Gus" Grissom was a veteran of a hundred combat missions in Korea. Navy Lieutenant Commander Walter M. Schirra Jr. was another Korean War veteran, with ninety missions. Air Force Captain L. Gordon Cooper Jr. had served with a peacetime fighter-bomber squadron in Germany, practicing for a possible Soviet invasion. Navy Lieutenant M. Scott Carpenter had flown surveillance missions along the Russian and Chinese coasts during the Korean conflict.

And then there was Air Force Captain Deke Slayton, who was uncharacteristically talkative after his selection was announced. "We have gone about as far as we can on this globe," he reflected. "We have to go somewhere, and space is all that is left." Then he made a confession: "I would give my left arm to be the first man in space."

In later years, as the astronaut corps grew, these pioneers would be known as the Original Seven. But when they were notified of their selection in April 1959, they envisioned a short-term project lasting three years at most, after which they would return to their flying careers, while NASA moved on to other things. NASA originally suggested that they resign from the military and become civilians, but this proposal met fierce resistance. "Given the state of NASA and Project Mercury," recollected Slayton, "you'd have had to be an idiot to give up your Air Force or Navy career to join them."

Early in the development of Mercury, Gilruth asked Faget what would happen if the launch vehicle blew up.

"I don't know," Faget replied.

"Well, you'd better figure something out!"

Mercury might never have gotten off the ground had Faget not come up with an escape rocket, attached by a tower to the top of the space-craft, designed to pull the capsule away from an exploding rocket. This had to be done very quickly. A normal Mercury launch would expose an astronaut to a force of six to eight g's (one g equals the pull of gravity at Earth's surface). At eight g's, someone weighing 150 pounds would be pushed back with a force of 1,200 pounds, making it difficult to breathe and impossible to lift an arm. In an emergency, Faget's escape rocket would blast the capsule to safety at up to twenty g's. At that accelera-tion, an astronaut weighing 150 pounds would briefly weigh 3,000 pounds and could suffer internal injuries. The getaway would be brutal but worth it, as a conflagration engulfed the launch vehicle and every-thing around it.

Escape was less of a concern with the Redstone, which would be used for the initial suborbital flights. Von Braun and his team had de-signed the booster to be rugged and reliable. Atlas was a different story. Created for the Air Force to loft nuclear warheads a third of the way around the planet, it was the only available rocket that could get the Mercury capsule into orbit. Pushing the technical state of the art, Atlas was essentially a stainless-steel balloon packed with propellant and at-tached to three rocket engines. The structure was thinner than a dime and had to be pressurized to keep from collapsing under its own weight. Its innovative design was very much like an egg: The eggshell was the rocket body; the yolk and white were the fuel and oxidizer tanks, sepa-rated by a thin bulkhead. The whole structure was amazingly light and strong, if difficult to build.

On May 18, 1959, a little over a month after being introduced to the public, the seven Mercury astronauts were attending an Atlas test flight at Cape Canaveral. Wearing hard hats and standing a quarter of a mile away, the future space travelers watched with great interest as the count reached zero and the engines of the mighty missile ignited, built up thrust, and then the vehicle lifted off the pad and rose into the sky. It was a perfect launch—for about a minute. Then the vehicle tipped to one side and started to veer out of control. The range safety officer hit the destruct switch, producing a gigantic fireball, "like a hydrogen bomb going off right over our heads," recalled astronaut Glenn. Even though the fiery debris cloud was on a path taking it over the Atlantic, the astronauts instinctively ducked.

Al Shepard broke the stunned silence: "I sure hope they fix that."

Being test pilots and trained engineers, the astronauts expected to have a role helping to improve the Mercury hardware and develop the mission procedures. Therefore, they divided Project Mercury into areas where their input could be useful. Deke Slayton got the most unnerving assignment of all: Atlas. He could do nothing about the rocket's habit of exploding, so he focused on the problem of joining a complicated spacecraft to a noisy, shaking, temperamental missile. Looking back on 1960, his first full year as an astronaut, he felt like he had experienced the Fourth of July run amok: "I spent most of my time that year at the Cape, watching Atlases take off and blow up."

Atlas wasn't the only rocket that was blowing up. This is a Juno II going out of control in 1959.

A Russian manned rocket leaves for space.

16

THE VICE PRESIDENT FINDS
A SPACE CHIEF

Fall 1960 featured a hotly contested presidential election, pitting Eisenhower's vice president, Richard Nixon, against Massachusetts senator and war hero John F. Kennedy. The Cold War was on everyone's mind, and one of the biggest campaign issues was the supposed "missile gap" between the United States and Soviet Union. Given the Soviets' intense secrecy, it was difficult to say how many nuclear-armed missiles they had. Kennedy cited an informed estimate that gave the Russians a roughly ten-to-one advantage. Eisenhower knew this was incorrect but couldn't say so publicly, since his information was based on intelligence sources that he didn't want to reveal.

Whatever the number of Russia's missiles, it was certain they were far more powerful than America's, as shown by the hefty satellites that these launch vehicles could put into orbit. The Soviets' very obvious superiority in space troubled many Americans, as did the spread of communism to places like Cuba, added to domestic problems such as the sluggish economy and the bitter struggle to end racial segregation and discrimination in the American South. Partly due to these anxieties, combined with the desire for change, Kennedy and his vice-presidential running mate, Lyndon Johnson, won in a very close race.

After he took office, Kennedy was much more focused on military and foreign affairs than on space policy, which he left to Johnson. Possibly because he was a Texan steeped in stories of the taming of the frontier, the vice president was genuinely enthusiastic about conquering space. As a senator responding to Sputnik in early 1958, he had painted a dire picture of America's fate if it did not answer Russia's space challenge. "Control of space means control of the world," he proclaimed. "From space, the masters of infinity would have the power to control the Earth's weather, to cause drought and flood, to change the tides and raise the levels of the sea, to divert the Gulf Stream and change temperate climates to frigid."

Johnson exaggerated, as he often did, but his commitment to the cause made him the obvious person to find a successor to NASA administrator Glennan when the Kennedy administration took power in January 1961. Surprisingly, no one of sufficient stature wanted the job. The problem appeared to be that no one knew where America's space program was going and whether NASA, a brand-new organization, would survive to lead it.

●

"I don't think I'm the right person for this job," Jim Webb said to Hugh Dryden as they waited for the vice president. "I'm not an engineer and I've never seen a rocket fly."

Dryden was still the deputy administrator of NASA and was there at Johnson's request to help persuade Webb to accept the position that so many others had turned down.

"I agree with that. I don't think you are either," Dryden confided.

"Well, can you tell the vice president?"

"I don't believe that he wants to listen to me on that."

Webb had been summoned, in part, because of his connection to Robert Kerr, the Democratic senator from Oklahoma who had inherited Johnson's chairmanship of the Senate space committee. Since leaving government service in 1953, Webb had run a company for Kerr's oil empire, and the senator thought very highly of him, noting that Webb had "the greatest . . . capacity for sustained mental and physical effort of anyone I know."

Just then, another of Webb's acquaintances entered the room. Frank Pace had been Webb's successor at the Bureau of the Budget and was now working for the company making the Atlas missile.

Webb explained his predicament. Pace agreed that Webb was probably not the right man and promised to try to talk Johnson out of it when the vice president arrived, which he soon did. As Webb and Dryden waited in an adjoining room, Pace had a few words with Johnson and was immediately thrown out of his office. Webb now had to face the music. Johnson tried his usual arm-twisting, but Webb insisted on a meeting with President Kennedy. While this was being arranged, he called a friend who was handling the presidential transition.

"Can you get me out of this?" he implored.

"Ha-ha, I've been recommending you! I am not going to get you out of it."

At the White House that afternoon, the president told Webb the reason that he, and not a rocket scientist or space expert, was the right person to head NASA: "You've had experience in the Bureau of the Budget and the State Department," Kennedy said. "This is a program that involves not science and technology so much as large issues of national and international policy, and that's why I want you to do it."

Webb felt that he couldn't refuse a direct request from the president of the United States. On February 14, 1961, this soft-spoken North Carolinian was sworn in as NASA's second administrator.

President John F. Kennedy (left) greets his new NASA administrator, Jim Webb, 1961.

One of Webb's first problems was what to do about Project Mercury. Kennedy's space advisory committee during the transition had issued a critical report, calling NASA's human spaceflight effort "marginal."

"We mean it's a sick program," a committee member explained to the press. "It was marginal from the beginning, and we should take a hard look at it before we decide to continue it."

With visions of Vanguard exploding on the launchpad and Atlases blowing up in midair, the committee was concerned that "a failure in our first attempt to place a man into orbit, resulting in the death of an astronaut, would create a situation of serious national embarrassment." An even more gruesome spectacle would unfold if an astronaut went

crazy in weightlessness, got stuck in orbit and asphyxiated, or was in-
cinerated due to a malfunction on the way down.

Just four days after taking charge of NASA, Webb had to decide
whether to go ahead with the launch of an unmanned Mercury capsule
atop an Atlas. An identical test the previous July had crashed into
the Atlantic. Fretting about the reputation of their Atlas missile and
fearing that it might be portrayed as a laughable threat by the Soviets,
the Air Force asked Webb to postpone the flight until a sturdier version
of the rocket could be substituted. Webb checked with his technical
staff, who assured him that the previous problems had been fixed. So
he gave the okay. Using a Marine Corps metaphor, he put it this way:
"My philosophy has always been . . . if you've got to take that island,
you'd better get in there and take it."

On February 21, 1961, the Mercury-Atlas flew flawlessly.

Webb was not only pressing ahead with Mercury, he was also laying
plans for the future. Max Faget had already sketched out a more advanced spacecraft—a three-person ship called Apollo (named by NASA
manager and mythology enthusiast Abe Silverstein, who had also chris-
tened Mercury). Faget decided that three astronauts made the most
sense for long missions, since they could rotate on watches in the same
way that a naval crew does.

Like Mercury, Apollo was a god with celestial connotations, notably
for driving the chariot of the Sun across the sky each day. Of course, no
one was thinking of sending astronauts to the Sun, but the Apollo spacecraft would be well suited for a variety of missions, such as ferrying
astronauts to a space station in Earth orbit or carrying them on a
voyage around the Moon. Hardly anyone was advocating *landing*

astronauts on the Moon, but Apollo could be adapted to do that, too. Apollo would require a much larger rocket than Atlas, and von Braun's team was currently working on a powerful family of launch vehicles called Saturn that would serve this purpose.

The president made no commitments, but he gave Webb permission to continue looking at advanced missions. Next, Webb had to convince Kennedy's advisers that it was finally time to launch an astronaut aboard Mercury. After all, the first few manned flights would be up-and-down suborbital trips on von Braun's Redstone, not the far riskier orbital journeys on an Atlas. But the advisers counseled delay. They wanted to be absolutely sure of the astronaut's safety, particularly during weightlessness, and insisted on additional test flights with animals. Events soon made them regret this demand.

●

On April 12, 1961, long-range radar operated by the United States near the Soviet Union's southern border detected a satellite launch. Twenty minutes later, as the satellite passed over a listening post in Alaska's Aleutian Islands, radio operators heard a human voice, saying in Russian: "I feel splendid, very well, very well, very well. Give me some results on the flight!"

Thirty-five minutes after that, as the vehicle approached the tip of South America, Radio Moscow in the Soviet capital announced: "The world's first satellite-ship, *Vostok*, with a human on board was launched into an orbit about the Earth from the Soviet Union. The pilot-cosmonaut of the spaceship satellite *Vostok* is a citizen of the Union of Soviet Socialist Republics, Major of Aviation Yuri Alekseyevich Gagarin."

Major Gagarin landed in Soviet territory after one orbit. He reported that he was in excellent health and took a congratulatory call from his nation's leader. During their conversation, Premier Khrushchev couldn't resist taunting America: "Let the capitalist countries catch up with our country!"

Round two of the space race had just gone to the Soviets.

A Soviet cosmonaut raises a hammer and sickle, the symbol of the Soviet Union. The text reads: "Long live the Soviet people—the space pioneers!"

President Kennedy, his wife, Jackie, and advisers nervously watch the televised launch of astronaut Alan Shepard. Vice President Lyndon Johnson is at far left.

17

"LIGHT THIS CANDLE"

On April 30, 1961, President Kennedy's first hundred days were up, and they had been a disaster. Americans liked the youth and vigor he brought to the presidency but were dismayed by his handling of the Cold War.

During the campaign, Kennedy had promised to do something about the recently established communist government in Cuba, headed by Fidel Castro. "Those who say they will stand up to Mr. Khrushchev have demonstrated no ability to stand up to Mr. Castro," he said, referring to his opponent in the election, Vice President Nixon.

In a debate with Nixon, Kennedy hammered the point home: "The communists have been moving with vigor—Laos, Africa, Cuba—all around the world today they're on the move. I think we have to revitalize our society. I think we have to demonstrate to the people of the world that we're determined in this free country of ours to be first—not first if, and not first but, and not first when—but first."

Now that he was president, Kennedy's promises were turning to dust. After Major Gagarin orbited the planet, the Soviet Union's claim to be first in technology suddenly looked pretty strong. Then five days after the flight, Kennedy gave the go-ahead for an invasion that was supposed to redeem his Cuba pledge. A U.S.-sponsored force of Cuban rebels landed on the island to retake it from Castro. But the invaders were quickly defeated, giving Kennedy another humiliating setback. Meanwhile in Southeast Asia, communists were gaining ground in Laos, and Kennedy felt forced to negotiate a hasty settlement with the rebels' Soviet backers.

Amid these disasters, who could blame Kennedy if he was nervous about Project Mercury? If his decision to proceed ended up killing an astronaut, his presidency might as well be over.

Ever since the Mercury astronauts were announced, the press had been speculating about who would make the first flight. Would they draw straws? Would it be the most qualified? Would Kennedy make the choice? The press favored John Glenn because of his easy charm, which was very much like the president's. But Bob Gilruth, head of the Space Task Group, chose Al Shepard due to his superb mastery of the Mercury spacecraft. Glenn would be Shepard's backup, and Slayton would be the primary capcom—the capsule communicator who would keep in radio contact with Shepard during the mission. Shepard picked *Freedom 7* for the name of his Mercury capsule in tribute to Kennedy's trademark celebration of freedom. The number seven was used because the capsule was the seventh in the test sequence, but in the public mind it stood for the solidarity of the seven Mercury astronauts.

After a series of delays, Shepard's liftoff was scheduled for early May. Even though this flight was suborbital and would last only fifteen minutes (Gagarin's lasted 108 minutes), the NASA press office was prepared for every contingency. If Shepard died during launch, they had an announcement ready: "Rescue units on the scene report that Astronaut

Shepard has perished today in the service of his country." Similar statements were on file to cover mishaps at every other stage of the mission.

As launch day approached, Kennedy fretted about whether to go ahead. The reality of putting a human atop a rocket was starting to sink in, and it struck him the way it did most Americans: it was crazy. Some of his advisers thought so, too, and tried to get him to postpone the flight at least until the furor over Cuba and Laos died down. But Webb assured the president that every precaution had been taken. Another space official was even more optimistic: "Why postpone a success?" he asked.

Still anxious, Kennedy sought additional assurance and had his press secretary call Cape Canaveral to discuss the details of the Mercury escape system. Clearly, visions of exploding rockets haunted him.

●

On launch day, May 5, 1961, Shepard was almost as cool as the liquid oxygen in the Redstone's oxidizer tank. When the count was stopped with barely two minutes to go, he had been sitting in the capsule for over four hours, waiting through delay after delay as one problem after another cropped up. This was the last straw.

"All right, I'm cooler than you are," he said testily. "Why don't you fix your little problem . . . and *light this candle*."

Shortly after, the count resumed.

It reached zero.

"Liftoff!" called Slayton over the radio link.

Only Gagarin had ridden a missile into space before, and he had said little publicly about the experience, due to the Soviet government's preference for secrecy. So Shepard didn't know exactly what to expect. To a Navy pilot used to being catapulted off aircraft carriers, liftoff was surprisingly smooth—"a subtle, gentle, gradual rise off the ground," he later recalled. It was not as noisy as he expected either. One oddity was that the cockpit altimeter showed rapidly increasing altitude—40, 50, 60 thousand feet—something every fighter pilot was familiar with. But the craft never leveled off, as an aircraft would have. It just kept climbing and climbing. This was a brand-new experience for the pilot.

About two minutes into the flight, at 70,000 feet, the Redstone broke the sound barrier. Shepard was experiencing 3 g's at this point. Half a minute later, he was passing through 100,000 feet—almost 20 miles up—and feeling 5 g's. He was traveling close to 5,000 miles per hour.

The Redstone exhausted its propellant and the engine cut off. Acceleration dropped to zero and Shepard was weightless. *Freedom 7* separated from the Redstone, turned its blunt end forward, and continued to soar higher against the pull of Earth's gravity, impelled by the tremendous boost given by the rocket. Zero g would last about five minutes, as the spacecraft arced to an altitude of 115 miles—well into space—and then began its plunge back to Earth. Shepard found weightlessness pleasant. As he dropped through 50 miles, the thin atmosphere began slowing the ship and he felt the renewed tug of g-forces. These quickly built to almost twelve times the pull of Earth's gravity, which was the peak g-force during his flight. The heat shield began to glow and flake off, dissipating the energy of reentry. Two minutes later, the main parachute deployed, and *Freedom 7* drifted slowly to the ocean, landing almost 300 miles east of Cape Canaveral, just a quarter of an hour after launch.

Except for one malfunctioning light in the cockpit, the mission had gone off without a hitch. Nervously, President Kennedy watched the television coverage from the White House. Relieved at the happy ending, he called to congratulate Shepard when he was aboard the recovery ship.

In a sense, Shepard's mission had been little more than the stunt described so honestly by Hugh Dryden—not unlike "shooting a young lady from a cannon." But the soaring flight of *Freedom 7* had also been a test in preparation for something far bigger. It had proved the two most crucial operations of any space mission, launch and reentry, which are comparable to takeoff and landing in an airplane. What would come in between—the actual mission—would have to wait.

Alan Shepard lifts off, on his way to becoming the first American in space, May 5, 1961.

Photomosaic of the Moon, assembled from telescopic images, 1966

18

GO TO THE MOON

For all its success, Shepard's flight was frustratingly like Explorer 1. Both missions paled in comparison to the Russian triumphs. Shepard had shot up like a V-2 and then come back down a few hundred miles away, while Gagarin had traveled completely around the globe. As for Explorer 1—it had been a third-place finisher that weighed only a fraction as much as the two Sputniks that preceded it. America had been badly beaten in the first two rounds of the space race.

Still, Al Shepard was a national hero, and his success perhaps foretold a change in the president's fortunes. At least that was the way *Time*, the nation's most influential news magazine, saw it: "The blaze of Alan Shepard's Redstone rocket was a bright light on a dark, Cold War horizon," the magazine wrote. "It was a first step in John Kennedy's fight back from the personal and political Pearl Harbors of Cuba and Laos."

Kennedy was determined to use this piece of good news to reset the country's priorities. A week after Gagarin's flight, he had asked Vice President Johnson to confer with Webb and other space advisers and answer this question: "Is there any . . . space program which promises dramatic results in which we could win?" Now, the jaw-dropping answer came back: it was time to go to the Moon.

The Moon may seem like an easy goal to reach. It's up in the sky where you can see it, and even a small telescope shows details of its rugged landscape, making it appear very close. But the Moon is extraordinarily distant: 240,000 miles away, equal to thirty times Earth's diameter or more than 2,000 times farther than the high point reached during Shepard's flight. The rocket and propellant needed to get astronauts to the Moon and back would have to be at least a hundred times more massive than the Mercury-Redstone. If observers of the Explorer 1 launch, which used a modified Redstone, were awed by the "tremendous jet burst from the base of the rocket" and the terrific "thunder of the rocket engine," then imagine the scene at the launch of a Moon rocket!

Also imagine how difficult it is to go to the Moon, which is a moving target (traveling over 2,000 miles per hour), land safely amid the countless craters, step outside in the complete vacuum to explore an unknown and potentially dangerous world, and finally find your way back to Earth, reentering the atmosphere at more than five times the top speed of *Freedom 7*. Nothing remotely like this had ever been done. However, Webb's advisers assured him and the president that it was possible—expensive, yes, but possible. Webb made doubly sure, since he was a cautious man. "When you decide you're going to do something and put the prestige of the United States government behind it," he said later, "you'd better doggone well be able to do it."

Kennedy was appalled by the price tag, which some experts put at 40 billion dollars. That was four times the combined cost of the B-29 and atomic bomb projects, which were the most expensive weapons systems ever built. He desperately wanted America to take the lead in space, but he also wondered if a less expensive goal than landing a man on the Moon would do. His advisers said no. The Soviets' current advantage in large rockets meant they could accomplish many interim goals in space, but they did not yet have a rocket that could send humans all the way to the Moon and back. America stood a decent chance of beating them to it.

A Moon voyage was a dream as old as humanity. It was also a dream that America could make happen. To anyone who had lived through World War II, daunting tasks were routine. In the weeks following Japan's attack on Pearl Harbor, the Japanese had seized control of the

President Kennedy tells Congress that America will go to the Moon, May 25, 1961. He is the tiny figure at the podium.

western Pacific. At the same time, Nazi forces occupied most of continental Europe. But with the United States in the war, even with its early setbacks, there was never any doubt that the Allies would win, and that America's industries, organizational genius, and fighting spirit would play a decisive role.

America's goal—
240,000 miles
distant

On May 25, 1961, three weeks after the flight of *Freedom 7*, Kennedy stood before a joint session of Congress to reenergize his presidency. His speech was full of new initiatives—in economic, domestic, and foreign policy, and in military affairs—all designed to combat Soviet power. Half an hour into the address, as senators and representatives may have been nodding off, he woke them up with a startling challenge: "I believe that this nation should commit itself to achieving the goal, before this decade is out, of landing a man on the Moon and returning him safely to the Earth."

Kennedy's speechwriter was in the hall and noted the audience's stunned reaction. The president continued: "No single space project in this period will be more impressive to mankind, or more important for the long-range exploration of space; and none will be so difficult or expensive to accomplish."

The president picked up on the air of doubt in the room and departed from his text to encourage the assembled politicians to rise to the challenge and vote in favor of supplying the necessary funds. He closed: "I have not asked for a single program which did not cause one or all Americans some inconvenience, or some hardship, or some sacrifice."

With this, he was echoing the most quoted line from his inaugural address, a patriotic call that had stirred the nation: "Ask not what your country can do for you—ask what you can do for your country." The Moon-landing program would call for the support of every citizen.

When they tuned in to the speech, Jim Webb and Bob Gilruth were flying to a meeting aboard a World War II–era transport from the old NACA fleet. The plane was noisy, but they could hear the president's distinctive Boston accent over the radio.

Webb knew what Kennedy was going to say, but Gilruth was shocked when he heard the president's deadline: "before this decade is out." Webb was relieved, since the original deadline had been 1967—the fiftieth anniversary of the Communist Revolution, which was widely assumed to be the Soviets' target date for their own Moon landing, although that was just a guess. Webb had asked the president's advisers for more time. The end of the decade seemed urgent enough but also possible. It was also conveniently vague: it could mean either 1969 or 1970, eight or nine years away, depending on where you started counting. In practice, the deadline came to be considered December 31, 1969.

But one of the managers who had to meet the deadline was sitting right next to Webb, and he was not so confident. Bob Gilruth later said, "I was always a guy that looked at all the things that could go wrong." After tallying that frightening list: "I was sort of aghast."

For the rest of the flight, Webb chatted away about the president's speech, while Gilruth was lost in thought. Below, a small part of planet Earth passed beneath them. A quarter of a million miles away, the Moon beckoned.

A page from the reading text of President
Kennedy's Moon speech

67

Space is open to us now; and our
eagerness to share its meaning is not
governed by the efforts of others. We
go into space because whatever mankind
must undertake, _free_ men must fully
share.

I therefore ask the Congress,
above and beyond the increases I have
earlier requested for space activities,
to provide the funds which are needed
to meet the following national goals:

First, I believe that this nation
should commit itself to achieving the
goal, before this decade is out,
of landing a man on the moon and
returning him safely to earth.

Kennedy honors Shepard after his flight.

Kennedy delivers his Moon
speech to Congress.

The Moon speech, continued

68

No single space project in this period
will be more ~~exciting, or~~ more
impressive, or more important for the
long-range exploration of space; and
none will be so difficult or expensive
to accomplish. Including necessary
supporting research, this objective
will require an additional $531 million
this year and still higher sums in the
future. We propose to accelerate
development of the appropriate lunar
space craft. We propose to develop
alternate liquid and solid fuel
boosters of much larger than any now
being developed, until certain which
is superior.

BRIEFING:
The President's Speech

Several years before he ran for president, John F. Kennedy was having dinner with Doc Draper in Boston. As head of the MIT Instrumentation Lab, Draper wanted to get the promising young politician interested in spaceflight. Kennedy made light-hearted fun of the idea, probably thinking of the science-fiction comics he saw in the newspaper. No one would have predicted that one day he would stand before Congress and launch history's most audacious space project.

The key to it, in President Kennedy's mind, was freedom—a concept that had a very special meaning during the Cold War. Eighteen months after the end of World War II, President Truman had invoked freedom again and again in a speech that was a call to arms against Soviet aggression. In his Moon-landing speech, President Kennedy followed suit, mentioning freedom nearly two dozen times, posing this challenge: "If we are to win the battle that is now going on around the world between freedom and tyranny, the dramatic achievements in space which occurred in recent weeks"—meaning the space-flights of Gagarin and Shepard—"should have made clear to us all . . . the impact of this adventure on the minds of men everywhere." He concluded that something as bold as a Moon landing would make the case for freedom. He was worried that the feats of Soviet scientists and engineers made the Soviet Union look like the most progressive society on Earth.

Kennedy didn't say that the Moon landing would be the realization of an age-old dream, or that humans are born explorers, or that the project would produce unimagined technological innovations or hundreds of thousands of jobs—all of which would have been true. Instead, he appealed to the most powerful idea motivating Americans at the time: freedom.

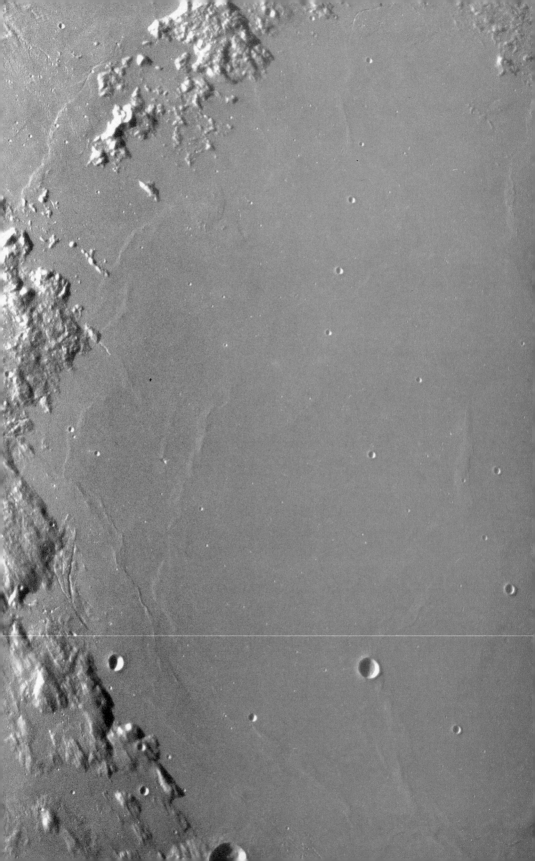

PART 4
THE PLAN

So much happened and it happened so fast. It was almost like being in an accident.

—Rocco Petrone, manager of Saturn V launch operations

The Moon's Sea of Serenity through a telescope

Wernher von Braun stands at the back end of his Moon rocket, with its giant F-1 engines.

19

PIECES OF THE PUZZLE

Thanks to Max Faget, Kennedy's Moon-landing venture already had a name and a design. Faget's three-man Apollo spacecraft could be adapted for landing by adding more rocket motors and other equipment. But what were the other steps? How do you put together the puzzle pieces for a lunar voyage? How do you even know what the pieces *are*? Like generals planning an invasion, Webb's top staff began devising a strategy. NASA's third-in-command, Robert C. Seamans Jr., remembers looking up at the Moon during this period and wondering "if we were all crazy. Intellectually, I believed we could do it. Each step seemed to make sense; yet when I grasped the enormity of the job, I wondered."

Over the next few months, Seamans and his colleagues came up with a plan:

1. Build a Moon rocket

Task number one was building a monstrous rocket that could carry astronauts to the Moon and back. The key component was already under development: a rocket engine called the F-1, designed to produce 1.5 million pounds of thrust—meaning it could lift anything weighing up to 1.5 million pounds. This amount of thrust was equal to nineteen Redstones firing simultaneously. For his Saturn family of rockets, von Braun envisioned boosters that clustered as many as four or five F-1s in the first stage, and he had designs for a behemoth called Nova that would use up to eight F-1s at launch.

These colossal machines could send significant payloads to the Moon. However, one of the big problems was moving them around on Earth. Simply putting one together would be a daunting task, since the completed vehicle would be taller than the Statue of Liberty. Assembly was best done in an enclosed space, out of the weather. Given the need to have several Moon rockets being worked on at the same time, the hangar would have to be the world's largest building by volume. When the rocket was ready, it would need to be moved several miles to the launchpad, since a mishap like the Vanguard explosion would pack the power of a small nuclear bomb.

Von Braun and his team were responsible for the Moon rocket. And a U.S. Army lieutenant colonel named Rocco Petrone was charged with creating the facilities—the assembly building, rocket transporter, launchpad, and other structures—that would send the titanic missiles on their way. These would include the cavernous firing room, where hundreds of engineers would control every aspect of the countdown and launch.

2. Hire a big boss

Webb and Seamans discussed appointing von Braun to head the entire Apollo effort. No one had pushed the dream of a lunar voyage harder than the German rocketeer or done so much to make it happen. But when NASA's long-serving deputy administrator Hugh Dryden heard

Early concept of the Moon rocket

the idea, he said he would rather resign than see the ex-Nazi lead America's greatest technological adventure.

So Webb and Seamans searched elsewhere. They settled on D. Brainerd Holmes, a brilliant engineer who had managed the development of the billion-dollar missile early warning system designed to detect Russian missiles coming over the Arctic region from the Soviet Union. He was an expert organizer of huge, complicated projects, and he looked like the perfect fit for heading not just Apollo, but all U.S. human spaceflight.

3. Expand NASA

In 1961, NASA had 18,000 employees at its centers plus 58,000 contract employees at companies all around the country. This was not nearly enough to mount an expedition to the Moon. The numbers would almost double within a year—the lion's share being contract workers designing and building rockets, spacecraft, and other hardware. The labor force would keep growing until it was at the strength of a major invasion during World War II, topping out at 411,000 workers by 1965.

In addition, a new NASA facility called the Manned Spacecraft Center was being planned to house Gilruth's rapidly expanding Space Task Group. In consultation with Kennedy, Webb selected Houston for the site. Houston met all the requirements, but more importantly, it was in Texas—the home state of Vice President Johnson as well as several top congressional leaders with influence over NASA's budget. (Years later the Manned Spacecraft Center would be renamed the Lyndon B. Johnson Space Center.)

4. Get spaceflight experience

When Kennedy announced that America was going to the Moon, the U.S. had all of fifteen minutes of manned spaceflight experience. Imagine if after the Wright brothers' first flight in 1903, lasting less than a minute, they had announced they were planning a flight around the world! They would have needed a much more sophisticated aircraft and vastly more piloting experience to do it.

NASA was in much the same position. Their Moon ship was in the works, but they needed veteran spacefarers who were familiar with the disorienting effects of takeoff, weightlessness, and reentry; who knew how to navigate by the stars, change orbits, rendezvous and dock with another ship, land on an alien surface, function outside in a pressure suit; and who could cope with other conditions, as yet unknown.

Furthermore, the space travelers had to stand up to these challenges for the full eight days of a round-trip lunar voyage.

Unfortunately, Project Mercury was only able to give astronauts the first three experiences: takeoff, weightlessness, and reentry. Mercury missions were expected to extend into 1963, including orbital flights lasting a day or so, but they would provide no practice in the more sophisticated aspects of spaceflight needed for a lunar voyage. Since Apollo wouldn't be ready for its first Earth orbital missions until 1965 at the earliest, an interim ship was essential. Project Gemini was designed to fill this gap. Named for the constellation that depicts twins from classical mythology, the Gemini spacecraft would carry two astronauts—the "twins"—on orbital missions that would test some of the major challenges of a Moon voyage. One was the maneuver called "rendezvous and docking," in which a spacecraft approaches another and links up with it. It sounds simple, but in space it's tricky and counterintuitive. During Apollo, rendezvous and docking was likely to be an important step for transferring crews, refueling, or other crucial operations.

NASA was also ready to choose the next group of astronauts. Anticipating many Gemini and Apollo flights—at two or three astronauts per mission plus backup crews—officials knew they would need quite a few spacefarers.

5. Reconnoiter the goal

If the Wright brothers really had decided to fly around the world, at least they would have known what they were getting into. Except for the poles, the Earth had been thoroughly explored by the twentieth century. The same was not true for the Moon. The nature of the lunar surface was a major mystery. One prominent scientist argued that billions of years of bombardment by meteorites had ground the Moon's surface into a thick layer of dust. Astronauts attempting to land, he said, would sink out of sight.

To settle this question and answer others, NASA planned three separate programs of robotic exploration to pave the way for Apollo:

- **Ranger**: Designed to plunge kamikaze-like into the Moon, these spacecraft would take pictures until the last instant, relaying them live to Earth while showing closer and closer views of possible landing areas.
- **Surveyor**: This series of automatic landers would come down much like the Apollo spacecraft, firing a braking rocket and settling gently onto the lunar surface, where they would test the soil properties and relay images.
- **Lunar Orbiter**: With the goal of mapping the entire Moon, these spacecraft would go into lunar orbit and use declassified spy-satellite cameras to photograph lunar craters, plains, valleys, and mountain ranges.

6. Develop astronavigation

One of the biggest hurdles facing Apollo astronauts was navigating to the Moon and back. NASA gave this problem such high priority that its first Apollo contract went to the firm best equipped to solve it: the Instrumentation Laboratory at MIT, headed by Doc Draper, who had worked with Jim Webb on defense projects during World War II.

The problem of astronavigation boiled down to designing an onboard guidance system—a gyroscope teamed with a sextant and a computer—that could tell astronauts exactly where they were at any given time, where they needed to be in the next phase of their trip, and what adjustments to make in their trajectory to get there. This information had to be independent of data relayed from Mission Control, since the spacecraft could lose radio contact at any time. In other words, the spacecraft had to be able to navigate on its own like a ship at sea. The difference was that the Apollo ship would be traveling a quarter of a million miles from home.

In 1961, Webb and others at NASA pressed Draper several times about whether his system would really work. He assured them it would. To prove it, the sixty-year-old professor volunteered to make the Moon voyage himself! (His application was politely turned down.)

There was no end to the Apollo to-do list. For example, giant dish antennas needed to be upgraded, as did the techniques for communicating with spaceships at lunar distances. The danger posed by meteors and high-energy solar particles in deep space required study. So did the risk of any hypothetical alien microbes that might be returned to Earth from the Moon. Also, the procedures for the new techniques of mission control had to be perfected; the astronauts would have so much to do, they would require substantial help from the ground. Indeed, the mission controllers would be as much a part of the flight as the crew.

But there was one gigantic piece of the puzzle that hadn't been settled. This was the size of the Apollo spacecraft and the sequence of steps in a mission. Would a single spacecraft proceed directly to the Moon, land, and then return, as in the movies? Or did a piecemeal approach make more sense?

In the early months of the Apollo program, this debate would become surprisingly heated.

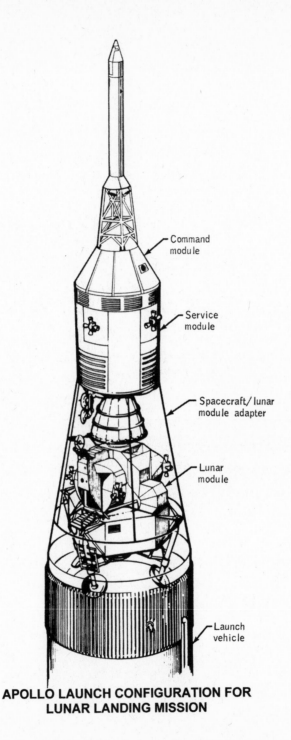

Command
module

Service
module

Spacecraft/lunar
module adapter

Lunar
module

Launch
vehicle

**APOLLO LAUNCH CONFIGURATION FOR
LUNAR LANDING MISSION**

The Lunar Module (LM) nestles behind the Command and Service Module (CSM) at the
top of the Saturn V. After launch, the CSM turns around and docks with the LM.

20

HOW TO GET TO THE MOON, AND BACK

"**Y**our figures lie!" shouted Max Faget. He had just seen a presentation by fellow NASA engineer John C. Houbolt, who was passionate about a cost- and time-saving plan for getting to the Moon.

"He's being misleading," Faget explained to the audience, which included Seamans, von Braun, and other top NASA officials.

Von Braun was also dubious. "No, that's no good," he said about the scheme.

Such united opposition from the nation's chief spacecraft designer and premier rocket scientist should have killed Houbolt's idea cold.

But it didn't.

The most crucial step in a round-trip to the Moon is the journey back. You must be absolutely sure that you have enough propellant to take off from the Moon and return to Earth. Therefore, mission planners often started their calculations by examining the return journey. How big a rocket does it take to get a given spacecraft, consisting of a crew cabin and its support equipment, off the Moon? The bigger the spacecraft sitting on the Moon, the more rocket power is needed to get home.

After you've made this calculation, you can work backward, figuring out how big a braking rocket is needed to land this contraption on the Moon and therefore how big a launch vehicle is required back on Earth to get the whole package traveling at 24,200 miles per hour—the launch speed needed to reach the Moon.

When these calculations were run with Faget's three-person Apollo spacecraft, they showed that the launch vehicle would have to be the largest on von Braun's drawing board: the Nova, packing eight F-1 engines in its first stage, each producing 1.5 million pounds of thrust.

The big assumption here is that you're going to the Moon the way it's done in the movies: leave Earth, land on the Moon, return. This approach is called "direct ascent," and while engineers love it for its simplicity, it's not the only way to go.

Direct ascent made von Braun nervous. He loved building big rockets, but the Nova was too big even for him. So he came up with an alternate strategy, called "Earth-orbit rendezvous." His plan was to use two or more smaller launch vehicles—still enormous but smaller than Nova—to assemble the expedition in Earth orbit. One rocket might send up the complete spacecraft, with its lunar descent and ascent stages attached. Another might launch the fully fueled propulsion unit. The two parts would dock, the propulsion unit would ignite, and off they would go. Other combinations were possible, such as launching a space tanker to "gas up" the Moon ship.

As far as NASA was concerned, Apollo would use one of these two approaches: direct ascent or Earth-orbit rendezvous. Both involved landing the entire Apollo spacecraft on the Moon, with its heat shield, parachutes, and other features intended solely for reentry into Earth's atmosphere. No one saw a practical way around this drawback—except Houbolt.

When Columbus arrived in the New World, he didn't sail his flagship onto the beach only to have to push the massive vessel back into the water on his departure. No, he anchored offshore and climbed into a rowboat that he then used to reach the shore. This was the essence of Houbolt's plan. There was no need to take the entire spacecraft down to the Moon, only to have to lift it off the surface to return to Earth. A small, specialized landing craft—a space rowboat—could do the job, shuttling from the mother ship in lunar orbit, down to the Moon, and back.

Called "lunar-orbit rendezvous," the plan broke down the Apollo spacecraft into modules. Houbolt didn't invent this approach, but he became its tireless champion. As they were later named, the modules became the command module, the service module, and the lunar module.

The command module (CM) is Faget's Apollo capsule, the crew compartment that sits like a nose cone atop the launch vehicle and serves as home to three astronauts. It is the only piece of hardware that returns to Earth, and therefore the only part that needs a heavy heat shield for protection during the scorching reentry into the atmosphere— which, from a lunar voyage, is even faster and hotter than the return from Earth orbit.

Behind the CM is the service module (SM), housing a rocket engine, propellant tanks, a power supply, breathing oxygen, drinking water, and communications equipment. Since the CM and SM remain attached until just before reentry, they can be considered a single unit, called the CSM.

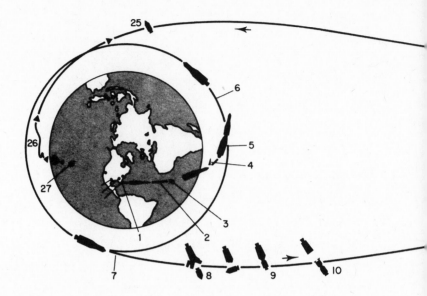

Apollo's Steps to the Moon

The Earth and Moon are not drawn to scale.

1. Saturn V lifts off
2. First-stage burn
3. Second-stage burn
4. Escape tower jettisoned
5. Third-stage burn
6. Earth orbit
7. Relight third stage to leave for Moon

8. CSM separates from LM shroud
9. CSM docks with LM
10. Third stage is cast off
11. Midcourse correction
12. Enter lunar orbit (dashed lines indicate loss of Earth communications)
13. Two astronauts enter LM
14. CSM and LM separate

The lunar module (LM, pronounced "lem") is the rowboat. During launch it is stored behind the CSM, surrounded by a protective shroud. After the firing of the third stage, when the Apollo spacecraft is Moon-bound, the CSM detaches from the top of the shroud, turns around, and docks with the LM, becoming one spacecraft. The third stage and shroud are then cast off. On arrival near the Moon, the CSM fires its engine, putting the combined CSM-LM ship into lunar orbit. Then two

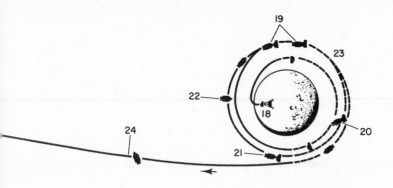

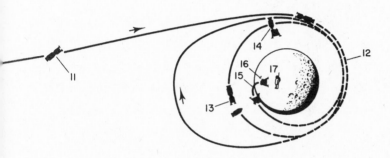

15. LM descent
16. Touchdown!
17. Explore surface, set up experiments
18. LM ascent stage lifts off
19. Rendezvous and docking with CSM
20. LM crew enters CSM
21. CSM detaches from LM

22. Crew prepares for return to Earth
23. CSM fires rocket to leave lunar orbit
24. Midcourse correction
25. CM separates from SM
26. Reentry
27. Splashdown!

astronauts enter the LM through a tunnel, detach from the CSM, and fire the LM's descent rocket, leaving behind the third astronaut in the CSM—the mother ship—to mind the store. They descend to a landing, go outside, and explore the Moon.

Ready to head home, the Moon explorers would climb back aboard the LM and fire its ascent rocket, leaving the descent stage behind on the Moon. Returning to lunar orbit, they dock with the mother ship and rejoin their comrade. The three astronauts then detach from the LM's ascent stage, leaving it behind, and fire the CSM rocket for return to Earth. Just before reentry the CM and SM detach. The CM plummets through the atmosphere (as does the SM, which burns up), roasting the CM's heat shield to a fiery red. In the lower atmosphere, parachutes deploy for a gentle landing in the ocean.

This sounded dangerously complicated to many NASA engineers. They were especially worried about a hair-raising moment of high risk: the rendezvous and docking of the LM ascent stage and CSM in lunar orbit, something that had never been done even in Earth orbit, much less around the Moon. As one NASA official put it, "Houbolt has a scheme that has a 50 percent chance of getting a man to the Moon and a 1 percent chance of getting him back."

Houbolt argued that this wisecrack greatly exaggerated the risk and that no one could dispute the cost-saving. Thanks to the shedding of weight as the flight progressed, a single-launch vehicle with five F-1 engines in its first stage, plus state-of-the-art second and third stages, would suffice for a complete Apollo mission. By contrast, two such boosters were needed for von Braun's preferred Earth-orbit rendezvous plan.

To Houbolt, lunar-orbit rendezvous "offered a chain reaction of simplifications," which significantly streamlined "development, testing, manufacturing, launch, and flight operations." As soon as he encountered the idea, he realized, "Oh my God, this is it! This is fantastic! If there is any idea we must push, it is this one."

After all concerned studied Houbolt's plan, they began to come around. Even Faget and von Braun joined the consensus, recognizing lunar-orbit rendezvous as the most elegant solution to a very difficult problem. It made the most with the least.

It helped that the astronauts far preferred lunar-orbit rendezvous. With the other two approaches, they had to bring a towering spaceship to a landing on the Moon while lying on their backs, watching a televised view of where they were going. The feat would be like backing a Mercury-Atlas onto the pad. By contrast, with Houbolt's plan they got a small, maneuverable lunar module that they could fly like a jet fighter, which naturally appealed to test pilots.

For their part, administrators liked lunar-orbit rendezvous because it avoided the complication of multiple launches and provided the best chance of meeting Kennedy's deadline of a landing by the end of 1969. And so, on July 11, 1962, NASA announced that lunar-orbit rendezvous would be America's path to the Moon. The rocket to start the journey would use five F-1 engines and would be called the Saturn V.

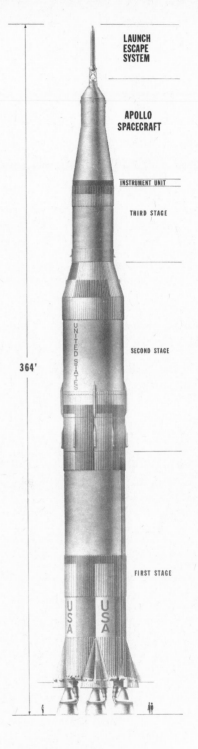

LAUNCH ESCAPE SYSTEM

APOLLO SPACECRAFT

INSTRUMENT UNIT

THIRD STAGE

SECOND STAGE

364'

FIRST STAGE

The Saturn V. (See page 158 for the positions of the CSM and LM.)

Three Russian cosmonauts with Premier Khrushchev (far right), 1963. Left to right: Yuri Gagarin, Pavel Popovich, and Valentina Tereshkova, the first woman in space.

21

THE RACE HEATS UP

Before they were selected as astronauts, the Original Seven were put through the most rigorous medical tests that doctors could devise. All were in superb physical condition. Testing continued during their training as they were subjected to bruising experiments designed to discover how much punishment the human body could take in launches, landings, gyrating space capsules, and other ordeals. Researchers were amazed at their endurance. Then, on the same day that NASA announced the lunar-orbit rendezvous decision, Americans were stunned to learn that Deke Slayton was being grounded due to a heart condition.

The subtle abnormality—irregular heartbeats—showed up briefly about every two weeks. No doctor could say why. Slayton paid no attention to these episodes until he was hooked up to a heart monitor before a training session. A technician noticed the problem and expressed concern. The nation's top heart specialists examined Slayton and found him fit in every way, except this. Just to be safe, they recommended that he be grounded.

Pilots are grounded every day, but this was big news. The Original Seven had been reduced to six. Newspapers treated it almost like a death, reporting in somber detail Slayton's sixty-three bombing missions over Europe and Japan during World War II, his test pilot career, and his memorable quote on joining Project Mercury: "I would give my left arm to be the first man in space." Now it seemed he wouldn't even be the hundredth.

In the summer of 1962, Mercury had come a long way since Shepard's flight a little over a year earlier. Eleven weeks after the launch of *Freedom 7*, Gus Grissom repeated Shepard's suborbital journey in a mission that went perfectly—until the hatch accidentally blew open after splashdown. The capsule sank and Grissom barely escaped with his life. But the perils of rocket flight, as opposed to recovery, appeared to be conquered.

Two weeks after Grissom's quick trip, the Russians countered with their second human spaceflight: seventeen orbits lasting a full day. The headline of one New York paper proclaimed, "Red Spaceman Lands! Covered 434,960 Mi. Can U.S. Still Win Race to Moon?" A British expert on spaceflight didn't think so. He predicted a Russian manned landing on the Moon in 1966 or 1967, and he expected a lunar reconnaissance flight with a dog to pave the way.

Gilruth reacted decisively by canceling the remaining suborbital flights and scheduling the next Mercury mission as Earth-orbiting. John Glenn, who had been backup to both Shepard and Grissom, got the assignment. His capsule, *Friendship 7*, flew on February 20, 1962, giving Glenn the first ride on the trouble-plagued Atlas. The booster behaved beautifully. His main worry during the five-hour, three-orbit trip was a warning light that blinked on at Mission Control, signaling that the

John Glenn heads for orbit aboard an Atlas, February 20, 1962.

capsule's heat shield had come loose. The identical light in Glenn's cabin was off. Mission Control suspected their reading was false, but they couldn't be sure, leading to some anxious moments and a hastily improvised change in the reentry procedure. Had the warning been correct and the heat shield had come off, Glenn would have burned up. Instead it was a faulty sensor, and Glenn had never been in danger. Even so, it was a reminder of the importance of getting every switch, sensor, and other component absolutely right.

America's second orbital mission was supposed to have been Slayton's. But he was grounded and Scott Carpenter took the flight, orbiting the world three times, just like Glenn, in May 1962.

Human spaceflight was soaring. In the following months, Slayton would watch jealously as the other Mercury rookies strapped into their capsules and took off: Wally Schirra for six orbits in October 1962, and Gordo Cooper for a wearying twenty-two orbits lasting thirty-four hours in May 1963.

●

Cooper's flight was the final Mercury mission and might have set an endurance record, except the Russians had already sent up two manned capsules at the same time, with each cosmonaut staying up more than twice as long as Cooper. More impressively, their orbits brought them within visual range of each other, a difficult feat in spaceflight that was the first step toward rendezvous and docking. A month after Cooper splashed down, the Russians extended their duration record to five days. This was also a dual mission, with the second capsule carrying the first woman in space, Valentina Tereshkova.

Premier Khrushchev crowed. "Bourgeois society always underlines that woman is the weaker sex," he said at a welcome-home rally for the two cosmonauts. "Our Soviet woman showed American astronauts a thing or two. Her flight was longer than that of all the American astronauts put together. There is your weaker sex!" he bellowed as the crowd erupted in cheers.

Khrushchev hit a sore point with American women. In the Soviet Union, females had a more equal status with men and played a major role in technical professions such as engineering. In the United States, a look at the NASA workforce, which was overwhelmingly male, showed that there was a lot of ground to make up. But the men in charge didn't seem to realize it. A prominent female author and politician named Clare Boothe Luce caught America's ambivalent mood in an editorial for *Life* magazine: "News reports after Valentina's blastoff said that women were dancing in the streets of Moscow while men hurled compliments and showered kisses upon them. Not so in America. The flight has become a source of bitter argument between the sexes."

U.S. officials (all male) were either dismissive or defensive. One of New York's senators made a joke about the first woman in space. "It is carrying romance to a new high," he quipped. The commander of military launches at Cape Canaveral called the achievement "merely a publicity stunt," as did a prominent champion of civil rights in the House of Representatives, who labeled it "a sort of stunt." Other critics pointed out that Tereshkova wasn't even a pilot. One NASA official said that the idea of female astronauts "makes me sick at my stomach." Meanwhile, astronaut John Glenn, now a national hero after becoming the first American in orbit, tried to calm the waters by explaining NASA's reasoning: "We felt the qualifications we were looking for . . . were best taken care of by men."

Glenn was right, but only because the deck was stacked. NASA's prime qualification for astronauts was test pilot experience in high-performance jets—a career path open only to men. On the other hand, NASA was loosening the requirement—slightly. As of 1963, non–test pilots could apply to the program, but they would need substantial experience flying military jet fighters—again, something only males were trained to do at the time. The accelerating pace of Apollo, combined with NASA's success with the first group of astronauts, inclined Webb to leave the system as it was. Another factor was that astronauts were on the committee to select new astronauts and tended to prefer their own kind.

Looking ahead, Senator Clinton Anderson of New Mexico remained optimistic. "We will train some women astronauts for sure," he predicted. He was right, but the first American female astronauts wouldn't fly until long after Apollo.

Wernher von Braun (center) explains the Saturn launch system to President Kennedy at Cape Canaveral, 1963. NASA Associate Administrator Robert Seamans is at left.

22

THE GREAT ESCAPE

In the summer of 1963, moviegoers were flocking to see
The Great Escape. With an all-star cast headed by Steve McQueen, it
told the true story of captured Allied airmen who engineer an elaborate
bid for freedom during World War II. Confined in a Nazi prisoner-of-war
camp designed to be escape-proof, they execute a plot involving multiple tunnels and ingeniously forged documents and uniforms. Their
audacious goal is to break out with hundreds of their fellow prisoners.
The climactic scene, involving a motorcycle chase through the German
countryside, made McQueen famous.

Audiences of the day were obsessed with stories about the war,
which had been America's finest hour. The war had been over for almost twenty years, but its memory lingered as a consolation against
distressing headlines in the news—about increasing U.S. involvement
in Vietnam, violent resistance to racial integration, the pernicious
health effects of nuclear testing, military coups abroad, and most up-
setting of all, the Cuban Missile Crisis the previous fall, which had been
a terrifying close call with possible nuclear war, instigated by Russia's

installation of nuclear missiles in Cuba. Fortunately, Kennedy and Khrushchev settled the crisis.

●

In this climate of unease, even America's vaunted space program was starting to draw fire. The most stinging criticism came from former president Eisenhower. This career military man put it bluntly: "Anybody who would spend 40 billion dollars in a race to the Moon for national prestige is nuts."

In fact, Webb's cost estimate for getting astronauts to the Moon and back was half that: 20 billion dollars. As an experienced Washington bureaucrat, he had good reasons for this number. After various rough guesses made the rounds, including some as high as 40 billion dollars, NASA's technical experts came up with a rigorous estimate of 8 to 12 billion. Webb thought this was unrealistic for a project with so many unknowns, so he added an "administrator's discount"—a fudge factor that would provide a cushion for the inevitable setbacks. He told Kennedy he needed 20 billion. No one had ever flown to the Moon before, so Kennedy and Congress accepted the figure, and Webb stuck to it.

Webb was able to get the money from Congress in yearly appropriations thanks to carefully nurtured contacts. He was shrewd in other ways. Bob Gilruth wanted the two-man Gemini program because it was critical for astronaut training. Webb agreed, but he also saw the public relations benefit of keeping human spaceflight in the news during the multiyear gap between Mercury and Apollo. Furthermore, he regarded Gemini as an insurance policy against unpleasant surprises with Apollo. He explained: "If we had an insuperable obstacle and had to stop Apollo, if our equipment wouldn't work or it is too difficult a

The Vehicle Assembly Building under construction, 1965. When completed the following year, it was the largest building in the world by volume. At right are three mobile launchers for the Saturn V.

job, if we really didn't see how to overcome some difficulty in getting to the Moon, we would have still done the next most important thing."

A few years later, two astronauts training for Gemini at the Cape had a premonition of just such a scenario. During time off, David Scott and Neil Armstrong decided to go look at the Apollo buildings under construction. "We walked into the firing room," Scott recalled, which had a sea of 450 consoles designed to control every facet of the Moon rocket.

By contrast, Gemini had about twenty consoles. Scott shook his head: "No way! There's no way this is going to work!" Next, Scott and Armstrong went into the mammoth Vehicle Assembly Building, where the Moon rocket would be put together. They were dumbfounded. "It ain't gonna work!" Scott repeated. "It is too big! It is just too big!"

Apollo, which dared to surmount the obstacles that confine us to our planet, would be humanity's Great Escape—if it worked.

Webb knew that his honeymoon with Congress, the press, and the public could only last so long. In the summer of 1963, Apollo hit its first rough patch. Sir Bernard Lovell, a prominent British scientist, returned from a visit to the Soviet Union reporting that technical advisers to the Soviet space program didn't think a manned lunar journey was feasible. "There are two problems which greatly concern them," Lovell told the press. First was the unpredictable rain of high-energy radiation from the Sun, which could kill Moon voyagers. Second was that once on the Moon, "there may be no solution to getting a man back to Earth safely."

Webb wondered if the Russians were trying to undermine public support for Apollo by painting it as impractical and not a goal they were pursuing. The Central Intelligence Agency (CIA) had advised him there was more than a fifty-fifty chance that the Soviets were, in fact, in the Moon race. Their manned flights, automatic lunar probes, and ambitious launch site construction (photographed by spy satellites) all seemed to support this conclusion.

Webb was also starting to have trouble with his top manager for Apollo. Brainerd Holmes was going behind his back to appeal to Kennedy for more money for the program. This might sound like a good thing, but it undermined Webb's relationship with the president and Congress, and it was an obvious sign that Holmes wanted Webb's job.

Furthermore, to Webb, it signaled that Holmes was running an inefficient operation that couldn't make do with the generous support Apollo was already getting.

When Kennedy asked why he shouldn't listen to Holmes, Webb was frank: "Look, if you want someone else to run the program, I don't know where you'll come out. If you and I stick together we'll both come out all right."

The president was persuaded: "I'm going to stick with you."

With that, Webb fired Holmes and searched for a new manager, ultimately hiring a highly regarded engineer with a knack for running a tight ship. Looking more like a professor than a hard-charging executive, George Mueller (pronounced "Miller") started work on September 1, 1963. Following standard business practice, he asked his staff for "a candid assessment of the real status" of Apollo. President Franklin Roosevelt had done much the same at the outset of World War II, when he asked for a realistic report on what it would take to win the war. The resulting Victory Program for the war was astonishingly farsighted— and successful.

Mueller also got a farsighted report, and it was bad news. Kennedy's goal was a man on the Moon by the end of 1969 at Webb's price tag of 20 billion dollars. There is "no way you're going to be able to do that," Mueller was told. He reviewed the findings with Bob Seamans, who listened quietly. At the end of the meeting, Seamans abruptly told Mueller to destroy the report. "Find out how to do it," he ordered. This was exactly what Mueller wanted to hear, and he spent the rest of that fall putting a new plan into action.

In November, Mueller had the chance to brief President Kennedy. It was a day of show-and-tell for the commander in chief, taking place at Cape Canaveral. Sitting in the firing room flanked by NASA's top brass, Kennedy watched intently as Mueller gave the big picture on the human spaceflight schedule. Particularly impressive were the scale models of

George Mueller gives a briefing to President Kennedy (front row center, with his hand on his chin). Just left of Kennedy is Jim Webb. On his other side are Hugh Dryden and Wernher von Braun.

the assembly building and Saturn V, both several years from completion. At the same scale was a Redstone. Compared to the Saturn V, it looked like a telephone pole next to a skyscraper.

"This is fantastic," Kennedy marveled, probably realizing for the first time the true immensity of Apollo. Mueller talked for about fifteen minutes. Then von Braun led the group out to the launchpad, where a Saturn I was being prepared for a test in a few weeks' time. If all went well, it would orbit a payload far exceeding the Soviet's current weight-lifting record. Kennedy loved that.

Before the end of the month, the launch center that the president had just toured would be renamed the John F. Kennedy Space Center, and the location would be called Cape Kennedy. This sudden honor was due to a tragedy that traumatized the nation. On November 22, 1963, less than a week after his visit to Florida, Kennedy was killed by an assassin in Dallas, Texas.

Once considered controversial, wasteful, and even crazy, the Apollo program would continue with more support than ever as a memorial to a fallen leader.

President Kennedy gazes up at a Saturn I, November 16, 1963. Six days later he would be assassinated.

The first Saturn V inside the Vehicle Assembly Building, 1967

23

GENERAL PHILLIPS JOINS THE TEAM

Raised in the tight-lipped American West, Sam Phillips was a man of few words—the type who would sum up his greatest experience in World War II with three syllables: "Surviving." Fourteen months as a fighter pilot escorting bombers through hailstorms of flak had taught him to speak sparingly, focus on the mission at hand, and ignore risks he had no way to control. His motto: "Results are what count."

After the war, Phillips stayed in the Air Force and rose through the ranks as a virtuoso manager of high-technology programs. As the Cold War heated up, new weapons became even more complex than the most monumental defense projects of World War II. New approaches were needed to make these superweapons work and get them finished on time and on budget.

After serving as project officer for the gargantuan B-52, the successor to the B-29, Phillips was assigned the nearly impossible task of producing and deploying a three-stage solid-propellant missile called

Sam Phillips as a major

Sam Phillips gets his general's star at a ceremony with his wife and three daughters, 1960.

Minuteman in just three years. He drew on a discipline called "systems engineering" to coordinate the many complex pieces of the job and meet the deadline. Along the way, he earned a general's star. At 39, he was the youngest general officer in the U.S. Armed Forces.

Before joining NASA as Brainerd Holmes's replacement, George Mueller had worked at one of the contractors for Minuteman. Through colleagues, he heard about the missile's miracle-working program manager, General Phillips. Now that Mueller oversaw human spaceflight, he needed his own miracle to get Apollo back on track, and he knew just who to call. Mueller wanted General Phillips as his deputy. The young general would remain in the Air Force but be on loan to NASA, where his sole responsibility would be Apollo. Although he would report to Mueller, Phillips would effectively be the big boss of the Moon-landing effort.

As Phillips was getting ready for his first day at NASA, a total eclipse of the Moon was in progress. Celestial mechanics brought the Sun, Earth, and Moon into line, so that Earth's shadow swept slowly across the lunar orb, turning it from its dazzling full phase into a gigantic, dark rock suspended in the sky—which is exactly what it is. That forbidding and alien world was General Phillips's new goal.

At end of 1963, lunar-orbit rendezvous had been the official plan for going to the Moon for a year and a half. Its major parts were all in the works: the three stages of the Saturn V rocket plus the Apollo spacecraft, composed of the CSM and LM. Each was among the most complex machines ever conceived. Chosen because it was a money- and time-saver, lunar-orbit rendezvous by itself was not enough to meet Kennedy's deadline. Apollo needed to be streamlined even more, and Mueller and Phillips came up with several measures to speed progress:

1. Reorganize NASA

NASA was like a medieval kingdom made up of warring provinces. The provinces were the old NACA facilities plus the new centers added since NASA formed in 1958. By 1963, the major turf battles over Apollo were between Gilruth's Manned Spacecraft Center in Houston and von Braun's rocket facility in Huntsville, with NASA Headquarters in Washington trying to make things run smoothly but not succeeding. Webb changed the chain of command, giving Mueller authority over Gilruth and von Braun. Mueller then decreed that everything having to do with Apollo would go through Phillips. Nothing would happen without the general's approval.

2. Simplify rocket testing

Multi-stage rockets like the Saturn V were always tested piecemeal. First, a series of launches perfected the first stage. When the first-stage kinks were worked out, a live second stage was added. More tests followed. Then a live third stage completed the process. But that wasn't how Phillips did it. With Minuteman, time had been so short that he followed an audacious strategy. He flew all three live stages on the very first launch. No one had ever done an "all-up" launch on the initial outing. It was considered "crazy" and likely to "blow up on the pad."

But it didn't. Phillips had so carefully managed design, construction, and quality control that everything worked perfectly. This was where systems engineering came in. So many things could go wrong with Minuteman that it would take forever to produce it with the trial-and-error methods used on earlier generations of rockets. Everything about the missile—components, computer programs, tests, timetables, and operations, along with supervising the teams—had to be coordinated like a symphony orchestra. In systems engineering, "if you do your piece right, and you hook it together, it will all work"—just as if you play your part correctly in a symphony, it will meld with all the other perfectly played parts to create beautiful music.

The general's all-up approach was so well known within the rocket community that by the time Phillips arrived at NASA, Mueller had already instituted it for Apollo. Von Braun, who was used to the painstaking, step-by-step German method, was appalled. All-up testing may have worked for Minuteman, he conceded, but for the even more fiendishly complex Saturn, it was likely to end in disaster. Other NASA insiders used words like *impossible, reckless, incredulous, harebrained,* and *nonsense*. But the decision stood.

3. Stop fooling with the design

Engineers love to design things. Perhaps even more, they love to *improve* their designs. Who could possibly object if they came up with a more efficient component for a rocket engine or an enhanced landing radar for the LM? But there is an old saying: "Better is the enemy of good." A change in one place inevitably leads to changes in everything connected to it, and this is rarely a good thing. Therefore, Mueller and Phillips instituted a rigorous system of configuration control, meaning that once a design was approved, any proposed changes faced a large hurdle. A review board had to approve all proposed modifications, taking into account their effects on the cost and schedule.

This policy rubbed Gilruth and other old NACA hands the wrong way, since they had grown up in an era when you built an airplane based on a set of calculations, flew it, tinkered with it, and then flew it again, improving it incrementally. Mueller considered those days over, especially where spaceflight was concerned. "The thing that really kills programs," he said, "is the changing requirements."

4. Meet daily milestones

As the father of two daughters, Mueller almost certainly had strict rules about homework, for he was like a demanding parent in his oversight of NASA employees. "Today's work must be done today," he insisted. The idea was that the path to what seemed like an unattainable goal could be divided into a series of daily tasks. If "we could operate in this fashion for six months we could substantially improve our schedule performance," he said. "And if we could do it for six months, we would find it easy to continue for a year and then two and then five." Mueller's can-do spirit would have done credit to Henry Ford. "We must accept in our minds and hearts that schedules can be met and that it is vital and important to meet them," Mueller urged.

5. Inspire the troops

Mueller practiced what he preached. His boss, Bob Seamans, was amazed. "George was a double whirlwind," he remembered. "The days of the week meant nothing to him. There were meetings on Saturdays and Sundays. George was indefatigable." He preferred to make his frequent trips around the country at night, so he could work all day, sleep on the plane, and then be ready for meetings with contractors or NASA center staff the next morning.

General Phillips was no less driven. A diary entry from his Apollo years records that he made fourteen phone calls, sent out three directives, responded to media, speaking, and congressional requests, and then caught an evening flight to Cape Kennedy, all on a day when he was at home sick.

The enthusiasm was infectious. One of Mueller and Phillips's employees, astronaut Neil Armstrong, noted, "You could stand across the street" from the Manned Spacecraft Center in Houston, "and you could not tell when quitting time was, because people didn't leave at quitting time ... People just worked, and they worked until ... their job was done, and if they had to be there until five o'clock or seven o'clock or nine-thirty or whatever it was, they were just there. They did it, and then they went home."

Thinking about how unusual it was to have this level of motivation, Armstrong added: "This was a project in which everybody involved was, one, interested, two, dedicated, and, three, fascinated by the job they were doing. And whenever you have those ingredients, whether it be government or private industry or a retail store, you're going to win."

ALL I ASK ...

DO GOOD WORK

MANNED FLIGHT AWARENESS

Gus Grissom

Astronaut Grissom's simple request—made into a poster

24

"DO GOOD WORK!"

World War II was won by soldiers, sailors, and pilots, but they couldn't have done it without the industries that supplied the equipment to fight the enemy. Two decades later, many of these same firms were producing the machines to take humans to the Moon, and many of the senior managers at these companies had been there since the early 1940s, moving up through the organization, indelibly shaped by the experience of working night and day to meet the national emergency of the war.

NASA Associate Administrator Bob Seamans had spent the war years at Doc Draper's Instrumentation Lab at MIT, perfecting military guidance and control systems for contractors such as Jim Webb's Sperry Gyroscope Company. His experience had been typical: "Like so many things for my generation," he said, "hard work and a belief in it went back to World War II."

"One year during the war," Seamans marveled, "Doc Draper said he thought it would be a good thing if we took Christmas day off! There were times when I would go to work in the morning, work through the night, then work all the next day in order to get something out on time. My generation built up a do-or-die work ethic. It amazes me when I look back."

●

Six months before America entered World War II, a young engineer named Harrison Storms took a job at North American Aviation in Los Angeles. His early projects included refining the aerodynamics of the P-51 Mustang and adapting the B-25 medium bomber so a squadron of them could take off from the short runway of an aircraft carrier, making possible the famous 1942 surprise attack on Tokyo known as the Doolittle Raid. After the war, Storms helped design the F-86 jet fighter used in Korea, and he was program manager for the X-15 rocket plane, whose elite pilots included Neil Armstrong. When Apollo came along, Storms led the North American teams that won the contracts for two major pieces of the Moon ship: the second stage of the Saturn V and the command and service module.

Alfred Munier came to work at Grumman Aircraft on Long Island in 1943, helping design the company's renowned Navy fighters. These planes had to be especially rugged to survive the stress of landing on an aircraft carrier at sea. Now Grumman was applying this expertise to the lunar module, which would be landing in a place no one had ever gone, under circumstances that were hard to predict. As the head of Grumman's space projects, Munier picked one of his best engineers, Thomas Kelly, to lead development of this unique flying machine.

Meanwhile, at a Boeing Company facility in Louisiana, a dapper, bow-tie-wearing executive named George Stoner was in charge of designing and building the first stage of the Saturn V, with the mighty F-1 engines being supplied by the rocket division at North American. During World

War II, Stoner had been a test supervisor for the dauntingly complex B-29 bomber.

Even a Manhattan Project scientist was involved with Apollo. Nobel Prize–winning chemist Harold Urey had perfected the method for enriching uranium to serve as an atomic explosive. Now he had branched out from chemistry to pursue a hobby: discovering where the planets came from. Convinced that the Moon was the key to this mystery, Urey was eager to get his hands on a piece of the Moon to study in his laboratory. Promising to grant his wish, NASA made him a member of its Working Group on Lunar Exploration.

For the NASA engineers who had started it all—Max Faget and Wernher von Braun—it was time to see their concepts turned into working machines. From here on, they would have a supervisory role only, overseeing the efforts of America's hard-driving, hypercompetitive aerospace industries.

Although these companies were in the business of making a profit, they reverted to their World War II outlook and attitude. National survival had been at stake then. It was not that desperate now, but the space program was still something big—something much larger and more important than making a living.

Astronaut Gus Grissom got a glimpse of this spirit when he was touring manufacturing plants during the Mercury program. On a visit to the Convair factory in San Diego that was building the Atlas rocket, Grissom was asked to address hundreds of engineers and staff assembled in the auditorium. He hesitated at this surprise request. Even more sparing with words than General Phillips, he gathered his thoughts and said, "Do good work!" That was it.

The audience reacted as if each and every one of them had been promised a month of paid vacation. They cheered wildly and wouldn't stop. They knew that Gus's message was quite the opposite—that long hours and weekends on the job were ahead as they ironed out the kinks in a vehicle that was all too prone to explode on the pad. But they were primed for the challenge and so inspired by Gus's "speech" that they had posters printed with his image, message, and signature. "Do good work" signs spread to contractors all over the country, putting a real face on the goal of hundreds of thousands of workers. They were doing their best not just for the space program but for Gus, since it was his life that was on the line.

If Grissom's listeners responded like athletes at a coach's pep talk, that was because many of them were barely out of college. Most were in their twenties. One Convair engineer remembered, "We carried responsibilities for very major aspects of the Mercury program . . . on our relatively inexperienced shoulders, and it didn't faze us . . . Atlases blew up, and the next day we went to work and we sat down and tried again." Many were unmarried and practically lived at their offices. Even those with families rarely saw them during daylight, except maybe on Sunday, since it was assumed they would all show up for work on Saturday.

Like a well-oiled machine, the space program was no longer running by fits and starts. It was moving at a fast clip toward Kennedy's goal. There was still much ground to cover and many hair-raising turns ahead, but things were starting to look up for America's race to the Moon. The best-oiled component of all was the astronaut office. As the Mercury program was winding down, it had a new boss, and he was using a system he had picked up during the war to prepare his pilots for a mission like no other.

A common scene during Apollo. Technicians carefully check out a piece of space hardware—in this case a two-man Gemini—to make sure it is ready for launch, 1966.

Map of Copernicus Crater by Pat Bridges

Margaret Hamilton with the
Apollo guidance software

Pat Bridges uses an airbrush on her Copernicus map.

Baerbel Lucchitta sits in a lunar rover trainer.

BRIEFING:
The Women of Apollo

Women may have been excluded from the American astronaut corps, but they filled other vital roles in Apollo.

In the mid-1960s, a mathematician named Margaret Hamilton heard that the MIT Instrumentation Lab was hiring computer programmers to write the software to guide astronauts to the Moon. Programming was a brand-new field, but she already had experience writing code to solve problems in weather forecasting and air defense, so she applied. Hamilton started at the bottom and soon established herself as an expert in the system code that made all the software pieces work together—which they had to do flawlessly. Her code was so error-free that she rose to be manager of command module software and later of all Apollo spacecraft software.

Patricia Bridges had a degree in fine arts and was working as a scientific illustrator for the Air Force mapping center. One day in 1959, her boss asked her to prepare a shaded-relief map of the region around Copernicus Crater on the Moon, based on telescopic images. Her rendering was so lifelike—and accurate—that she was made lead illustrator for a complete set of lunar charts to be used by Apollo planners, scientists, and astronauts.

Born in Germany, Baerbel Lucchitta grew up amid the chaos and devastation of World War II. A U.S. government scholarship brought her to America, where she earned degrees in geology in the early 1960s and went to work for the U.S. Geological Survey. She became an expert on lunar science and taught Moon-bound astronauts what they needed to know about their destination. After they got back, she analyzed the mission data to help redefine our understanding of Earth's far-off companion.

There were more women—in engineering, applied mathematics, rocket propulsion, and other technical fields. But Apollo was a project of its era, and its openness to the female sex was perhaps best symbolized by the near total lack of women's restrooms at Mission Control in Houston. It was still a man's world.

PART 5
CREWS

Any crew can fly any mission.

—Deke Slayton, motto

Kepler Crater (center), photographed by Lunar Orbiter 3

Chief astronaut Deke Slayton (right) and astronaut Mike Collins have just landed in the T-38 jet behind them.

25

SQUADRON COMMANDER

After Deke Slayton was grounded for an irregular heartbeat in 1962, Al Shepard discussed the situation with the other astronauts and then approached Bob Gilruth. They wanted Slayton to be their chief, Shepard said. Deke might be ineligible to fly in space, but he could run the astronaut office and serve as their supervisor, much like a squadron commander.

Gilruth liked the idea—and so did Slayton, since it would keep him on the scene until the day when his heart problem cleared up and he could finally put on a space suit.

One of his new duties was choosing the crews that would fly in space. It was easy enough with the last Mercury flight, since Gordo Cooper was the only one of the Original Seven besides Slayton himself who hadn't flown. Slayton felt that it was Gordo's turn, plain and simple. But ahead lay the complexities of the Gemini program.

Originally known as Advanced Mercury, Gemini would be a slightly roomier but much more advanced capsule, taking two men on missions in Earth orbit of up to two weeks. Ultimately, ten manned Gemini flights would be launched at roughly two-month intervals, from 1965 through 1966. Each mission required four astronauts: a prime crew who would fly, plus a backup crew who would go through identical training and be available in case illness, accident, or some other mishap put members of the prime crew out of action. The idea was that nothing would delay the schedule. In the end, Gemini involved twenty-one individual astronauts in prime and backup roles—some flying more than once. It was quite a scheduling puzzle for Slayton, and it would only get more complicated with Apollo, which had a crew of three.

The problem was much like assembling crews for bombing sorties during the war. Back then, the squadron operations officer took account of who was on flying status, the slots that needed filling (pilot, copilot, bombardier, etc.), whose turn it was for a combat assignment, and any special requirements for that mission. A well-run squadron rotated airmen at an orderly rate, kept the unit up to strength, and held frequent training exercises. Slayton ran the astronaut office the same way. One of his rules was "any crew can fly any mission"—just as with his bomb group in Italy. If you were accepted by NASA and made it through initial training, then, as far as Slayton was concerned, you were eligible for anything that came up. Not that you would necessarily be picked, but you were eligible.

To keep the astronaut office up to strength, NASA selected new groups of pilot-astronauts in 1962, 1963, and 1966—at which point there were some fifty astronauts, including a handful of scientist-astronauts chosen in 1965. The '62 and '63 groups formed the core of Gemini and Apollo crews and included:

Astronaut Group Two, 1962. Front row, left to right: Conrad, Borman, Armstrong, Young. Back row: See, McDivitt, Lovell, White, Stafford.

1962 Astronaut Group

Neil A. Armstrong, civilian
Frank F. Borman II, U.S. Air Force
Charles "Pete" Conrad Jr., U.S. Navy
James A. Lovell Jr., U.S. Navy
James A. McDivitt, U.S. Air Force
Elliot M. See Jr., civilian
Thomas P. Stafford, U.S. Air Force
Edward H. White II, U.S. Air Force
John W. Young, U.S. Navy

1963 Astronaut Group

Edwin E. "Buzz" Aldrin Jr., U.S. Air Force
William A. Anders, U.S. Air Force

Astronaut Group Three, 1963. Front row, left to right: Aldrin, Anders, Bassett, Bean, Cernan, Chaffee. Back row: Collins, Cunningham, Eisele, Freeman, Gordon, Schweickart, Scott, Williams.

Charles A. Bassett II, U.S. Air Force
Alan L. Bean, U.S. Navy
Eugene A. Cernan, U.S. Navy
Roger B. Chaffee, U.S. Navy
Michael Collins, U.S. Air Force
R. Walter Cunningham, civilian
Donn F. Eisele, U.S. Air Force
Theodore C. Freeman, U.S. Air Force
Richard F. Gordon Jr., U.S. Navy
Russell L. "Rusty" Schweickart, civilian
David R. Scott, U.S. Air Force
Clifton C. "C.C." Williams, U.S. Marine Corps

In addition to this nucleus of twenty-three astronauts, three of the Original Seven were still active in 1964: Gus Grissom, Wally Schirra, and Gordo Cooper. Like Slayton, Al Shepard had been grounded due to a medical problem, and he took a new job as Deke's deputy. John Glenn and Scott Carpenter were pursuing other interests.

Of the new astronauts, all in the '62 group were experienced test pilots in the mold of the Original Seven. The '63 group featured a mix of test pilots, operational fighter pilots, and fighter-pilot-scientists. Interestingly, 80 percent of all NASA astronauts had been Boy Scouts in their younger years, and 16 percent had achieved the top rank of Eagle Scout.

Being an astronaut was a dangerous business. Four astronauts were killed in plane crashes before they had a chance to fly on Gemini or

Apollo. Three others would perish in an accident that almost derailed the Apollo program (recounted in a later chapter). For the '63 group, the loss rate was particularly high. More than a quarter died on the job, a mortality rate that was comparable to that of a combat tour with a bomber squadron during the war.

As new missions approached and Deke announced the crew assignments, astronauts tried to figure out his system. They understood that the key was to get a backup slot, which would clear the way for a seat on a future mission. But how did they land that coveted first assignment? Did buttering up the boss help? Did showing off their flying skills? Most applied the motto of Bill Anders from the '63 group: "Work your tail off, and someone will notice." But that did little to distinguish them from all of their equally ambitious colleagues. If only they had spent

Boy Scout Neil Armstrong (front row, standing next to the scoutmaster), around 1942

time in the operations tent back in southern Italy during the war, they would have understood Deke Slayton's art and science of assembling a crew.

Like a good squadron operations officer, Deke had a method. He always picked the commander first. The commander was the captain of the ship with the authority to make decisions during the flight, subject only to instructions from Mission Control; he also called the shots during training. Slayton gave careful thought to which astronauts would excel in this position. The other slots were filled through private consultation with the commander, aided by Deke's observations of who worked well together. But his principle that any crew could fly any mission meant that in theory anyone could fit in. After all, these were highly motivated professionals who would get the job done even if they didn't like each other.

Slayton also created a rotation system. If you were on a backup crew, you could usually expect to be tapped for a prime crew on the third mission after your backup assignment. For example, the Gemini 3 backup crew became the prime crew for Gemini 6, and the Gemini 4 backups took the prime slots for Gemini 7. A subordinate astronaut who did especially well on his mission could be promoted to commander on a later mission.

Always at the forefront of Slayton's thinking was that he was building a squadron with the skills and working relationships to go to the Moon.

Outside of NASA, Slayton's key role went largely unnoticed. Many reporters regarded him as a slightly sad figure. They could see he was staying in shape and keeping up with training in hopes of returning to flight status. But that seemed a forlorn hope, since more and more younger astronauts were coming on board. The press knew he was in charge, but they considered his administrative job a bureaucratic chore.

Furthermore, in interviews Deke made odd comments like, "Going to the Moon is going from point A to point B in a transportation system." There was no poetry or passion to him. Little did they realize, but this ineloquent man was directing the greatest spectacle ever made. He was choosing and coaching the men who would embark on history's most astounding adventure.

One journalist who did get a glimpse behind Slayton's deceptively dull surface was Oriana Fallaci, a feisty Italian writer who jetted around the world interviewing famous people. Like everyone else, she wanted to talk to Shepard and Glenn, but Deke was the chief astronaut, so she had to talk to him first. Naturally, she asked him how it felt to be kicked off his Mercury flight.

"Forgive me for bringing it up," she added.

"Everybody brings it up," he said with resignation. Then he recited the story he had told so many times, about his anger over the decision and his futile attempts to get it reversed.

Searching for another topic, Fallaci got him onto the subject of flying.

Slayton brightened up. "Anything that flies, I'll use it. I'd use an umbrella if an umbrella could fly." Astronauts were famously ignorant of current events, but this remark showed a surprising familiarity with popular culture, since the Disney movie *Mary Poppins* with its umbrella-piloting nanny was about to be released.

He continued: "I've been flying for twenty years. I was nineteen when I was a bomber pilot flying over Italy—"

Fallaci broke in: "Wait, wait, Italy?! And where were you bombing?"

"Here and there, everywhere. Naples. Tuscany. Florence, I remember. In October of '43."

Fallaci had a sick feeling. "Florence? In October of '43?"

"Yes. That cursed railroad."

Fallaci knew it too well. She had been there as a fourteen-year-old girl. Her house had been destroyed, and she had injured her foot getting away.

Slayton was shocked. "I'm sorry. I'm very sorry. It was my job."

"It was the war," she said. It was her turn to be resigned.

And they bonded over this tragedy. Oriana offered Deke a cigarette. He had given up smoking, but he accepted. Like millions of soldiers, he had smoked incessantly during the war. Now, for a moment, he was back, reliving the horror with one of war's innocent victims.

Cosmonaut Alexi Leonov makes history's first space walk, March 18, 1965.

26

THE MOON COMES INTO FOCUS

Sometimes NASA officials felt like the Union Army in the Civil War. During much of that conflict, Union forces in the East were outfoxed again and again by Confederate General Robert E. Lee, whose aggressive style invariably beat them to the punch. At his wit's end, President Lincoln sent for an officer who had been successful in another theater of the war, Ulysses S. Grant, and put him in charge of turning the tide against Lee.

Grant's first job was to convince his demoralized troops that Lee was not invincible. "Oh, I am heartily tired of hearing about what Lee is going to do," he scolded them. "Some of you always seem to think he is suddenly going to turn a double somersault, and land in our rear and on both of our flanks at the same time. Go back to your command, and try to think what we are going to do ourselves, instead of what Lee is going to do."

A century later, the Soviet space program was a lot like General Lee. Invariably, they beat Americans to the punch. They were the first to launch a satellite, the first to send a human into space, and the first to orbit two manned spaceships simultaneously. By 1963, they were in first, second, third, *and* fourth places in the duration of manned missions. (Gordo Cooper's Mercury flight was in fifth place.)

Soviet secrecy kept everyone guessing about their next moves, but one thing was certain: they were reading American newspapers. Alerted by reports of the planned two-seat Gemini spacecraft, they got the jump on the U.S. by launching *three* cosmonauts into orbit some five months before Gemini's inaugural flight (with Gus Grissom and John Young on Gemini 3 in March 1965).

They also knew about NASA's plans for a much-anticipated space spectacular—the moment when an astronaut in orbit would open the hatch and drift out into the void, protected only by a space suit and attached to his craft by a tenuous lifeline. This science-fiction-like feat, popularly known as a space walk but which NASA called "extravehicular activity," or EVA, was scheduled for one of the later Gemini flights. Not only would the EVA provide glorious pictures of an astronaut floating above the blue planet, but it was an indispensable skill for eventually going outside on the Moon.

True to form, the Soviets struck again. They chalked up the world's first EVA in March 1965, eleven weeks before NASA achieved the same feat with Ed White on Gemini 4, advancing its own schedule to try to keep up with the Russians.

"The Russians upstage us every time," an American astronaut lamented.

Premier Nikita Khrushchev was no longer on hand to taunt America. He had been deposed from power the previous year, but his enthusiasm for space lived on with the new leadership. One Soviet space official boldly hinted at the next step: "The target now before us is the Moon, and we hope to reach it in the not-distant future." Oddly enough, political tensions between the United States and Soviet Union were decreasing during this time, helped in part by the departure of Premier

Ed White floats above Earth on America's first space walk, June 3, 1965.

Khrushchev. But the competition in space was becoming fiercer than ever.

●)

The Soviets were not just first in manned spaceflight, they were also leading the way in robotic missions. In September 1959, they were the first to hit the Moon with a probe. A month later, they were the first to photograph the far side of the Moon. The photos from the far side mission highlighted the amazing power of space probes, for the images showed the hemisphere of the Moon that is permanently turned away from Earth—something impossible to see without flying hundreds of thousands of miles, taking a series of pictures, and then relaying them by radio signal to Earth, which is exactly what the Soviet probe did.

Although America seemed permanently in second place, its efforts were nonetheless starting to pay off. After six failed attempts, NASA's Ranger program achieved a success in the summer of 1964 when Ranger 7 crashed into the Moon's Sea of Clouds. On the way down it sent back a continuous stream of pictures as it hurtled toward a possible Apollo landing area. Ranger's close-up views were a thousand times better than those from the largest telescopes, and they held good news and bad. The good: lunar dust didn't seem nearly as thick as some scientists had feared. The bad: craters were present at all scales—craters on top of craters on top of craters. The nearer Ranger got, the more craters showed up. Obviously, finding a reasonably flat place to land would be challenging.

NASA adviser Harold Urey suggested the Sea of Tranquility for Ranger's next target. In February 1965, Ranger 8 duly dove into this region, finding it similar to the Sea of Clouds. One area near its southwestern edge offered an expanse of safe-looking terrain that seemed promising for an early Apollo landing site.

A final Ranger expedition took off in March 1965, two days before Grissom and Young's Gemini 3 flight. The highlight of this mission was not the science but the show, aired live on network television. The program put millions of viewers in the driver's seat of Ranger 9, watching the Moon get closer and closer, picture by picture, as the craft plummeted toward self-destruction. Americans viewing at home felt like participants in a thrilling voyage of discovery. Calling it "one of the dramatic moments in television history," an awestruck journalist wrote: "For the first time earthbound people found themselves figuratively transported through space and hurtling toward the Moon at 6,000 miles per hour."

Another newspaper looked ahead to the even more spectacular show to come. "The time is not distant," this reporter prophesied, "when

One of the first views of the Moon's far side—impossible to see from Earth—photographed by a Soviet space probe in October 1959

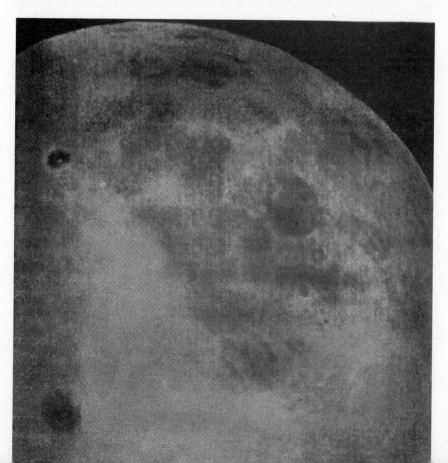

the first men will emerge from a spaceship, carrying cameras with them. Millions all over the world will be able to follow their progress on television as the lunar explorers take man's first step outside the terrestrial sphere. That will be the television show of the century." In his speech announcing the Apollo program, President Kennedy had promised, "In a very real sense, it will not be one man going to the Moon . . . it will be an entire nation."

●

Keeping up the pressure, the next year the Soviets were the first to soft-land a robotic probe on the Moon. Their craft set down in the Ocean of Storms, another of the Moon's bone-dry seas. A soft landing is the most difficult step of all in lunar exploration. Two months later, in April 1966, they scored another coup by putting the first satellite into orbit around the Moon. This would be a crucial maneuver for lunar-orbit rendez-vous.

As usual, America was not far behind. In early June, NASA's Surveyor 1 fired its braking rocket and made a gentle touchdown some 400 miles from the Russian landing site. And in mid-August, Lunar Orbiter 1 began circling the Moon, photographing the landscape below in search of more landing possibilities for Apollo. Additional Surveyors and Lunar Orbiters followed.

Also during this time, Gemini missions were going up at an unprecedented rate—an average of one every nine and half weeks—giving American astronauts crucial experience in the complex art of space-flight. Like General Grant in a much earlier contest, NASA was doing its best to turn the tide.

The American probe Lunar Orbiter 1 records the far side of the Moon, with the crescent Earth in the distance, August 1966.

After a near disaster in space, Neil Armstrong (right) and Dave Scott (left) sit inside their Gemini capsule, assisted by the rescue team, 1966.

27

NEIL ARMSTRONG'S WILD RIDE

During the first few Gemini flights, space rendezvous proved trickier than astronauts had expected. As pilots, their instinct was to accelerate when catching up with a target. But in space, putting on the gas causes the spacecraft to rise to a higher orbit, where it moves *more slowly* than the target. (The higher the orbit, the slower a satellite travels, since gravity grows weaker with distance.) The correct procedure is to *decelerate*, dropping to a lower and therefore faster orbit than the target. When the spacecraft catches up, it must adjust its orbit to be exactly the same as that of the target. Furthermore, the rendezvous must take place under the right lighting conditions, which requires careful timing. The astronauts had trained for all of this, but they still found it frustratingly difficult.

Another difficulty was that Gemini's unmanned target vehicle, a specially adapted Agena rocket stage, was having technical problems. Launched separately from Gemini, Agena was the proxy command module to Gemini's lunar module, designed to re-create the rendezvous and docking circumstances that astronauts would encounter around

A Gemini spacecraft in orbit, photographed from another Gemini during the first space rendezvous, 1965

the Moon. On its much-delayed first launch, Agena blew up. Undaunted, the Gemini astronauts practiced rendezvous—but not docking—with another Gemini spacecraft that had been launched on a separate mission. Not until Gemini 8, the sixth piloted mission, in March 1966, did an Agena finally arrive in orbit, ready for the first rendezvous-and-docking attempt.

Gemini 8 was commanded by Neil Armstrong, teamed with copilot Dave Scott. Aided by radar and a simple onboard computer, Armstrong made rendezvous and docking look easy. After executing a series of precise orbital changes by firing thrusters with a hand controller, he closed in on

Piloted by Neil Armstrong, the Gemini 8 spacecraft approaches an Agena rocket stage (center) prior to the first docking in space, March 1966. Shortly after, the linked vehicles began to gyrate out of control.

Agena during Gemini's fourth revolution around the Earth. Given the final go-ahead, he nudged the spacecraft's nose into Agena's docking collar until capture latches engaged. Announcing, "We are docked!" he added with test pilot nonchalance, "Yes, it's really a smoothie." Back in Houston, mission controllers cheered. This was a space first for America.

Armstrong was relieved that his hardest task of the mission was over. Then, half an hour later, Scott noticed that the two linked vehicles were starting to gyrate slowly. Armstrong righted the situation with his hand controller, but then it started again, growing worse. Assuming the problem was with Agena's control system, which he had been warned about, Armstrong undocked. This only made the oscillations increase, and the Gemini spacecraft soon began tumbling at a rate that approached one revolution per second—about the speed of a figure skater, with arms outstretched, at the start of an Olympic-class spin. Like the skater, Gemini's rotational speed seemed headed for a dizzying finale.

"We have serious problems here," Scott radioed the ground.

Armstrong explained, "We're rolling up and we can't turn anything off. Continuously increasing in a left roll." Both men sounded eerily calm.

Scott later described the event as "like being on a theme-park ride which thrills passengers by spinning at high speed, except theme-park rides don't spin so fast or for so long—if they did, too many passengers would black out."

Close to blacking out themselves, the astronauts diagnosed the problem as a malfunction in their maneuvering system, which consisted of sixteen small thrusters arrayed around the spacecraft. One of the thrusters was stuck and wouldn't stop firing. Fighting vertigo and tunnel vision, and with checklists and other loose items plastered against the walls of the spacecraft from centrifugal force, Armstrong managed to shut down the entire system and activate special thrusters for orienting the spacecraft during reentry. Using these, he gradually got the capsule under control. Mission rules required that they now return to Earth, since they couldn't risk losing more reentry fuel.

And so the flight of Gemini 8 ended prematurely but with two big accomplishments: rendezvous and docking had been demonstrated for the first time, and two coolheaded astronauts had solved the most serious crisis yet in space.

It had been a close call. On the ground, mission controller Bob Carlton, a slow-talking engineer from Alabama who rarely got excited about anything, quickly grasped that the astronauts had been fighting for their lives. "I thought they were gone," he said afterward, calling it one of the most terrifying experiences of his career. Three years later, Carlton would have another hair-raising moment with Armstrong.

●

Gemini 8 was followed by four more Gemini missions. Surprisingly, the entire Gemini manned program—ten flights stretching from March 1965 to November 1966—took place without a single spaceflight by Soviet cosmonauts. The Russians had preempted the first Gemini mission by a few days with their spectacular space walk, but then they launched no manned missions for the next two years. Given their previous pace of activity, this pause was hard to understand—but nonetheless welcomed, since NASA was now starting to take the lead in the space race.

The agency racked up multiple successes with rendezvous and docking, and also large orbital changes using the Agena engine to propel the docked spacecraft to new heights. Both were crucial techniques for a lunar mission, and the Soviets had done nothing like it. Project Gemini also bested the Russians with the longest-duration spaceflight to date (two weeks, proving that astronauts could survive the minimum eight days of lunar landing roundtrip without ill physical effects); record-breaking space walks (paving the way for lunar field trips); demonstrations of guided reentry (the only way to reduce g-forces to a survivable level when returning from the Moon); and an altitude record of 850 miles (only a third of a percent of the way to the Moon, but a dizzying height for the time).

●

Even while Gemini was under way, Apollo missions were lining up in the schedule. Deke Slayton had assembled six crews to handle the first three manned Apollo missions, projected for 1967. None would yet go to

Gemini 12—the last of the Gemini series—blasts off in November 1966. Apollo missions were due to start in early 1967.

the Moon, since these early missions would be test flights in Earth orbit of various crucial components. But it was a good guess that Deke's prime crew for the eventual first lunar landing would be picked from among these eighteen astronauts. With the commander listed first, the crews were:

Apollo 1
Prime crew: Gus Grissom, Ed White, Roger Chaffee
Backup: Wally Schirra, Donn Eisele, Walt Cunningham

Apollo 2
Prime crew: Jim McDivitt, Dave Scott, Rusty Schweickart
Backup: Tom Stafford, John Young, Gene Cernan

Apollo 3
Prime crew: Frank Borman, Mike Collins, Bill Anders
Backup: Pete Conrad, Dick Gordon, C.C. Williams

Based on the importance that Slayton placed on the commander, the top-ranked astronauts in his calculations were Gus Grissom, Wally Schirra, Jim McDivitt, Tom Stafford, Frank Borman, and Pete Conrad. Grissom and Schirra were both Mercury and Gemini veterans; Stafford and Conrad had each flown two Gemini missions; and Borman had commanded the record-breaking two-week Gemini flight. The other twelve astronauts were half Gemini veterans, half rookies.

Under Deke's rotation system, a backup crew could expect to skip ahead three missions to the next prime assignment, while the original prime crew became the backup for that mission. In theory, the six crews could keep rotating like this through Apollos 4, 5, 6, and beyond, honing their skills as the hardware was put through its paces in Earth orbit, then near the Moon, and finally on the Moon. Slayton had the option of changing the crews as the Moon landing got closer, sidelining some members and choosing replacements from the remaining pool of astronauts. The important thing was that he now had the system in place to deliver a flight-ready crew for the first lunar landing whenever it was needed—just as during the war his squadron could deliver well-trained crews for any combat mission assigned by headquarters.

Conspicuously missing from his Apollo roster was the heroic commander of Gemini 8: Neil Armstrong.

Apollo 1 crew. Left to right: Gus Grissom, Ed White, and Roger Chaffee.

28

"FIRE IN THE COCKPIT"

Ever since Project Mercury, the media had warned about all the ways that spaceflight could kill astronauts. Launch was the most obvious danger, but reentry was just as risky, and Armstrong and Scott on Gemini 8 had experienced the perils of a minor malfunction in orbit—a simple stuck thruster—that nearly doomed them. At NASA, astronauts, engineers, managers, public affairs officials—everyone—was primed for a tragedy sooner or later, but no one expected the disaster that came.

●

Oxygen is one of the essential requirements for human life. We get it from the air, where it is only one-fifth of any given breath we take; the rest is mostly nitrogen, which we don't need. In a spacecraft, the simplest solution is to skip the nitrogen and fill the cabin with oxygen only—pure oxygen.

A big advantage to this approach is that the cabin pressure can be greatly reduced from ordinary sea-level pressure, since pure oxygen at a lower pressure still gives you all you need. The payoff is that lower cabin pressure means the spacecraft structure can weigh less, since it doesn't have to withstand fifteen pounds per square inch (sea-level pressure) against the vacuum of space. So like the Mercury and Gemini capsules before it, Apollo was designed for a pure-oxygen environment at five pounds per square inch.

The disadvantage of pure oxygen is an increased risk of fire. Most materials need oxygen to burn, and they burn hotter and faster in pure oxygen. However, this problem seemed to be offset by the peculiar behavior of fire in space. Studies suggested that a fire would quickly burn itself out, because the convection currents that feed it don't operate in weightlessness. Just to be safe, NASA ordered that flammable materials be kept to a minimum in the Apollo capsule.

Therefore, fire wasn't on anyone's mind on January 27, 1967, when Apollo 1 astronauts Gus Grissom, Ed White, and Roger Chaffee were sealed into the command module for a simulated countdown at Cape Kennedy in preparation for Apollo's first manned mission—a two-week test of the CSM in Earth orbit, set for the following month. The biggest worry was a frustrating series of equipment problems that had to be worked out before launch day.

The CSM sat atop von Braun's Saturn IB, the largest rocket yet to carry humans, although it was a baby compared to the Saturn V. The rocket was not fueled that day, so the test was not considered hazardous. It should have been, since the cabin was filled with pure oxygen, not at the five pounds per square inch to be used in space, but at the fifteen pounds per square inch at sea level. In fact, the pressure was set a bit higher than sea-level pressure to reveal any leaks in the spacecraft. It was an explosive situation. At seventeen pounds per square inch, practically anything will burn in pure oxygen, even aluminum metal. All it takes is a spark.

Every Mercury and Gemini had been tested on the launchpad with high-pressure oxygen. But they were much smaller spacecraft, much simpler, and with far less wiring.

Somewhere in Apollo's thirty miles of wire a spark jumped between two bare leads where insulation had broken off. In the oxygen-saturated atmosphere, nearby Velcro strips and nylon netting ignited like tissue paper. The netting, which was designed to catch fallen objects, extended throughout the cabin and acted like a trail of spilled gasoline. The fire spread so quickly that the astronauts barely had time to react.

"We've got a fire in the cockpit," one reported tersely. Two of them immediately scrambled to open the hatch, which was impossible against the rising pressure generated by the blaze. Seconds later, all three lost consciousness from the toxic gases and died soon after, thankfully before the raging inferno burned through their space suits.

By the time rescue workers reached the scene, the capsule had burst open and was spouting flames and smoke. The responders did their best to save the crew, but it took five minutes to unbolt the hatch. One glance inside told them it was too late. A reporter who saw the spaceship afterward said it looked like "the cockpit of an aircraft in World War II that took a direct hit."

Aviation veterans were reminded of a catastrophe twenty-four years earlier. In 1943, another mammoth technological project had suffered a similar gruesome setback when a prototype of the B-29 bomber

The burned-out
Apollo 1 cabin,
January 1967. The
astronauts' bodies
have been removed.

crashed in Seattle, killing thirty-one people. Straining to produce
enough power, one of the engines on the super-bomber had burst into
flames. With World War II under way, America badly needed advanced
weapons, but critics thought the B-29 was impossibly complicated and
recklessly being rushed into production.

Now, many felt the same way about Apollo. In the wake of the fire,
there were calls to slow down the Moon-landing program or even end
it. Walter Lippmann, the most influential newspaper columnist of the
day, argued that the success of robotic probes like Ranger and Surveyor proved that humans were not needed in space. "We should abandon the idea of landing a man on the Moon by some arbitrary date," he
wrote, "and we should put our minds on the use of machines, already
spectacularly promising, to increase our knowledge of the Moon and
the space around it." J. William Fulbright, a powerful senator from Ar-
kansas, shared this view. He blamed the fire on "the inflexible, but
meaningless, goal of putting an American on the Moon by 1970" and
demanded a "full reappraisal of the space program." A handful of
others in Congress agreed with him. They were the voices of common
sense that had been resisting the lure of human spaceflight since the
beginning.

Jim Webb and other top NASA officials were at a diplomatic event in Washington on the day of the accident. President Lyndon Johnson had zealously backed the space program since he assumed the presidency after Kennedy's assassination, and on January 27 he happened to be hosting the signing of an international treaty on the peaceful uses of outer space, marking an easing of Cold War tensions. News of the fire arrived as post-signing celebrations were under way. Everyone was stunned. Some stayed for dinner, but General Phillips and Bob Gilruth immediately left for the Cape to get the full story, while Webb, Seamans, and Mueller went to NASA headquarters to handle the crisis. One badly shaken aerospace official observed, "This is the dreadful price you have to pay in a business like this."

That evening, Webb held a press conference: "We've always known something like this would happen sooner or later," he said, "but it's not going to be permitted to stop the program." Then he brought up the circumstance that made the blow so much worse: "Although everyone realized that someday space pilots would die, who would have thought the first tragedy would be on the ground?"

Astronaut Frank Borman thought the same thing. One of Slayton's Apollo commanders, he later recalled how the accident affected him and his colleagues: "Three superbly trained pilots had died, trapped during a supposedly routine ground test that shouldn't have been any more dangerous than taking a bath. I don't think the grief would have been any less if they had perished in space, but at least it would have been more logical and half-expected."

At Webb's direction, Bob Seamans assembled a review board to investigate the fire. Seamans tapped Borman to represent the astronaut corps and Max Faget to cover spacecraft engineering, together with seven other experts. The night after he inspected the burned-out capsule for the first time, Borman was so overcome that he went out drinking with Faget and Slayton. The three disciplined, dignified men offered toast after toast to Gus, Ed, and Roger. They perhaps overdid it. The agile Faget decided to demonstrate handstands, and they ended the evening by throwing their glasses against the wall.

"It was right out of a World War I movie," Borman wrote. "The only thing we left out was the bravado toast, 'Here's to the next man to die.'"

The review board discovered that work on the command module had been hasty, with large and small problems piling up. It was an impressive ship—in theory. At North American Aviation, the prime contractor, they proudly referred to it as "a labyrinth of systems more complicated than an aircraft carrier packed into a stainless-steel phone booth." But like the B-29 before it, the CM was pushing the state of the art and courting trouble.

At Faget's suggestion, ground operations from then on would be

Max Faget (foreground) and Frank Borman inside a command module mock-up during their investigation of the Apollo 1 fire, 1967

The Apollo 1 command module under construction at North American Aviation, 1966

conducted in nitrogen-rich air, which is far less of a fire hazard. In space, the capsule would operate, as designed, with pure oxygen, but made safer by more stringent rules about flammable materials and wiring. The board also recommended a new hatch that would be much easier for the crew to open.

But the most significant change was something not mandated by the board: a renewed commitment to perfection by all 400,000 people working on Apollo. The new spirit was summed up by Chief Flight Director Gene Kranz. "Spaceflight will never tolerate carelessness, incapacity, and neglect," he told his Mission Control team. "Somewhere, somehow, we screwed up . . . We were rolling the dice, hoping that things would come together by launch day, when in our hearts we knew it would take a miracle . . . From this day forward, Flight Control will be known by two words: *tough* and *competent. Tough* means we are forever accountable for what we do or what we fail to do . . . *Competent* means we will never take anything for granted." He closed by ordering that their two watchwords—*tough* and *competent*—be written on every blackboard in every office. "Each day when you enter the room these words will remind you of the price paid by Grissom, White, and Chaffee."

Saturn V emerges from the Vehicle Assembly Building. Note the three workers along the railing at lower right.

29

"GO, BABY, GO!"

"The guys who are going to fly the first lunar missions are the guys in this room." As usual, Deke Slayton was getting right to the point. It was Monday, April 10, 1967—ten weeks since the fire. Deke had called a meeting of his six Apollo crews to get them ready for the tasks ahead.

With the death of Grissom's crew, Slayton had moved their backups into the prime slot for the first manned Apollo mission and readjusted the other assignments. At the end of the line, he added a new crew, picking three astronauts he had been holding in reserve: Neil Armstrong as commander, teamed with Jim Lovell and Buzz Aldrin. The eighteen potential Moon explorers sat around the small conference room, keeping their thoughts to themselves. Gene Cernan was awed but psyched. Walt Cunningham felt at "the climax of a grand competition." Both John Young and Neil Armstrong believed their boss was simply stating the obvious. "Who else would be doing it, flying the first lunar missions, besides us?" wondered Young.

But one thing was certain: in the entire history of exploration, no one had been able to make a promise like this—until now.

Issuing his standard warning—"Be flexible, this stuff will change"—Slayton outlined the schedule. A series of unmanned flights up through Apollo 6 would test the Saturn V, the command and service module, and the lunar module before hazarding a manned Apollo flight with the improved CSM, to be designated Apollo 7. Slayton sketched the goals and announced the crew assignments:

Apollo 7
Prime crew: Wally Schirra, Donn Eisele, Walt Cunningham
Backup: Tom Stafford, John Young, Gene Cernan
Mission: Run the CSM through its paces in Earth orbit. Test the Apollo navigation system and guidance computer.

Apollo 8
Prime crew: Jim McDivitt, Dave Scott, Rusty Schweickart
Backup: Pete Conrad, Dick Gordon, C.C. Williams
Mission: Test the CSM and LM in Earth orbit, to be launched separately by two Saturn IBs (later reassigned to a single Saturn V).

Apollo 9
Prime crew: Frank Borman, Mike Collins, Bill Anders
Backup: Neil Armstrong, Jim Lovell, Buzz Aldrin
Mission: Simulate a lunar mission with the CSM and LM in a high Earth orbit, scheduled to be the first manned flight of a Saturn V.

If all went well, then the next mission, Apollo 10, could conceivably be the first lunar-landing attempt, giving the prize to Stafford's crew, assuming that the three-mission rotation system was followed. However, the achievement of Kennedy's goal was more likely to happen on

Apollo 11, 12, 13, or 14. Enough hardware was being ordered for missions through Apollo 20.

The CSM and LM could be perfect in every way, but if the Saturn V didn't work, the Moon landings were off. Webb and Mueller pressed for a test flight as soon as possible to show Congress that Apollo was back on track.

At the time of the Apollo 1 fire in January 1967, all three stages of the first Saturn V were at the Cape to be checked out. Problems kept cropping up. Repairs, new checks, and more modifications extended into the summer. Then much of the fall was taken up with an elaborate rehearsal of the countdown. Only in early November was the Saturn V finally ready for its maiden flight—a risky trial of all three stages at once, carrying an unmanned CSM. This all-up approach was General Phillips's brainchild and George Mueller's decreed policy, designed to save time. Although von Braun went along with it, he was still worried that the tactic courted disaster.

Saturn V (lower right) leaves the assembly building on its 3.5-mile journey to the launchpad.

Phillips and von Braun had had their differences before. During World War II, Phillips piloted an escort fighter on a bombing raid over von Braun's rocket base. Now, the former enemies were colleagues and friends, with utmost respect for each other's dedication and organizational abilities. On the morning of November 9, they stood together in the firing room as the countdown approached 7:00 a.m.—launch time for an event that would make them either heroes or scapegoats. The Saturn V was three and a half miles away. At that distance, you could reach out your arm and blot out the Moon rocket with the width of your little finger. This was the closest that observers were allowed to get to a missile that packed the explosive power of a small atomic bomb.

A few seconds before the count reached zero, the base of the rocket erupted in billowing fire, signaling the start of the ignition sequence. On television, the brilliant light flooded the sensors of the TV camera, making it look like a catastrophic explosion. Then at zero, the mighty rocket started to lift off the pad, propelled by seven and a half million pounds of thrust. It took ten seconds to clear the launch tower—"the longest ten seconds of my life," recalled von Braun, who was shouting, "Go, baby, go!" in his German accent.

At this point, the sound waves from the rocket reached the launch center and press viewing area: "a continuous, pulsating clap of deep thunder," wrote one reporter. With it came bone-rattling vibrations like those from an earthquake.

"My God, our building's shaking!" Walter Cronkite of *CBS Evening News* exclaimed over live television. As ceiling tiles rained down and soft-drink bottles clattered to the floor, Cronkite pushed against the plate-glass window to hold it in place.

He couldn't keep his eyes off the spectacle outside. "Look at that rocket go!" he yelled. "Into the clouds at 3,000 feet! The roar is terrific!"

Upward it went, devouring kerosene and liquid oxygen at a rate of fifteen tons per second. Growing lighter as it ascended, while its thrust stayed nearly constant, the thirty-six-story-tall vehicle gained speed. After just over a minute, it was traveling Mach 1 at an altitude of four and a half miles. It would need to go twenty-five times faster and higher before it reached Earth orbit.

At two and a half minutes, the first stage ran out of propellant and dropped away. The second stage ignited, burning liquid hydrogen and liquid oxygen, one of the most potent combinations known. The Saturn V was a hybrid of old and new, with its first stage of five F-1 engines drawing on technology from the 1950s, while its upper stages used more innovative engines designed to handle liquid hydrogen, which is even colder than liquid oxygen. The challenge of developing the second stage had led to long delays before Saturn V's test flight. Developed by North American Aviation, under Harrison Storm's direction, the second stage behaved beautifully, burning for six minutes and taking the ship to an altitude of over a hundred miles.

At this point, the rocket stack was traveling parallel to Earth's surface, 900 miles downrange, at nearly 90 percent of orbital velocity. The third stage ignited for two and half minutes to push the vehicle into orbit. Then it shut off.

On a lunar mission, the CSM and third stage, with the LM nestled between them, would make an orbit and a half. Then the third stage would fire again, propelling the stack to the Moon. On this flight, there was no LM, but a crucial goal was to test the restart capability of the third stage. It reignited and put the CSM into a highly elliptical orbit for the final challenge—a simulation of Apollo's return to Earth. With

an additional boost from the service module engine, the spacecraft plunged back into the atmosphere, reaching a top speed of 25,000 miles per hour, subjecting the heat shield to temperatures double those experienced by reentering Mercury and Gemini capsules.

The test flight ended as the charred but intact command module parachuted to an on-target landing in the Pacific Ocean, almost nine hours after liftoff.

●

Marvin Miles, aerospace editor for the *Los Angeles Times*, had witnessed nuclear explosions and ridden with pilots breaking the sound barrier, but he had never experienced anything like this. He summed up what was at stake: "Had the critical test failed in a giant burst of flame equivalent to one million pounds of TNT, it would have obliterated all U.S. hope of landing astronauts on the Moon by 1970, surrendered the space lead to Russia, and dealt a staggering blow to American technology and national prestige."

Instead, it had dazzled the world, renewed public confidence in NASA, and proved the wisdom of the all-up strategy. And it had taken place the week of the fiftieth anniversary of the Communist Revolution in Russia— the supposed target date for the Soviets' own Moon landing. There was still much to do before America reached that goal, but Russia appeared to be far behind.

"Apollo is on the way to the Moon," proclaimed Sam Phillips. The normally impassive general could hardly stop smiling.

The first Saturn V takes off just after dawn on November 9, 1967.

New NASA manager Tom Paine holds a model of the lunar module, 1968.

30

THE SUBMARINER TAKES CHARGE

After World War II, the fearless submariner Tom Paine was assigned to help disarm enemy subs. During this time, he visited Hiroshima and Nagasaki, the two cities destroyed by atomic bombs. "If you can visualize a molten streetcar," he wrote his parents, "or an area miles square with no object bigger than a fireplace log in it, where it is impossible to tell where the streets and buildings were located, where some 80,000 people were living one second and completely disintegrated along with all their buildings the next, if you can visualize this, you can imagine the process of the atomic bomb." This powerful memory stuck with him for life.

Paine's duties included boarding Japanese submarines, still bristling with weapons as they came into port to surrender. In one case, his small boat approached a sub larger than any in the world. This was the I-400 class, a superweapon able to carry three airplanes. It could maneuver close to a target, surface, and launch a surprise air attack. America had nothing like it. The Japanese planned to use four such vessels to bomb the Panama Canal, the U.S. Navy's vital link between the Atlantic and Pacific oceans. In the end, the Japanese realized that attacking the canal would make no difference in the war, and the supersubs never saw action.

Captured Japanese supersub *I-400*, which Tom Paine navigated from Japan to Hawaii at the end of World War II

A nautical romantic, Paine said that inspecting the supersub was like "carrying out a classic naval 'boarders, away!' operation." "Boarders away!" was the traditional order to scramble aboard an enemy ship. In the old days, the boarding party was armed with cutlasses and pistols. Paine's operation was not quite so dramatic, but it had its elements of suspense. As he and his men toured the giant vessel, they were "wary of the impassive Japanese who stiffly greeted us, curious about the unfamiliar aircraft handling equipment all around us, delighted to be directly involved in this historic finale of the undersea war, and concerned about both the technical and human problems involved in carrying out our orders to disable her torpedo, ordnance, and radio gear before bringing her in." The operation culminated in a 4,500-mile voyage, delivering one of the supersubs to Pearl Harbor. During the journey, Paine was second-in-command, which was his highest military posting—"a fitting finale to my career in the Submarine Service," he wrote.

Twenty-three years later, in 1968, he found himself second-in-command of an even more thrilling enterprise.

In the months after the Apollo 1 fire, NASA deputy administrator Bob Seamans felt he was no longer trusted by his boss, Jim Webb. Traumatized by the deaths of the three astronauts, Webb wanted to make sure it didn't happen again, and he sought out any institutional weaknesses at NASA. If anything, Seamans was a tower of strength, but he knew he had lost his close working relationship with Webb, who blamed part of the negligence that had led to the tragedy on him. Therefore, Seamans resigned to go back to teaching at MIT. The search for his replacement turned up a brilliant executive at the General Electric Company: Tom Paine.

Since his submarine days, Paine had held a series of important jobs at General Electric. Most recently, he headed its innovative think tank, TEMPO, which concentrated on social and technological problems of the future and how they might be solved. When offered the number two spot at NASA, he said yes, in part because he felt the tug of something familiar about the organization. He couldn't put his finger on it, but his wife, Barbara, did.

They had fallen in love during the war, when she was a ground controller for the Royal Australian Air Force in Perth, his submarine's home port. After Barbara and Tom's first tour of NASA installations, she pointed out how the total commitment in the space program was the same spirit they remembered from the war. "These are the RAF types who have just come back from battling the Luftwaffe," she said, "these are the young submariners in Perth," thinking only of the next mission, "taking risks and fighting odds and really doing exciting things."

"It was absolutely true," Paine said later. The experience of working at NASA was "a great recharging of my battery."

Paine was nominated to be NASA's deputy administrator almost exactly a year after the fire. In Jim Webb's mind, it was just a matter of time until Paine filled his own shoes. Webb hadn't told anyone, but he was planning to retire from government service. It may seem odd to leave when the organization you have nurtured for seven difficult years is on the verge of its greatest accomplishments, but Webb had mixed feelings about staying. President Johnson had told him he would not be running for reelection in 1968. Whoever was elected that fall would see Webb as Johnson's man and want him replaced. It was vitally important to Webb that someone of Paine's caliber succeed him, and the former submariner had a good chance of being promoted to the top job by the new president, whoever it was.

Plus, the inquiry following the fire had worn Webb down. Congress and the press had searched under every rock for a scandal connected to him. Inevitably, some contracts and political deals were questioned.

They were typical of Webb's no-holds-barred management style, which made him so effective in Washington, where it is notoriously difficult to get things done. Nothing came of these probes. Still, the intense scrutiny meant that Webb had lost his clout with Congress. His turn to resign had come. Privately, he told Johnson he wanted to leave on his sixty-second birthday, October 7, 1968. When the day came, Paine took charge as acting administrator.

A month later, John F. Kennedy's old antagonist, Richard M. Nixon, was elected president in a close contest with the Democratic nominee, Vice President Hubert H. Humphrey. As Nixon's administration was settling in during the following spring, the new secretary of defense, Melvin Laird, called the new secretary of the Air Force, none other than Bob Seamans, and asked him whether Tom Paine should officially be made NASA administrator.

"I can give you a very straightforward, simple answer," Seamans told Laird. "Ask the president if he wants to carry out the lunar landing this year. If he does, make Tom Paine the administrator. But if he wants to run the risk of not going this year, then bring in somebody else."

Tom Paine got the appointment.

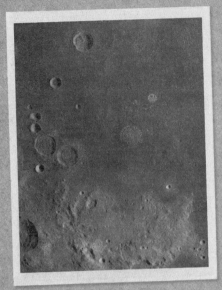

Western Sea of Tranquility from Lunar Orbiter 4, 1967. Apollo Landing Site 2 is in the lower right quadrant. This image is 165 miles across. (Note Moltke Crater at the lower right, also visible in the photos on pages 290 and 291.)

Ranger 8 on its death dive into the Sea of Tranquility, 1965. The two large craters at left are also in the Lunar Orbiter image above.

Ranger 8 two seconds before impact. The image is less than a mile across. The strip of static at right marks the end of transmission on crashing.

Surveyor 5 takes a surface photo from the Sea of Tranquility, 1965.

BRIEFING:
Lunar Reconnaissance

When automatic probes began arriving at the Moon to scout promising landing sites for Apollo, they concentrated on the band along the lunar equator. This region is easier to reach from Earth than are the higher latitudes. Therefore, robotic spacecraft searched there first.

Fortunately, some of the dark areas of the Moon, called lunar "seas," overlap the equator. Telescopic observations showed that these areas are flatter and less heavily cratered than the bright, rugged highlands, and so would make better landing sites, particularly for the crucial early missions. The designation "seas" traces to the pioneering era of telescopes, when the dark spots were thought to be bodies of water. Eventually, it was realized they are dry land, but the original term stuck.

From 1965 to 1967, four Ranger missions successfully crashed into the Moon, five Surveyors soft-landed, and five Lunar Orbiters circled, providing thousands of photographs at all scales. The Apollo site-selection board zeroed in on five potential landing zones that seemed to pose the fewest hazards. Moving from east to west, two were in the Sea of Tranquility, one was in the Central Bay at the Moon's geographic center, and two more were in the Ocean of Storms.

For a variety of reasons, the landing site in the western sector of the Sea of Tranquility was the best option. The selection board called it Apollo Landing Site 2. The automatic probes had found plenty of candidates for more challenging and geologically intriguing missions, once astronauts had a couple of successful landings to their credit. But for the purpose of achieving Kennedy's goal, Landing Site 2 looked like the place to go.

PART 6
THE MOON

"12 02 alarm! 12 02, what's that?"
—Mission controller during Apollo 11 landing, 1969

The surface of the Moon

Apollo 8 mission patch

31

A NEW MISSION TAKES SHAPE

"**A**re you out of your *mind*?" Webb shouted into the receiver.

Two months before he retired as NASA administrator, Jim Webb received a phone call from Apollo program director General Sam Phillips. The normally levelheaded general had floated an idea that made Webb question his sanity.

For his part, General Phillips was grateful that the conversation was taking place by long distance. "If a person's shock could be transmitted over the telephone," he recalled, "I'd probably have been shot in the head."

Also on the line was deputy administrator Tom Paine, who agreed that Webb was "horrified."

What was up?

That summer of 1968, Kennedy's goal of putting a man on the Moon by December 31, 1969, was looking more and more doubtful, since work on the lunar module was falling behind. The LM was unique. No one had ever designed a manned vehicle to land on another world. Not surprisingly, problems kept cropping up, delaying the crucial first manned flight of the LM. This test of the LM's systems, scheduled to take place in Earth orbit on Apollo 8, was now postponed until the winter of 1969, delaying other milestones that had to be reached before humans could walk on the Moon.

These other goals included perfecting techniques for navigation and communications between Earth and the Moon, testing the procedure for entering and leaving lunar orbit, certifying the safety of Apollo landing sites by visual observations from orbit, and demonstrating manned reentry into Earth's atmosphere at 24,200 miles per hour, the speed of a spacecraft returning from the Moon.

However, one NASA official saw the LM's troubles as an opportunity to skip ahead in the schedule and do something truly spectacular. George Low, Apollo spacecraft manager in Houston, proposed forgetting about the LM for Apollo 8 and launching a command and service module by itself on a mission around the Moon and back using a Saturn V. The CSM and Saturn V both appeared to be on track. The CSM still had to prove itself on Apollo 7, set to launch in the fall; and the Saturn V had run into problems on its second test flight earlier in the year, but von Braun was confident his rocket team could fix them. Obviously, the astronauts would be unable to land on the Moon without a LM, but they could test the procedures for traveling there and possibly even for going into lunar orbit, while getting the first close-up look at Earth's nearest neighbor.

Low approached Phillips with the idea. He loved it and checked with Paine, who was equally enthusiastic. When they called Webb, who was with Mueller at a conference in Europe, he hit the roof. Apollo had not yet sent a crew into Earth orbit, and now they were talking about going to the Moon!

Standing from left to right: George Low, Sam Phillips, and Deke Slayton, during an Apollo launch, 1969

But aside from streamlining the schedule, there was another very good reason to attempt this feat. Recent activity by the Russians strongly suggested they were planning to do it themselves.

The path to the Moon, around it, and back is relatively simple. Essentially, it is just an elliptical orbit (really a figure eight) with the Moon at one end. All that's needed is a spacecraft with supplies for several days, a booster that can accelerate the ship to 24,200 miles per hour, and a heat shield that can withstand reentry into Earth's atmosphere at that speed. During the Gemini program, one never-pursued idea called for modifying the Gemini capsule and using a more powerful rocket for exactly this purpose.

The danger of such a circumlunar mission is that once you are outbound, you can't change your mind and come back—a least not without expending more rocket power than you probably have. You are essentially committed to a six-day voyage to the Moon and back. This could be disastrous if you ran into a problem. Nonetheless, the simplicity of the trajectory makes it the poor man's Moon mission. You don't go into orbit around the Moon, you don't land, but you get to see the Moon from roughly a hundred miles away. In a sense, you can say you've been there.

In the summer of 1968, this was what the Soviets were clearly gear-

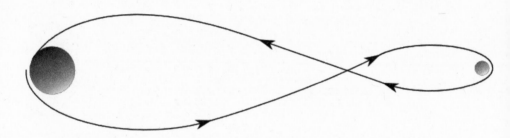

Figure–eight trajectory from Earth (at left) to the Moon and back (not drawn to scale)

ing up to do, and Low was worried that many people would not see the difference between going around the Moon and landing on it. The poor man's Moon mission might easily upstage Apollo. Then it wouldn't matter who landed on the Moon first, because the race would be seen to be over. This would be especially ironic if the Russians had never been in the man-on-the-Moon race in the first place. No one outside the Soviet Union knew whether they had their own Apollo program or not, but their intention to send a cosmonaut crew around the Moon and back had been hinted at by an unusual unmanned flight earlier in the spring.

Meanwhile, events were moving quickly in the Apollo program. Starting in October, the space agency was poised to launch manned missions at roughly two-month intervals, just as during Project Gemini. Apollo 7 took off on October 11, commanded by Wally Schirra, with copilots Donn Eisele and Walt Cunningham. Conducting the postponed Apollo 1 mission from nearly two years earlier, except on a redesigned spacecraft, Apollo 7 orbited Earth for eleven days and showed that the CSM was a superb spacecraft, ready for more ambitious missions.

Since Webb had retired on October 7, the decision about how ambitious the next flight would be fell to the acting administrator, Tom Paine. He was characteristically bold. "After a careful and thorough examination of all of the systems and risks involved," he told the press, "we have concluded that we are now ready to fly the most advanced mission for our Apollo 8 launch in December, the orbit around the Moon."

In other words, the next mission, Apollo 8, would carry out the most daring version of George Low's plan. It would not just fly out to the Moon and back. When it started to round the Moon on its elongated trajectory, it would fire the service module's rocket engine and enter lunar orbit, exactly as it would do when there was a lunar module attached. The CSM would then circle the Moon ten times and finally relight its engine and accelerate to the speed needed to return to Earth.

Paine added, "Frank Borman and his crew and all of our engineers are unanimously in favor of selecting this mission." As far as the astronauts were concerned, this unprecedented journey posed no unreasonable risks. "This will be within the normal hazards of test pilots flying experimental craft," Paine stressed.

Apollo 8 crew. Left to right: Bill Anders, Frank Borman, Jim Lovell.

Many NASA insiders felt that if Webb had still been in charge, he would have been too cautious to authorize such a plan, haunted by memories of the Apollo 1 fire. But Paine was more willing to take a chance. Though he looked like a risk-averse insurance salesman, underneath he was a swashbuckling submariner.

The new mission prompted Deke Slayton to juggle his crews. He wanted Apollo 8's original commander, Jim McDivitt, to stick with his crucial job of flying the first manned test of the LM. That mission would now become Apollo 9. Apollo 9's commander, Frank Borman, was moved to Apollo 8. His original crewmates were Mike Collins and Bill Anders, but Collins had been grounded for a spinal operation and was replaced by his backup, Jim Lovell.

These adjustments had a ripple effect. As Borman's backup, Neil Armstrong was now in line to command the flight three missions after Apollo 8—namely, Apollo 11. Although it was just a number at this point, Apollo 11 would become the most famous manned spaceflight of all time.

Russia's answer to Apollo: the Soyuz spacecraft, seen head-on as it orbits Earth

32

"IN THE BEGINNING"

After a mysterious break during America's Gemini missions, the Soviet manned space program was back in the news in 1967 and 1968. It was a rocky return. One of the reasons for their pause was they were building an advanced capsule called Soyuz. With room for a crew of three, Soyuz was their equivalent of the Apollo command and service module. On its maiden flight in April 1967, Soyuz was piloted by a single cosmonaut—the space veteran Vladimir Komarov. After launch, Komarov faced problems with critical equipment, and the flight director ordered the mission to be cut short. At the end of the eighteenth orbit, Soyuz fired its retrorockets to return to Earth. Unfortunately, the parachute system failed and the ship plummeted to the ground, crashing and killing Komarov instantly. This tragedy took place three months after the Apollo 1 fire.

A year later, in the spring of 1968, a redesigned Soyuz took off on an unmanned flight called Zond 4, which used a new rocket. Although not nearly as powerful as the Saturn V, this booster could send large payloads to the Moon. Zond 4 went nearly as far as the Moon and then returned to Earth, again malfunctioning during reentry.

Then in September 1968, Zond 5 took off, and for a time it seemed there might be a cosmonaut aboard, since a British ground station picked up a voice in Russian calling out instrument readings. It turned out to be a recording for testing communications at lunar distances, clearly in preparation for a manned flight. After passing behind the Moon, Zond 5 returned to Earth. Once again, reentry did not go well, but the craft managed to land intact in the Indian Ocean. It was the first-ever round-trip between Earth and the Moon, and the Russians announced that its cargo included two tortoises and several plants, all of which survived. Also that fall, the Soviets launched another unmanned lunar Zond, as well as an Earth-orbiting Soyuz piloted by a cosmonaut. All objectives were met on both missions, according to Soviet news reports.

The Russians now appeared to be poised for a manned lunar flight. Like a war that flares up after a long lull, the space race had reignited. *Time* magazine caught the mood on the cover of its December 6, 1968, issue, which showed an illustration of two spacemen, one Soviet, one American. They were sprinting toward the Moon over a caption that read, "Race for the Moon."

Queried by a reporter, Wernher von Braun conceded that the Soviets had a good chance of beating Apollo 8 to the Moon. As for who would be the first to land, he predicted it would be "a photo finish."

Missions to the Moon have to be launched during specific periods, called launch windows. These fleeting opportunities depend on the location of the launch site, the location of the tracking stations, the lunar phase when the spacecraft is supposed to arrive at the Moon, and the region on Earth where the spacecraft is supposed to land at the end of the mission. If at all possible, launch and landing should take place during daylight.

For the Soviet Union, these stringent requirements meant that the December 1968 launch window opened on the 8th of the month. For the United States, it didn't open until the 20th. Apollo 8 was scheduled to launch the next day, but no one knew what the Soviets' plans were. Therefore, the first part of December was tense with anticipation. On Saturday, December 7, the day before the Russian launch window opened, the newspaper for the town adjoining the Kennedy Space Center ran the headline, "Moon Shot for Soviets Sunday?" When Sunday came, there was nothing to report. Nor on Monday or Tuesday. When the window closed on Thursday, December 12, the Soviets' only space activity had been a routine satellite launch on the 10th. As usual, they said nothing. The following week, on the day before Apollo 8's scheduled takeoff, one of Russia's senior cosmonauts made this remark to journalists: "It is not important to mankind who will reach the Moon first and when he will reach it—in 1969 or 1970."

Had the Russians thrown in the towel?

Apollo 8 launched precisely on time, with Earth-shaking power that once again rattled Walter Cronkite's broadcast booth three and a half miles away. So smooth and steady was the Saturn V's rise that Cronkite guessed the astronauts were less jostled than his camera crew on the ground.

Far from it! Frank Borman, Jim Lovell, and Bill Anders were being whipped around like "a rat in the jaws of a big terrier," remembered Anders. The giant F-1 engines at the base of the Saturn V swiveled to keep the rocket upright and avoid knocking into the launch tower, which would have been catastrophic. This feat was like balancing a yardstick vertically in the palm of the hand; tiny movements at the base translate into large fluctuations at the tip—which were what the three astronauts were experiencing.

No one had ever ridden a rocket like this, and the crew could only compare it to a form of transportation they knew from their youth: a freight train. The Apollo astronauts were all children of the Great Depression. Some had hopped freights in their younger days for free rides. Others had held summer jobs on the railroad. Most had ridden troop trains at some point, which had few of the comforts of passenger trains. One astronaut likened the experience on a Saturn V to "a runaway freight train on a crooked track, swaying from side to side."

Then there was the "train wreck," as another astronaut described the instant when the first stage cut off. This happened two and a half minutes after liftoff, as the F-1 engines were burning the last of the first-stage propellant. At this point, the vehicle was 40 miles high and increasing its speed by almost 90 miles per hour every second, as if a racing car could go from 90 to 180 to 270 miles per hour in less time than it takes to read these words. The acceleration pinned the astronauts against their seats with four g's. When the engines quit, the acceleration suddenly dropped to zero and the crew lurched violently forward as if in a head-on collision.

"I suddenly felt like I'd been sitting on a catapult and somebody cut the rope," recalled Anders. In fact, he was experiencing the recoil of the rocket body as it responded to the abrupt loss of thrust, like a spring being released after it is compressed.

Then the second stage kicked in with its hydrogen-oxygen engines, throwing the space travelers back into their seats, this time with a gentler one g, which slowly built to two g's. From here on, the ride was less traumatic except for a periodic back-and-forth oscillation called

The first stage of the Saturn V drops away at an altitude of forty miles.

"pogo," named for the spring-loaded jumping stick. Pogo was one of the problems that von Braun had promised to fix, and his rocket team had been able to reduce it to a safe level but not eliminate it entirely. Therefore, Borman was relieved when the jittery second stage finally shut down and the smoother third stage took over, giving the vehicle a final push to orbital speed—17,500 miles per hour.

They were now in a low, temporary orbit, 119 miles high. Borman, Lovell, and Anders had two to three orbits to check out the spacecraft and confirm it was safe to proceed to the Moon, three days away. After verifying that all was well, they got the okay from Mission Control and relit the third stage for a little over five minutes. For the first time ever, explorers were leaving the Earth behind. No one had ever been on an expedition like this!

The view from Apollo 8, four and a half hours after launch. South America is at the bottom. North America is covered in clouds. No humans had seen the full Earth before.

When Apollo 8 lifted off, more than thirty humans had been into space. But no one had seen our planet from farther away than 850 miles, which was the high point reached during Gemini 11 in 1966. Less than two minutes after the third stage shut down, Apollo 8 beat that record, and half an hour later they were already 7,500 miles from Earth. Frank Borman radioed the ground: "We see the Earth now, almost as a disk."

Jim Lovell filled in the details. "We have a beautiful view of Florida . . . And at the same time, we can see Africa. West Africa is beautiful. I can also see Gibraltar at the same time I'm looking at Florida."

Two and a half days later, the astronauts were so far from their home planet that they couldn't see it at all without carefully orienting the CSM until Earth drifted into view in one of the windows, so small that they could blot it out with a thumb. Anders, who had attended the Naval Academy, said the feeling of isolation was "like being on the inside of a submarine."

Apollo 8 was on a "free-return" trajectory, meaning that if the astronauts did nothing, the CSM would curve around the Moon and return to Earth. As they neared the Moon, they rechecked their systems and confirmed that everything was working properly for the next step: entering lunar orbit. Making sure the CSM was turned so that its big rocket engine was facing backward, they counted down and fired the engine for four minutes, allowing the Moon to capture their craft. Twenty hours later, they would turn the other way and fire the engine again to escape and go home. But for now, they could look down on the Moon from a distance of only seventy miles. Automatic space probes had visited the Moon and taken pictures, but nothing prepared Borman, Lovell, and Anders for what they now saw: a world that was battered beyond belief—"like a war zone," recalled Anders. And it was utterly without color.

"The Moon is essentially gray," Lovell radioed back. "It looks like plaster of Paris or sort of a grayish beach sand." The lack of an atmosphere meant there were no clouds, haze, or suspended dust. Neither was there any sign of water or life.

The far side of the Moon from Apollo 8. The picture is about ninety miles across.

"It's a vast, lonely, forbidding-type existence, or expanse of nothing, that looks rather like clouds and clouds of pumice stone," Borman announced, "and it certainly would not appear to be a very inviting place to live or work."

Like millions of others, Anders had been conditioned by decades of science-fiction movies to expect a landscape of sharp relief, with jagged mountains, ridges, and canyons resembling those in the American West or Swiss Alps. The movie *2001: A Space Odyssey*, one of the most popular films of 1968 and one that every astronaut had seen at least once, was the most realistic depiction of spaceflight ever attempted, and it showed the Moon in exactly this way—which was wrong.

"Let me tell you," Anders said later, "it's sandblasted."

Apollo 8's ten orbits lasted a little less than a day. By the fixed timetable of the December 1968 launch window, that day happened to be the 24th, Christmas Eve. Aboard the CSM was a simple black-and-white television camera, and NASA had instructed the astronauts to do a live broadcast on their next-to-last orbit, which corresponded to prime time in the eastern half of the United States. The content of the program was up to them, but the men were cautioned that they would probably have the largest television audience in history.

When the time came, Borman, Lovell, and Anders focused on the Moon, training the camera out the window and trying to convey the nature of this strange place that had become the object of America's crazy quest.

As the lunar-science specialist on the mission, Anders led the tour, pointing out the changing topography and naming the craters and seas passing below. He interspersed his commentary with long pauses. Lovell and Borman contributed their own commentary, and they used enough scientific jargon to create an aura of esoteric mystery.

Toward the end of the transmission, Anders noted that they were passing over the Sea of Tranquility, "one of our future landing sites," he explained, referring to the prime target zone called Apollo Landing

Site 2. Then, as the camera recorded the lengthening shadows of the approaching lunar night, he began to wrap things up. "For all the people back on Earth," he announced, "the crew of Apollo 8 has a message we would like to send you."

Flying over a world of primordial chaos on Christmas Eve, these men, who were direct witnesses to the wonders of the cosmos, began reading the account of creation from the book of Genesis.

Anders recited, "In the beginning, God created the heaven and the Earth. And the Earth was without form and void; and darkness was

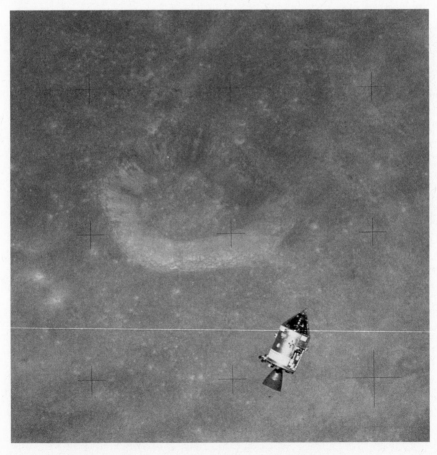

Apollo command and service module over the Moon (made on Apollo 17)

upon the face of the deep. And the spirit of God moved upon the face of the waters. And God said, 'Let there be light,' and there was light."

Taking turns, they read to the end of verse 10, which is just before the creation of life. Then Frank Borman concluded, "And from the crew of Apollo 8, we close with good night, good luck, a merry Christmas, and God bless all of you, all of you on the good Earth."

Earthrise from the Moon, photographed from Apollo 8 on December 24, 1968

33

EARTHRISE

On their fourth orbit of the Moon, Frank Borman was turning the spacecraft to get photographs of features of interest to scientists. Quite by chance, the Earth happened to be rising over the lunar horizon—something the astronauts hadn't seen yet. Bill Anders caught sight of it out his window.

"Oh, my God!" he said. "Look at that picture over there! Here's the Earth coming up. Wow, is that pretty!"

"Hey, don't take that," Borman teased him, "it's not scheduled." In fact, it was true: they had almost no time to depart from the schedule, which booked practically every moment of the trip, but this was an exception. Anders got off several shots that showed the brilliant blue Earth suspended over the ashen lunar landscape.

"It was the most beautiful, heart-catching sight of my life," Borman later wrote. "It was the only thing in space that had any color to it. Everything else was either black or white, but not the Earth. It was mostly a soft, peaceful blue, the continents outlined in a pinkish brown.

And always the white clouds, like long streaks of cotton suspended above that immense globe."

Lovell was also overcome, calling Earth "a grand oasis in the big vastness of space."

After they relit their service module engine and returned home, their hundreds of photographs were developed and distributed to scientists and the press. One of Anders's Earthrise pictures struck a chord. For the first time, ordinary people had the startling experience of seeing their world as an interplanetary visitor would.

It dawned on Anders that the long years of training, focused entirely on the Moon, had led the astronauts, in the end, to discover Earth. "Here we came all this way to the Moon, and yet the most significant thing we're seeing is our own home planet."

The year 1968 had been unusually difficult for the inhabitants of Earth. In the United States, two political assassinations shocked the nation. In April, the great civil rights leader Martin Luther King Jr. was gunned down. And in June, Senator Robert F. Kennedy, the brother of the slain president, was killed. The other great trauma for the U.S. was the ongoing Vietnam War, which was proving to be America's most deadly and costly conflict in the Cold War. Events were no less tumultuous abroad, where France was seized by nationwide unrest, and Czechoslovakia, a Soviet ally, saw its brief experiment in political freedom crushed by Soviet troops in the largest military operation in Europe since World War II. Amid all the chaos, Apollo 8 was a breath of fresh air. In thanks for redeeming 1968, *Time* magazine named Borman, Lovell, and Anders its "Men of the Year," a prestigious journalistic honor.

"For all its upheavals and frustrations," *Time*'s editors wrote, "the year would be remembered to the end of time for the dazzling skills and Promethean daring that sent mortals around the Moon. It would be celebrated as the year in which men saw at first hand their little Earth entire, a remote, blue-brown sphere hovering like a migrant bird in the hostile night of space."

The coming year, 1969, marked the deadline for President Kennedy's quest. Thanks to Apollo 7 and 8, NASA was back on track. If Apollo 9 and 10 were similarly successful, then the first Moon landing attempt would probably fall on Apollo 11, sometime in the summer. According to Deke Slayton's rotation system, that job should go to the Apollo 8 backup crew: Neil Armstrong, Buzz Aldrin, and Fred Haise (Haise joined Armstrong's crew when Jim Lovell moved to the Apollo 8 prime crew to replace the ailing Mike Collins).

Deke's mantra was "any crew can fly any mission." But the first lunar landing was special, and he was ready to break his rotation system for this history-making crew. Had Gus Grissom been alive, Slayton would have preferred him for commander. Gus was just the gutsy flyer who could pull it off; plus, as one of the Original Seven, he had seniority. But Gus was dead, so Slayton had been grooming two other astronauts as potential commanders for the first lunar landing: Frank Borman and Jim McDivitt.

Unfortunately, Borman was out of the running. Before Apollo 8 flew, he told Deke it was his last mission. Managing redesign of the command module following the Apollo 1 fire and then training for Apollo 8 had kept him away from home for almost two years. He felt his family deserved to have him back. When he heard speculation that he could have the first Moon landing, he sensibly pointed out that there wasn't time for him to train on the lunar module, since he was a command module specialist.

Jim McDivitt *was* a lunar module specialist, but he was leading the shakedown cruise of the LM on Apollo 9, due to launch into Earth orbit in the winter of 1969. As commander of Apollo 10, Tom Stafford was next in line. He was scheduled to take a CSM and LM out to the Moon on a mission that could conceivably land. But NASA managers wanted to use it as a dress rehearsal for Apollo 11, testing procedures down to an altitude of 50,000 feet. If delays caused Apollo 10 to slip into the fall, then it could go all the way.

Given all the *if*s—*if* the LM didn't run into problems, *if* pogo didn't return in the Saturn V, *if* the countless other critical systems didn't fail—Slayton decided to stick with his tried-and-true system and assign command of Apollo 11 to the next man in the rotation: Neil Armstrong. If his mission didn't land, then Pete Conrad, the probable commander of Apollo 12, would get a shot. "This is like handling a squadron of fighter pilots," Slayton remarked. "You've got a mission to do and you've got so many flights to fly and you assign guys to fly them." It was that simple.

Mike Collins was healed from his spinal surgery and back in the rotation. Deke had special sympathy for pilots who had been medically grounded, like himself, so he assigned Collins to one of the other seats on Apollo 11. Logically, the third slot belonged to Buzz Aldrin. (Fred Haise was less experienced than either Collins or Aldrin and would stay on backup status for the time being.) Yet Deke had his doubts about Aldrin. Buzz was an expert pilot, a brilliant engineer, and he had flown a flawless mission on Gemini 12. But many of the other astronauts found it hard to get along with him. Personality clashes shouldn't matter; however, Slayton gave Armstrong the option to switch Aldrin for Jim Lovell, who was just coming off duty from Apollo 8. Lovell famously got along with everyone. Armstrong thought it over and decided it wouldn't be fair to Lovell, who deserved a command of his own, much less to Aldrin, who had worked well with Armstrong on the backup crew for Apollo 8.

On January 6, 1969, Deke called the three men into his office. "You're it," he said. Armstrong would command the mission and fly the lunar module. Collins would pilot the command module and stay in lunar orbit, standing by to rescue the LM in an emergency. Aldrin would accompany Armstrong down to the Moon as the lunar module pilot—in reality the copilot, with the all-important job of running the computer and relaying the flight data to Armstrong. In effect, he would talk Neil down to a safe landing—or try to.

Apollo 11 crew, 1969. Left to right: Buzz Aldrin, Neil Armstrong, and Mike Collins.

NASA officials after the launch of Apollo 11. Foreground, from right to left: Sam Phillips, George Mueller, and Wernher von Braun (with binoculars).

34

GO FEVER

The Apollo 1 fire led to a new term, "go fever," which is the tendency to make mistakes while rushing to get a job done, especially when things are going well. Go fever had killed three astronauts aboard Apollo 1. Now, with the near-perfect flights of Apollo 7 and 8, some at NASA worried about go fever in the rush to meet Kennedy's deadline. A truly spectacular disaster was possible—an atomic-bomb-scale explosion on the launchpad, a lunar crash landing, a crew stranded in interplanetary space.

Apollo 8 astronaut Frank Borman knew the risks and worried about the public's reaction to a new catastrophe. "I do not submit that there won't be further tragedy in this program," he cautioned, "but I do say that it's worth the price we have to pay." His remark seemed intended to prepare the public for something frightful.

Since the fire, NASA had tightened contractor management and set up new safety procedures. Still, there were roughly 6 million parts in a typical Apollo mission: 3 million in the Saturn V, 2 million in the CSM, and 1 million in the LM. If those parts were 99.9 percent reliable, that would still mean an average of 6,000 failures per flight. To keep the failure rate even lower than that, every contractor followed Wernher von Braun's advice to encourage "an almost religious vigilance and attention to detail on the part of every member of a development team."

NASA administrator Tom Paine had his own way of dealing with go fever. Starting with Apollo 8, he flew down to the Cape before each mission and had dinner with the crew. He kept it informal, starting out with relaxed conversation. He had two goals. First, he wanted to open a direct channel of communications to the astronauts in case they had concerns they were reluctant to share with their immediate bosses. Second, during dessert or as he was saying goodbye, he had an even more important message. Don't take any unnecessary chances, he told them. "If you don't like the way things look," he said, "come on home and I'll guarantee you three the next flight to try again."

It was a generous offer and one that took some of the pressure off. But it was advice the astronauts were not likely to heed. All the astronauts had been in flight situations where the bad omens kept multiplying, but they had stuck with the mission, intent on solving the problems, which they eventually did. The fact that they were still alive proved they were good at it, and that was why they were chosen as astronauts. To them, a bigger concern than staying alive was not disgracing themselves in the eyes of their peers by playing it safe and aborting a mission needlessly. They prided themselves on having what author Tom Wolfe later labeled "the right stuff," which Wolfe defined as "the ability to go up in a hurtling piece of machinery . . . and have the moxie, the reflexes, the experience, the coolness, to pull it back at the last yawning moment."

That was not what Paine meant when he said not to take unnecessary chances.

●

No one personified the right stuff more than Neil Armstrong. His crewmate Mike Collins compared him to a gourmet who savors perilous situations like fine wines, "rolling them around on his tongue . . . and swallowing at the very last moment." On May 6, 1968, Armstrong had been practicing solo lunar landings in a training vehicle nicknamed the "flying bedstead." It resembled a giant bed frame equipped with a vertically mounted jet engine. Officially called the Lunar Landing Research Vehicle, or LLRV, it was the only way, realistically, to simulate landing on the Moon. And if flying it was extremely hazardous, then that only added to the realism. Armstrong had made several successful landing approaches that day, and he was going up for another practice run. Suddenly, no more than 200 feet in the air, the control system went haywire and the LLRV began tipping over.

"Neil held on as long as he could, not wanting to abandon an expensive piece of hardware," Buzz Aldrin wrote. "At the last possible moment, he realized the thruster system had completely malfunctioned, and he pulled his ejection handles." He was so low that his parachute barely had time to open fully before he hit the ground.

Later that morning, astronaut Al Bean arrived at work and was told, "Do you know that Neil bailed out of the LLRV this morning?"

Bean said, "No way!" He checked Armstrong's office, where he found him sitting calmly at his desk, shuffling some papers.

"Those guys out in the office said you bailed out of the LLRV this morning," Bean reported.

Armstrong gave a distracted reply: "Yeah."

"That was all he said, 'Yeah,'" Bean recalled in amazement. "This

The LLRV, also known as the "flying bedstead," the only realistic practice for landing on the Moon. The pilot is at right.

guy had been a second and a half from being killed. That was it! He didn't say, 'I nearly got killed!'—'Yeah.' That was it!"

Bean himself had a personal connection with crashes, since he had been promoted to an Apollo crew after the death of C.C. Williams, another astronaut. Williams, too, had been in an aircraft that lost control. He, too, had held on and ejected low. But he had been too low.

Armstrong's luck ran out on another mission. Fortunately, it was an Earthbound simulation. The Apollo 11 crew spent hundreds of hours in simulators that mimicked the real spacecraft and real mission in every

Neil Armstrong parachutes to safety after ejecting from a malfunctioning LLRV, 1968.

way possible. Mike Collins recalled that on one of these imaginary flights, "Neil and Buzz had been descending in the LM when some catastrophe had overtaken them, and they had been ordered by Houston to abort. Neil, for some reason, either questioned the advice or was just slow to act on it, but in any event, the computer printout showed that the LM had descended below the altitude of the lunar surface before starting to climb again. In plain English, Neil had crashed the LM and destroyed the machine, himself, and Buzz."

Armstrong later claimed he had been testing the limits to see how Mission Control would respond. This attitude worried Houston. The influential director of flight operations, Christopher C. Kraft Jr., questioned Armstrong's commitment to the rule that Mission Control's orders must be obeyed. And Chief Flight Director Gene Kranz complained that Armstrong obviously "had set his own rules for the landing. I just wanted to know what they were."

Kranz judged that when the moment of truth came, "my gut feeling said he would press on, accepting any risk as long as there was even a remote chance to land."

As for Armstrong, not even Aldrin standing next to him in the LM knew what he was going to do.

Apollo 9 launched into Earth orbit in March and returned with some 150 failures, practically all minor, for a reliability rate of 99.999975 percent. Apollo 10, which went to the Moon in May, was just as trouble-free, with the biggest glitch occurring during preparation for firing the LM's ascent-stage rocket, as a lunar landing crew would have to do to take off from the Moon and rejoin the CSM. On Apollo 10, this test of the maneuver took place in lunar orbit. An incorrectly set switch in the LM caused a tense moment when the LM started tumbling, recalling Armstrong and Scott's harrowing experience with a stuck thruster on Gemini 8. Piloting the LM, Mission Commander Tom Stafford quickly regained control. In less expert hands, the incident might have ended in disaster. It was a lesson in how little room there was for error.

Apollo 11's launch was set for July 16, timed for a landing four days later just after lunar sunrise on the southwestern edge of the Moon's Sea of Tranquility—Apollo Landing Site 2. Inspecting the target area from 50,000 feet on Apollo 10, astronaut Gene Cernan described it as "pretty smooth, like a gummy grayish sand." Stafford warned, "There's still lots of small craters down there, but . . . if you've got hover time, you can probably make it." He added, "If you come down in the wrong area . . . you're going to have to shove off"—meaning Armstrong might have to abort the landing, cutting loose the LM's descent stage and using the ascent engine to rejoin the CSM in lunar orbit.

Deke Slayton awoke the crew on the morning of the 16th, had breakfast with them, and then accompanied them to the transport van after they suited up. On the way out to the pad, he got off at the firing room. There Slayton joined General Phillips, Wernher von Braun, Tom Paine, and other NASA staff. Max Faget usually skipped launches. "To watch a flight is not that big a deal," he often said. "It's just a lot of standing around to watch it go off." There's no record that he attended this one.

Neil Armstrong suits up on Apollo 11 launch day. Deke Slayton is at right.

Apollo 11 lifts off, July 16, 1969.

Outside on the VIP bleachers, Jim Webb stood with his former boss Lyndon Johnson. Warned about the possibility of delay or worse, the new president, Richard Nixon, wasn't attending and had sent his vice president, Spiro Agnew, instead.

As the count reached zero and the Saturn V rumbled to life, one word was in the thoughts and hearts of the breathless millions who watched.

"Go!"

Former President Johnson (center, in dark suit) watches Apollo 11 rocket skyward. Next to him on the left is Jim Webb. On the right (with the light jacket) is Vice President Agnew.

Mission Control at the moment *Eagle* landed on the Moon. Left to right: Deke Slayton, Charlie Duke (capcom), and Jim Lovell (Apollo 11 backup commander).

35

TRANQUILITY BASE

Apollo 11 wasn't the only vehicle headed for the Moon on July 16. The Russians had a head start with their surprise launch of an unmanned probe, Luna 15, which was only a day away from entering lunar orbit when Apollo 11 took off. Most experts believed Luna 15 was designed to grab some lunar soil and return to Earth ahead of the Americans, becoming the first mission to obtain samples of the Moon and doing it without an enormously expensive manned flight.

The press went wild with other theories. Some suggested that Luna 15 was a hostile probe designed to jam radio signals from Apollo 11, or that it was on a spy mission to learn how Apollo really worked, or that it was on an errand of mercy to rescue Armstrong and Aldrin if they got stranded.

Von Braun tried to bring reporters down to Earth. "This is undoubtedly quite a challenging mission, to soft-land a spacecraft on the Moon and scoop up a sample of lunar soil and fly it back to Earth," he explained. He even added a note of admiration: "It would show again that we have very competent competitors in this race . . . I am even quite glad that we are not alone in doing this thing."

But whatever its mission, Luna 15 was a dark horse lurking in the shadows as the most remarkable expedition in history unfolded for all the world to see.

Apollo 11 arrived in lunar orbit on July 19. The following day the CSM and LM undocked, with Collins staying in the command module, named *Columbia*, while Armstrong and Aldrin departed in the lunar module, called *Eagle*. Some 240,000 miles away, in Houston, astronaut Charles Duke was the capcom who would relay information and instructions from flight controllers during the landing attempt. The flight director for this crucial shift was Gene Kranz.

When the time came for Duke to give *Eagle* permission to fire its descent rocket and head down to the surface, he had trouble getting through.

Eagle in lunar orbit. Contact probes extend from the foot pads.

Buzz Aldrin in a composite of photos taken inside *Eagle* prior to landing. Armstrong's station is at the left triangular window; Aldrin's is at the right.

"*Eagle*, Houston," he radioed. "If you read, you're go for powered descent. Over."

The only reply was static. This was not a good sign.

Six seconds later, Collins, whose radio link was working fine, relayed the message to Armstrong and Aldrin: "*Eagle*, this is *Columbia*. They just gave you a go for powered descent."

If the communications stayed this bad, then the landing would have to be canceled for several reasons. One was that Kranz insisted on having as much telemetry as possible to determine what had gone wrong in case the astronauts crashed.

But thirty seconds later, after Aldrin readjusted *Eagle*'s antenna, his ship was back on the air. Five minutes after that, Armstrong lit the descent engine. They were at 50,000 feet and on their way down. Since there was no room for seats in the LM, the two astronauts were standing—as if they were in an elevator on a nine-and-a-half-mile plunge.

Anyone who has ever flown on a commercial jet knows what it's like to be tens of thousands of feet in the air. The ground is a long way down, and you thank your lucky stars that the pilots have plenty of experience landing the plane. Imagine, though, that you are at 50,000 feet—higher than most airliners fly—in a vehicle that *has never landed before*. This violates every rule of flight testing. When the Wright brothers made their first powered flight, they rose a few feet into the air and immediately set down. They repeated this process countless times, going incrementally higher and farther while making steady improvements in their vehicle and their technique. Every airplane ever designed and every pilot who has ever earned a license has gone through a similar process.

Western Sea of Tranquility from lunar orbit. *Eagle's* landing site is just right of center near the edge of darkness.

Not so the LM and its two-man crew. This vehicle had never gone through an actual landing, and neither had the astronauts. They had *simulated* a landing, and Armstrong had practiced the last few hundred feet in the flying bedstead, but no one knew how accurate these exercises were.

Moreover, landing on the Moon presents unique challenges. For one, there are few clues about the size of objects, since there are no cities, buildings, roads, rivers, trees, and certainly no airports to give a sense of how far away things are. There are only craters upon craters upon

The region southwest of *Eagle*'s landing site from 50,000 feet. The large crater is Moltke, four miles wide. On the opposite page, Moltke is barely visible just left of center (also in the top photo on page 246).

craters, of all sizes and all looking much the same. Furthermore, the Moon is considerably smaller than Earth—only one-quarter of Earth's diameter, which means the horizon is closer than it may appear. As you fly over the Moon, features come into view much more quickly than they do on Earth, giving the illusion that you are going faster than you really are. Confusing matters still more, the Moon has no atmosphere, which means that distant objects are not blurred by air. The landscape looks just as sharp from 50,000 feet as it does from 500. Combined with the lack of objects of known scale, this makes it doubly hard to judge distances.

The lack of air has another effect: the LM can't use air resistance to slow down and control its descent, as airplanes do. Apart from crashing like a meteorite, the only way to land on the Moon is to fire a rocket in the direction of travel and gradually slow the spacecraft to a safe landing speed, while using smaller control thrusters to orient the vehicle. This must be done all the way to the ground, and it takes a lot of fuel.

Therefore, you might think the LM would have plenty of gas to give the commander time to survey the landing area, circle it a couple of times, and pick an alternate site if things looked too risky. This was especially important for Apollo, since photos from lunar orbit didn't show features smaller than about six feet, meaning that dangerous boulders and small craters could lurk anywhere. Unfortunately, a properly cautious landing was out of the question. Stringent weight limits meant that the LM had only about a minute of hover time for the pilot to make up his mind.

These formidable hurdles were the reason that practically no one thought Apollo would succeed on its first landing attempt, least of all the flight controllers in Houston. When the inevitable problems accumulated past a certain point, the crew would have to abort, using either the LM's descent stage or the ascent-stage engine to rocket back to the CSM for return to Earth and another try.

Landing on the Moon would have been all but impossible except for two electronic devices: the onboard computer and the landing radar.

Computers in the 1960s were room-size machines that consumed enormous amounts of electricity. In a miracle of engineering devised by Doc Draper's Instrumentation Lab, the CM and LM each carried a suitcase-size computer that used very little power and yet served as the master control for navigation, propulsion, the automatic pilot, instrument readings, and command inputs, allowing the spacecraft to function independently of Mission Control. The computer's performance was similar to that of the earliest personal computers, which became available a decade later—and popularized such games as *Space Invaders* and *Lunar Lander*. Primitive by today's standards, the Apollo computer was so efficiently programmed that it could direct not a crude video game, but a real-life mission to the Moon.

The computer in the lunar module also controlled the landing radar, which told the astronauts their altitude above the surface and their velocity in three dimensions. These readings were crucial pieces of information that Aldrin would be feeding Armstrong.

The landing got off to a bad start. On top of the on-again-off-again communications, Armstrong discovered early in *Eagle*'s descent that he would miss the prime target by several miles, rendering futile all his time spent memorizing landmarks. This meant he was heading for the western end of the landing zone, which Tom Stafford had warned him was much rougher than the aim point.

Things soon got worse—much worse. As *Eagle* passed through 35,000 feet, it was traveling at the fast clip of a supersonic jet coming in for an emergency landing. Aldrin made a routine query to the computer when suddenly the astronauts heard a buzzing tone in their headsets. It was the caution and warning system, informing them there was a computer problem.

"Program alarm," said Armstrong in the crisp voice of a pilot reporting trouble.

He checked the computer display and read out the code: "It's a twelve-oh-two." Neither he nor Buzz had any idea what that meant.

In Houston, capcom Duke had a sinking feeling. A computer problem was a potential showstopper. He didn't know what the code meant either.

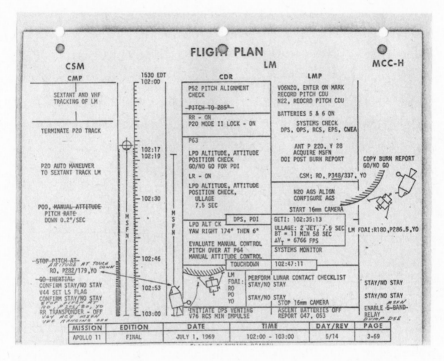

Minute-by-minute flight plan for Apollo 11. This page shows what Collins (CMP), Armstrong (CDR), Aldrin (LMP), and Mission Control (MCC-H) were doing during the landing phase. Everyone involved had this timeline.

Working in a back room, a group of computer experts were linked to Steve Bales, the guidance officer in Mission Control. One of them echoed Armstrong's call: "12 02 alarm!" then muttered, "12 02, what's that?" as he riffled the pages of his checklist.

Seconds passed. Up in the LM, Armstrong calmly radioed Houston.

"Give us a reading on the 12 02 program alarm"—meaning, "What the hell should we do?!"

By now, Jack Garman in the back room knew. "It's executive overflow," he told Bales. "If it does not occur again, we're fine . . . Continue."

Bales passed the word to flight director Kranz. "We're—we're go on that, Flight."

Kranz nodded to Duke, who immediately relayed the message to Armstrong and Aldrin. "We're go on that alarm!"

Twenty seconds later there was another 12 02 alarm.

Quietly observing at Mission Control, astronaut Walt Cunningham worried that the alarms "were creating doubt, one of a pilot's deadliest enemies." And in the press room, British journalist Reginald Turnill couldn't shake a feeling of "impending disaster." He knew enough to realize that problems were piling up. "They're crashing," he kept thinking.

"Okay, all flight controllers, hang tight," urged Kranz.

Executive overflow signaled that the computer had more to do than it could handle, so it stopped and restarted, cutting out less essential tasks. But then something overloaded it again. Fortunately, the computer's design allowed it to stop and restart almost instantaneously, although the vital navigation data disappeared momentarily. There was no time to figure out what the problem was. Garman deduced it was something they could live with as long as the machine's performance didn't degrade further.

Listening in at the MIT Instrumentation Lab in Massachusetts was Don Eyles, the programmer who had written the landing software. He knew the code inside and out, and was thinking, "If it were in my hands, I would call an abort." But he didn't have a direct line to Mission Control.

However, the man at the controls had come to the same conclusion as Garman. "There wasn't anything obviously wrong," Armstrong said afterward. "The vehicle was flying well, it was going down the trajectory we expected, no abnormalities in anything that we saw." He reasoned that "as long as everything was going well and looked right, I would be in favor of continuing, no matter what the computer was complaining about."

As luck would have it, Mission Control had recently run a simulation with another Apollo crew that involved a similar alarm. During that exercise, Bales overreacted and called for an abort. Worried about the mistake, Kranz ordered Bales and Garman to review every possible alarm and come up with the proper action to take for each. It was this list that Garman was consulting for Apollo 11.

Nevertheless, five alarms sounded over a period of four minutes. With their attention-grabbing buzz in the astronauts' headsets, the need to query the computer each time, and the interruption in the crucial navigation numbers, the warnings were hard to ignore.

"I licked my dry lips," Aldrin later wrote. "This was a time for discipline. But the tension had me rigid inside my suit. We *had* to trust Mission Control."

Mission Control responded "go" each time. At MIT, Eyles was practically having a nervous breakdown. "It is as though a terrible screech is coming from the front of your car, but the engine is still running, the steering still works, and you are getting very near your destination."

Duke inadvertently added to the confusion with a constant stream of reassuring chatter. Deke Slayton, who was sitting next to him, punched him in the side and said, "Charlie, shut up and let them land!"

"I think we'd better be quiet, Flight," Duke whispered to Kranz, who announced to the room, "Okay, the only callouts from now on will be fuel."

So far, *Eagle* was being guided by the autopilot, which theoretically could steer the ship all the way to the ground. Armstrong had the option of taking control at any time. After dealing with the computer alarms, he finally had a chance to look out the window. He didn't like what he saw. A mile ahead was a large crater, and the computer was targeting *Eagle* to its debris field, comprised of car-size boulders. When Armstrong activated the manual control to fly over it, the computer suddenly had less to do and the program alarms stopped. Characteristically, Armstrong didn't tell Mission Control—or Aldrin—what he was doing or why. "Pretty rocky area," was all he said—to himself.

At this point, controllers saw something strange on their screens. The data showed that "Neil was flying a trajectory that we'd never flown in the simulator," said Duke. "We kept trying to figure out, 'What's going on? He's just whizzing across the surface at about 400 feet.'"

Aldrin, whose eyes were glued to the instruments, noticed this, too, on the gauge that measured forward speed, which was stopped at its highest setting. Cool as ever, Buzz remarked, "Okay, you're pegged on horizontal velocity"—meaning, "Where the hell are you going?!" Neil didn't reply.

In the back row at Mission Control, Bob Gilruth and Chris Kraft were becoming increasingly edgy. "We could see on our displays that Armstrong was flying manually now and that fuel was getting low," Kraft wrote in his memoirs. "My worry level soared because he should have been descending. He needed an open spot to land, and my worst fear was that he couldn't find one . . . Bob Gilruth squeezed his eyes shut, then opened them with a deep breath. I don't remember if I was breathing or not."

Astronaut Al Bean understood Armstrong's situation as well as anyone, since he was the lunar module pilot for the next mission. He knew that the maneuver Armstrong was performing was wasting gas and must mean there was some kind of emergency. "I wonder if he's going to make it," he thought.

Meanwhile, sitting in Mission Control's viewing gallery, Max Faget had the same reaction: "If they keep doing this, they're going to run out of fuel."

●

There was one person completely untroubled by the dwindling fuel supply. "If I'd run out of fuel, why, I would have put down right there," Armstrong said later. In the flying bedstead, he often landed with just fifteen seconds of gas left.

"It would have been nice if I'd had another minute of fuel" in the LM, he admitted. "I knew we were getting short; I knew we had to get it on the ground, and I knew we had to get it below fifty feet. But I wasn't panic-stricken."

Aldrin wasn't panic-stricken either, but he was doing his best to convince Neil to land. "Ease her down," he said at an altitude of 270 feet. They were now almost clear of the boulder field.

"Okay, how's the fuel?" Armstrong responded.

"Eight percent."

"Okay. Here's a . . . looks like a good area here," Armstrong said. He had spotted a small crater about 400 feet ahead. Nearby was a reasonably clear patch. It was roughly a minute away.

A minute later, Armstrong was beyond the crater and still searching for a good spot. Aldrin was squirming inside his space suit. "Without wanting to say anything to Neil that might disrupt his focus, I pretty much used my body 'English' as best I could . . . as if to say, 'Neil, get this on the ground!'"

Charlie Duke called up in a tense voice: "Sixty seconds"—meaning a minute of fuel left. The flight surgeon's display showed Armstrong's heart racing at 150 beats per minute.

For millions of Americans watching on television, the networks provided animations, since there was nothing else to see. At this point, CBS showed a replica of the lunar module sitting triumphantly on the surface. According to the landing countdown clock projected on the TV screen, the astronauts should be down by now, and that was what viewers saw. But Buzz's voice continued to recite altitude and velocity figures. In other words, they hadn't landed yet! Neil and Buzz were still out there over the Moon, searching for a safe haven as Houston relayed increasingly alarming numbers on their decreasing fuel.

Flight controller Bob Carlton, who was keeping track of the fuel, had given up hope they would land. He just prayed they'd be able to abort

View out Aldrin's window from an altitude of 220 feet. Armstrong is using *Eagle*'s dwindling fuel supply to fly over the upper left crater, which is about 100 feet wide.

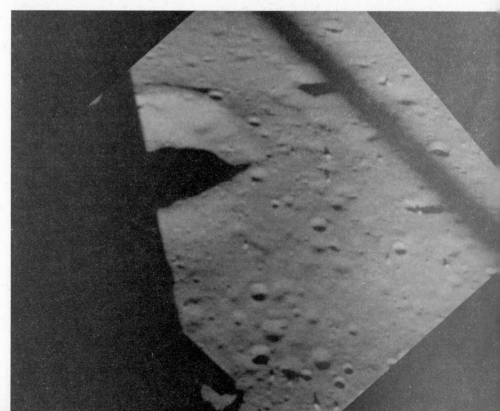

and keep from crashing. Meanwhile, tracking and data manager Bill Easter was spellbound. "It was like watching a man, some snake trainer, put his hand on a cobra; anything can happen any minute and probably will." Another controller, Ed Fendell, felt like he was levitating off his chair.

Garman had a different reaction. When Aldrin reported seeing dust kicked up by the rocket exhaust as they neared the surface, it hit him that this was actually happening, since dust was a detail that had never come up in a simulation. "My God, this is the real thing," he marveled.

●

The dust was all too real to Armstrong, who was now struggling with the disorienting illusion created by sheets of dust shooting in all directions. He compared it to "landing an airplane when there's a real thin layer of ground fog . . . However, all this fog was moving at a great rate, which was a little bit confusing." As Armstrong looked left, the dust was moving left, which gave the illusion that *Eagle* was moving right. So he instinctively fired the thrusters to push *Eagle* left. But then he glimpsed stationary rocks through the dust, which gave him a reference point. Having overcorrected, he fired the thrusters on the other side to neutralize his sideways drift.

"He's using a lot of RCS," said Bob Nance in the back room, referring to the reaction control system fuel that powered the thrusters.

"Thirty seconds," said Duke.

Armstrong's goal was to come straight down with a hint of forward motion. Too fast and the LM would tip over, but if he was moving in reverse he might back into a crater or boulder he couldn't see.

In his unruffled voice, as if he were helping Neil steer into a tight parking space, Buzz urged him on. "Drifting forward just a little bit; that's good."

Armstrong could see the spidery shadow of the LM growing larger and moving toward him to meet the contact probes dangling from *Eagle*'s footpads. A blizzard of dust engulfed everything.

"Contact light," said Aldrin briskly.

Armstrong intended to shut down the engine at this moment and drop the last few feet to the surface. There was a chance that blowback from the rocket exhaust would cause the engine to explode. Luckily, that didn't happen. Oblivious to the glowing contact light and Aldrin's announcement, Neil piloted *Eagle* to the gentlest possible landing.

"Shutdown," he said.

At Mission Control, they couldn't believe it. Aldrin read through some final instrument settings, then, breathlessly, Duke ventured, "We copy you down, *Eagle* . . ."

Armstrong had a proclamation ready: "Houston, Tranquility Base here. The *Eagle* has landed."

But Duke broke the formality with an expression of overwhelming, jubilant relief: "Roger, Tranquility. We copy you on the ground. You got a bunch of guys about to turn blue. We're breathing again. Thanks a lot."

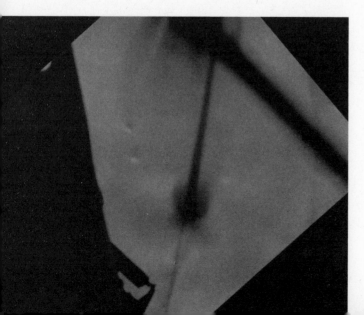

Seconds from touchdown, the shadow of one of *Eagle*'s legs reaches toward the ground.

Astronaut boot print on the Moon, July 20, 1969

36

ONE SMALL STEP

For most of the world, the main act in the Moon-landing drama was yet to come: the first step by a human onto the surface of the Moon. But to Neil Armstrong, that was an almost trivial part of the mission—"not something that I thought was really very important," he said years later. "It has always been surprising to me," he explained, "that there was such an intense public interest about stepping onto the lunar surface, let alone who did it first. In my mind, the important thing was that we got four aluminum legs safely down on the surface of the Moon while we were still inside the craft." On a difficulty scale of one to ten, Armstrong ranked walking on the Moon as a one, whereas "the lunar descent . . . was probably a thirteen."

When he was assigned to command Apollo 11, Armstrong almost certainly assumed that Aldrin would be the first down the ladder. NASA's practice in Project Gemini had been for copilots to make space walks. Science experiments were always the copilot's responsibility due to the heavy workload on the commander. Walking on the Moon was nothing if not a science experiment, and it made sense for the copilot, in this case Aldrin, to go first.

In fact, the original plan had been for the copilot to be the *only* astronaut to go outside. General Phillips felt strongly that a single, brief outing by a single explorer was a reasonable goal for the first landing. However, Bob Gilruth convinced him that both astronauts should go outside and be available to help each other, if necessary.

Neil Armstrong climbs down *Eagle*'s ladder in the television view watched live by 600 million people.

With both astronauts going out, the question then became: Who goes first? To someone like Neil Armstrong, it didn't matter. But to the press it mattered enormously. The first person to plant his foot on the Moon was the *first*—a historically unique individual, even if the second was right behind him.

Unfortunately for Aldrin, personality decided this issue. In a note to President Nixon, Frank Borman described his fellow astronauts this way: Armstrong was "quiet," "perceptive," and "thoroughly decent," while Aldrin was "aggressive," "hard-charging," and "almost humorless." Aldrin's pushy style had won him enemies at NASA. He was respected for his perseverance and intelligence, but top managers thought he was the wrong individual to wear the hero's mantle that the press would inevitably bestow on the first man on the Moon.

Therefore, Neil Armstrong got the assignment. Aldrin was not happy and tried to have the decision reversed, but without success.

On July 20, 1969, six and a half hours after he and Aldrin landed on the Moon, Armstrong backed out of *Eagle*'s hatch and onto the porch. Slowly, he made his way down the ladder. At the bottom, he was not yet on the Moon, since he was standing on one of the LM's broad footpads.

An important duty that went with taking the first step onto the Moon was saying something suitably memorable. People had been pestering Armstrong about this for weeks, asking him what he intended to say. He honestly hadn't decided, because there was a good chance he and Aldrin would have to abort the mission and he wouldn't have to say anything. But now the time had come.

After describing how the LM's footpad was depressed only an inch or two into the soil—an indication that he probably wouldn't sink out of sight as one scientist had insisted would happen—Armstrong said casually, "Okay, I'm going to step off the LM now." More than half a billion people on Earth watched the live television transmission as he leaned to his left—his right hand gripping the ladder just in the case the scientist was right—and took a tentative step into the dirt.

"That's one small step for man; one giant leap for mankind."

Buzz Aldrin climbs down shortly after Armstrong, who takes this picture.

Later, Armstrong said he had intended to say, "*a* man." But people tend to speak in poetic rhythms, and he naturally (and unconsciously) left out the extra syllable. It was actually better that way, since his statement became even more meaningful—contrasting humans as individuals or members of a group, with all of humanity throughout its history.

Fifteen minutes later, it was Aldrin's turn. He slowly slithered through the hatch. Houston had instructed him to close it partially when he was out. He made a sly joke, saying he would be careful not to lock it. Then he started down the ladder, jumped the last three feet from the bottom rung to the pad, leaped back up to test the difficulty of the return climb—an experiment Armstrong had also tried—and paused to take in the panorama.

Armstrong had picked a good landing spot. It wasn't smooth—no place on the Moon is smooth—but it was reasonably flat, amid a sea of small craters, depressions, mounds, and ridges in every direction. Alert to the geology, Aldrin had already looked out the window and described with great enthusiasm the variety of the different rock shapes. Now that he was outside, he felt a different kind of excitement. He blurted out, "Beautiful view!"

Buzz Aldrin stands on the Moon's Sea of Tranquility. Armstrong is the white figure reflected in Aldrin's visor.

Neil agreed. "Isn't it magnificent?"

Buzz summed it up: "Magnificent desolation."

Surveying the landscape, Armstrong said he was reminded of "the high desert of the United States." He was probably thinking of the area around Edwards Air Force Base, California, where he, Deke Slayton, and so many of the astronauts had been test pilots. "It's very pretty out here," he added. This surprised Eric Sevareid of CBS News. "I never expected to hear that word 'pretty,'" he remarked during the network's moonwalk coverage. "The scene he saw on the Moon, what we thought was cold and desolate and forbidding, somehow they found a strange beauty there that I suppose they can never really describe to us."

Armstrong, Aldrin, and later Moon explorers did describe it. One of the most striking things they noted was a sky blacker than any black on Earth, a velvety black you felt you could touch, but when you reached out your hand there was nothing there. No night sky on Earth was that black, even though Apollo landings took place in daylight, with the Sun low in the east, shining so brilliantly that it was impossible to look at it even for an instant. The black sky; the gray landscape sparkling in the dazzling morning Sun; the sharp features visible all the way to the horizon because there is no atmosphere, defeating any attempt to judge distances; and the absence of wind, clouds, sound, or any living thing. It's a breathtaking world of utter barrenness.

Magnificent desolation.

Then there was the joy of moving around. Astronauts were used to being weightless, and like everyone on Earth they were used to the one-g pull of terrestrial gravity, not to mention the multiple g's experienced during jet aircraft maneuvers and rocket launches. But the Moon gave them a totally new experience of gravity.

Standing near *Eagle*, Buzz Aldrin sets up an experiment to measure charged particles from the Sun.

The Moon is far smaller and much less massive than Earth. At its surface, gravity is six times weaker than on Earth. No one was quite sure how disorienting the experience would be, so Armstrong and Aldrin were instructed to move with great care to avoid falling. They quickly discovered that one-sixth g is very pleasant, and they were soon bouncing and skipping along. On television, they seemed to be moving in slow motion, and that was how it felt. "When you move" on the Moon, recalled Aldrin, "you just *wait* to be brought down to the surface . . . you've got a lot of time, which means that time slowed down, which gives you this sensation of slow motion . . . you're getting to observe a lot more, and you're aware that you're still not down yet."

Yet there was much to do. Their backpacks carried only four hours of oxygen and cooling water. To be on the safe side, Mission Control had limited their outdoor time to roughly half that. During this period, Armstrong and Aldrin had to set up experiments, collect rocks, take photographs, and explore the general area. Armstrong loped over to the small crater they had flown over in the final minute before landing. Craters are interesting for what they reveal about the geology beneath the surface, and he wanted to get photographs of the inside walls for scientists back home.

"Exploring this place that had never before been seen by human eyes, upon which no foot had stepped, or hand touched—was awe-inspiring," Aldrin later wrote. "But we had no time for philosophical musings." That would come later.

NASA did make time for several commemorative events. Armstrong and Aldrin planted an American flag. They took a short congratulatory call from President Nixon (who had requested that the national anthem be played, but Frank Borman talked him out of it because of the two and a half minutes it would deduct from the astronauts' frantic schedule). And Armstrong and Aldrin unveiled a commemorative plaque mounted between two rungs of the ladder. The plaque reads:

HERE MEN FROM THE PLANET EARTH
FIRST SET FOOT UPON THE MOON
JULY 1969, A.D.
WE CAME IN PEACE FOR ALL MANKIND

It is signed by all three Apollo 11 astronauts and by President Nixon—much as a president's name goes on the dedicatory signs for dams, bridges, post offices, and other federal projects.

Apollo 11's commemorative plaque, mounted on one of *Eagle*'s legs

Surmounting the inscription are the two hemispheres of Earth. Future visitors to the site need only look straight up and lean back a little to see the real thing, always in the same spot of the sky. It's not easy to do in a space suit, said Aldrin, who tried and just managed to catch a glimpse of "our marble-sized planet, no bigger than my thumb."

Earth suspended above *Eagle*. Because the Moon always keeps the same side turned toward Earth, our planet hardly moves in the lunar sky.

No one was celebrating until the astronauts got home, but the landing and moonwalk were feats that brought tears to the eyes of millions. Many people went outside and looked at the Moon while Neil and Buzz were there. It was in its crescent phase, and if you gazed at the center of the crescent, in the sunlit area near the boundary between light and dark—that was where they were. The familiar Moon, origin of myths and bright beacon in the night sky, suddenly looked different.

Like thousands of others who worked on Apollo, Ed Fendell was so busy with his job that he had no time to think about anything else. He had been at Mission Control when Apollo 11 landed. When the new shift came on duty, he stayed to watch the moonwalk. Then he went home to get some sleep. The next morning, he was having breakfast at his usual coffee shop. It was just like any other day. "Two guys walk in and sit down on the two stools next to me," he recalled three decades later. They were from a nearby gas station.

"They're waiting for their breakfast," Fendell went on. "They start talking . . . One of them says to the other one . . . 'You know, I went all through World War II. I landed at Normandy on D-Day . . . It was an incredible day, an incredible life, and I went all the way through Paris and on into Berlin . . . but yesterday was the day that I felt the proudest to be an American.'"

In the year 2000, when Ed Fendell was recounting this story to a NASA historian, it all came flooding back: the excitement, the wonder, the camaraderie, and the pride in being part of a unique adventure. "As you can tell," he said tearfully, "I'm getting a little choked up right now."

NASA managers in the back row at Mission Control celebrate Apollo 11's return to Earth, July 24, 1969. Foreground, left to right: Max Faget, Chris Kraft (with flag), George Low, and Robert Gilruth.

EPILOGUE
"WE MUST STOP"

The real test of John Houbolt's lunar-orbit rendezvous strategy came when Armstrong and Aldrin fired *Eagle*'s ascent-stage engine on July 21. Meticulously timed for a rendezvous with Mike Collins in the orbiting *Columbia*, this do-or-die maneuver was exactly like a Gemini spacecraft ascending to dock with an Agena, except it was happening a quarter of a million miles from Earth. The astronauts used to joke that a launch at the Cape took thousands of people, while the ascent from the Moon needed just two.

It worked. After two orbits, Armstrong and Aldrin rejoined Collins. Later the empty *Eagle* was cut loose and *Columbia* lit its engine for home. Ahead for the three explorers was a short period of quarantine to ensure they had brought home no alien microbes, then parades, speeches, and a lifetime of adulation, which has its frustrations for men who just want to be alone in the cockpit of an airplane. Wherever they went, Armstrong, Aldrin, and Collins said that they weren't the heroes; the American people were the heroes. Still, they had been given a demanding job to do, and they had done it—perfectly.

Shortly before Armstrong and Aldrin took off from Tranquility Base, Luna 15 began its long-delayed descent from lunar orbit. The automatic probe crashed more than 700 miles away. The Soviets put the best possible face on what was supposed to be a headline-stealing sample-return mission, announcing that Luna 15 "achieved the Moon's surface in the preselected area."

The following year, their next attempt, Luna 16, would succeed, returning a canister full of lunar soil to Earth. The Soviets claimed this was the extent of their lunar program and that they had never been in the man-on-the-Moon race to begin with. However, within five years

Tom Paine (left) and President Nixon wait to greet the Apollo 11 astronauts on the recovery ship in the Pacific Ocean.

researchers in the West made a convincing case that the Russians had
been in the race all along. Later disclosures showed that they had built
a monstrous rocket comparable to the Saturn V and secretly tested it
four times between 1969 and 1972. Each time it blew up. They had also
developed hardware similar to the Apollo CSM and LM, but they never
flew it with cosmonauts. Even so, they came close to beating Apollo 8
around the Moon with a less advanced version of their CSM, only to be
derailed by technical problems.

What probably doomed their efforts was that the genius behind the
Soviet space program, the man responsible for Sputnik, Yuri Gagarin's
flight, and the other early triumphs, died during surgery in 1966. Sergei
Korolev was the Soviets' Wernher von Braun, Max Faget, Jim Webb, and

New York City welcomes Collins, Aldrin, and Armstrong. Tom Paine is sitting in front
of Aldrin.

Bob Gilruth all rolled into one. That may have been the problem. The United States had a deep bench of talent. The Russians had Korolev—until they didn't.

After Apollo 11, NASA made six more manned lunar trips: Apollo 12 through 17. One was nearly a disaster. On the way to the Moon in April 1970, a main oxygen tank in Apollo 13's service module exploded due to a faulty switch. It took four days to get back, as vital supplies dwindled. Commanded by Jim Lovell, this mission is one of history's great survival stories. The other Apollo flights are equally notable as some of history's greatest scientific expeditions, which solved the secret of the Moon's origin and energized the field of planetary science.

However, NASA managers were getting nervous. Mindful of the close call on Apollo 13 and the millions of other things that could go wrong, Bob Gilruth lobbied to end the program. "We must stop. There are so many chances for us losing a crew. We just know that we're going to do that if we keep going." His colleague Chris Kraft felt the same way.

And so, in December 1972, three and a half years after Armstrong and Aldrin made history, America closed the book on its incredible lunar adventure with Apollo 17, even though hardware for more flights was available. No one has kicked up the lunar dust and gazed at the Moon's magnificent desolation since then.

By the end of the Apollo program, its total cost was just over 25 billion dollars. Taking inflation into account, this was a billion or so less than the 20 billion Jim Webb had said he needed in 1963—and that was just for a single Moon landing! In a way, this was Webb's proudest accomplishment. Landing a man on the Moon is difficult enough, but he had made it happen on time and on budget, which is a miracle in large-scale government projects. Ever since Apollo, advocates for any formidable goal—from curing cancer to solving global warming—preface their pitch with, "If we can land a man on the Moon . . ." What they really mean is, "If we only had Jim Webb . . ."

Wernher von Braun was the dreamer who realized before anyone else that a Moon voyage was possible. After Apollo 11, he tried to make the case for going to Mars. As usual, he had worked out all the details. But with the Vietnam War still raging and America's other problems, it was an impossible idea to sell. He was persuaded to leave his rocket team in Huntsville and take a strategic-planning job at NASA headquarters in Washington, where his promised authority never materialized. It was like tricking a wizard into giving up his magic wand. One of his associates described von Braun's fate this way: "Wernher is like a great conductor who has held the world in awe with his fabulous performances, and who suddenly finds himself without an orchestra, without players and their instruments, without a concert hall, and even without music-loving audiences. He still plays his own violin once in a while, but only few people listen to him."

After the launch of the first Saturn V, when the ground shook and the dawn sky was ablaze with what seemed like a second Sun, when Wernher von Braun yelled, "Go, baby, go!" and the most powerful rocket ever built left Earth for space, Apollo boss General Sam Phillips was asked what he thought. "I was impressed," he said simply. A military man to the core, Phillips reported to the Air Force for his next assignment after Apollo 11. He went on to other high-level posts, including Director of the National Security Agency, the military's intelligence arm, where his tight-lipped style fit right in.

In 1972, Deke Slayton's clean living finally paid off. His heart problem had cleared up and doctors put him back on flight status. As Director of Flight Crew Operations, Deke recommended himself for the next available mission, the docking of American and Soviet craft in Earth orbit, scheduled for 1975. This joint flight would mark a truce in the Cold War and a hoped-for era of cooperation. Using the last flightworthy Apollo CSM, the U.S. crew was commanded by Apollo 10 veteran Tom Stafford and also included Vance Brand, a rookie like Slayton. On their ride into orbit, the two rookies became the seventy-seventh and seventy-eighth persons in space. Deke Slayton had made it after all.

Tom Paine had the top job at NASA and a ringside seat during the exhilarating days of Apollo 7 through 13. He was instrumental in changing the mission of Apollo 8 from Earth orbit to lunar orbit, heading off the Soviet Union's best chance of beating America to the Moon. He presided over the fulfillment of Kennedy's goal, and he promoted an ambitious program of space exploration after Apollo, which was rejected except for the Space Shuttle and Space Station. Paine's account of this pivotal period would have been fascinating. But in retirement he chose to focus on something else: his submarine service during World War II. Paine wrote a memoir about his exploits and amassed a library of some 3,500 volumes on submarines, which was later donated to the United

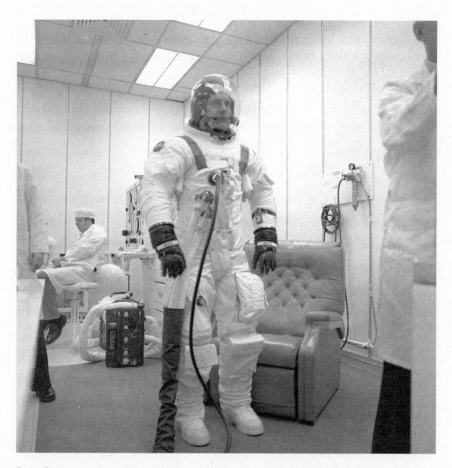

Deke Slayton suits up for the first joint U.S.–Soviet space mission, 1975.

States Naval Academy. Before Apollo 11's launch, he was given the chance to send a keepsake that would fly to the Moon and back with Armstrong, Aldrin, and Collins. He chose the gold dolphin pin that he had proudly worn as a U.S. Navy submarine officer.

Max Faget, the genius behind the Mercury capsule and the Apollo command module, went on to design the Space Shuttle. In fact, he may have missed the Apollo 11 launch because he was already deep into work on

Submarine officer's pin like the one carried aboard Apollo 11 for Tom Paine

the shuttle in the summer of 1969. Once asked how the U.S. got to the Moon so quickly, he told the story of his submarine, *Guavina*, during World War II. It was built in Manitowoc, Wisconsin, by a firm that specialized in ore haulers and ferries for the Great Lakes. "We weren't going to fight a war on the lake," Faget noted, so the company asked the Navy what kind of ship it needed. Submarines, came the answer. "They had never built a submarine before, didn't know the first thing about it," but they got the plans and worked around the clock to turn them out. "I rode on one, and they were beautifully built," he recalled. "When you've got a real burr up your rear end, boy, you're going to move. So we moved in World War II." Apollo was no different, and in the future, he added, "if we had a real crisis, we could respond a lot faster than you think."

Several years after the end of Apollo, Max Faget and Bob Gilruth were walking on the beach at Galveston, Texas, not far from the space center. The Apollo landings were receding into history, and Americans were starting to forget the anxiety and thrill of the space race, and their tremendous pride in Apollo 11.

This may have been on Gilruth's mind as he looked up at the Moon, shining over the Gulf of Mexico. "You know, Max," he said, "someday people are going to try to go back to the Moon, and they're going to find out how hard it really is."

Gazing up at that distant, glowing orb, Faget nodded. Yes, it had been hard. Most people had no idea how hard. That was the way it always was with a great achievement: in retrospect, it looked easy.

For those involved in Project Apollo—all 400,000 of them—it had been challenging, perplexing, nerve-racking. But for many of them, it was ultimately the most rewarding experience of their lives. Some called it a war without shooting. But it was the crisis of a real war that had made it possible. World War II had taught Faget, Paine, Slayton, Phillips, von Braun, Webb, and thousands of others how to do big things quickly. In submarines, cockpits, research labs, and defense plants, on the front lines and on the home front, they mastered the selfless teamwork that would one day achieve the seemingly impossible—a voyage beyond the atmosphere, through the vacuum of space, to the ultimate destination: the Moon.

Max Faget's submarine, built with speed and skill by a company that was new to submarines. Apollo would spark the same commitment.

Apollo landing sites on the Moon

Apollo 11 (1969)

Apollo 12 (1969)

Apollo 14 (1971)

Apollo 15 (1971)

Apollo 16 (1972)

Apollo 17 (1972)

BRIEFING:
Six Landing Sites

Between 1969 and 1972, the United States landed six Apollo missions on the Moon. Apollo 11 set down on a flat plain, where Armstrong and Aldrin spent barely two hours outside. Each successive mission went to a more challenging site, stayed longer, and explored farther. Unlike Apollo 11, they also made pinpoint landings near their objectives. By Apollo 15, commander Dave Scott was threading his LM between two high mountains to land at their foot next to a canyon as deep as Colorado's Royal Gorge. He and his copilot, Jim Irwin, stayed for three days, exploring the region in an electric moon buggy. "It's absolutely mind-boggling, because you cannot believe it is really that spectacular," Scott said afterward.

The geology during the missions was also spectacular. Practically any rock that astronauts picked up was as old as Earth's most ancient rocks, and many were far older. The specimens told a story of a primordial magma ocean, huge asteroid impacts, and the Moon's origin far back in time, when a rogue planet collided with the infant Earth.

In choosing the astronauts who went to the Moon, Deke Slayton stuck to his rotation system, except he let Al Shepard—America's first spaceman—jump to the head of the line after he was restored to flight status. Below is a rundown of the six landings and crews, with the commander listed first, followed by the command module pilot and lunar module pilot. Along with the crews of Apollo 8, 10, and 13, which flew around the Moon but did not land, these are history's first lunar explorers:

Apollo 11
Crew: Neil Armstrong, Mike Collins, Buzz Aldrin
Landing site: Sea of Tranquility

Apollo 12
Crew: Pete Conrad, Dick Gordon, Al Bean
Landing site: Ocean of Storms

Apollo 14
Crew: Al Shepard, Stu Roosa, Ed Mitchell
Landing site: Fra Mauro highlands

Apollo 15
Crew: Dave Scott, Al Worden, Jim Irwin
Landing site: Hadley Rille

Apollo 16
Crew: John Young, Tom Mattingly, Charlie Duke
Landing site: Descartes highlands

Apollo 17
Crew: Gene Cernan, Ron Evans, Jack Schmitt
Landing site: Taurus-Littrow valley

TIMELINE

1941

Japan attacks Pearl Harbor, Hawaii, bringing the U.S. into World War II.

1957

Sputnik 1, the first artificial satellite, is launched by the Soviet Union, using the world's largest rocket at the time. The space age begins.

1945

Germany surrenders. Three months later, the U.S. drops two atomic bombs on Japan, which surrenders, ending World War II.

1958

The U.S. launches its first satellite with a rocket developed from V-2 technology.

1962-1964

The Soviet Union launches five manned Earth-orbiting missions, versus four by America's Mercury program.

German V-2s—the first rockets capable of reaching space—are launched against England with high-explosive warheads.

The Cold War starts, pitting the U.S. and its allies against the Soviet Union and the communist bloc in a largely ideological conflict.

1947

Russian Yuri Gagarin is the first man in space. A month later, Alan Shepard is the first American in space. Shortly after, President Kennedy announces the goal of landing a man on the Moon by the end of the decade, which becomes Project Apollo.

1944

1961

1965

A Russian makes the first space walk. Months later, an American follows suit.

1968

Apollo 8 circles the Moon in a surprise mission, beating an anticipated Soviet manned circumlunar flight.

1966

America's Gemini program ends after ten successful manned spaceflights, including a near disaster for astronaut Neil Armstrong.

1972

Project Apollo ends with its sixth manned Moon landing, Apollo 17.

The Apollo 1 spacecraft is destroyed in a fire on the launchpad, killing the crew. A Russian also dies while testing a new spacecraft.
The first flight of the Saturn V Moon rocket is spectacularly successful.

Apollo 11 astronauts Armstrong and Aldrin become the first humans on the Moon, while their colleague Collins orbits the Moon in the mother ship.

The Soviet Union collapses, bringing an end to the Cold War.

1991

1969

1967

ACKNOWLEDGMENTS

When I was fourteen, I did a science-fair project on rockets that won an award from NASA. It was nothing brilliant, and there were over a hundred winners in the Great Plains states from Texas (where I lived) to North Dakota. We were all honored with a special conference at the then brand-new Manned Spacecraft Center (MSC) in Houston in August 1965.

As luck would have it, the Gemini 5 mission was delayed and ended up coinciding with our visit. Gemini 5 was the longest-duration human spaceflight yet and only the second time that MSC was being used as Mission Control for astronauts in orbit—a function it still serves as the rechristened Lyndon B. Johnson Space Center. Apollo planning was at its peak, and Gemini 5 was intended to show that humans could function in space for the eight days that a lunar-landing mission would take.

Back then, MSC had the look of an Old West boomtown. New construction was everywhere in the middle of what had formerly been ranch land. Our itinerary included tours, a visit to a Gemini press conference (where the big celebrities were the television correspondents we saw on the nightly news), and talks given by insiders such as Apollo spacecraft manager Joseph Shea and astronaut Charles Bassett, who spoke at our banquet on the last night.

Not long after, Bassett was chosen to fly on Gemini 9, scheduled for spring 1966. Tragically, he was to die with his mission commander, Elliot See, when their T-38 jet crashed in bad weather just three months before their launch date. Deke Slayton, head of Flight Crew Operations, said he had had "a lot of plans for Charlie Bassett." After his Gemini assignment, Bassett was slated to be an Apollo command module pilot. Given Slayton's rotation system, he would probably have commanded one of the later Apollo missions and walked on the Moon. T-38s also took the lives of Apollo astronauts Theodore Freeman and Clifton "C.C." Williams—also before they had a chance to fly in space. Astronaut Edward Givens Jr. died in an automobile accident—again before his first mission. In chapter 28, I recount the tragedy of the Apollo 1 fire, which killed three astronauts in a ground test. There were also fatal accidents in the Soviet space program. We should never forget these brave pioneers.

Many years have passed since my teenage visit to Houston, but I have never stopped marveling at the amazing adventure of Apollo. Most recently, conversations with David Michaud and Steven Bressler got me thinking about the importance of World War II to the Apollo program, which drew on the infrastructure, experience, and attitudes developed during the war. David and Steve are talented exhibit designers, and the three of us planned to produce a traveling exhibit on Apollo. It fell through, but the germ of our discussions grew into this book.

My first and closest connections to Apollo veterans have been with the late William R. Muehlberger of the University of Texas at Austin and James W. Head III of Brown University. Both were advisory geologists in the Apollo program, helping pick landing sites, plan exploration, and train the astronauts. Some years ago, I interviewed Jack Schmitt, who actually went to the Moon as a geologist and lunar module pilot on Apollo 17. I was interested in the parallels between the exploration of the American West and the Moon, which as a student of history and a native of New Mexico, Schmitt saw very clearly. Over the years, Apollo historian Andrew Chaikin has been an enthusiastic and indulgent sounding board. Exhibit projects with different museums and galleries allowed me to immerse myself deeply in Apollo images and artifacts. Lorraine Neilan of Mountview Middle School in Holden, Massachusetts, invited me to discuss Apollo with her science students. And Gale Free Library in Holden has been an indispensable resource, for which I thank library director Susan Scott and her superb staff. I am also grateful to space journalist and historian James Oberg for reviewing the manuscript and making a number of excellent suggestions. Any defects that remain are mine alone.

The author's name goes on the title page, but a book is really a joint effort. My collaborators at Roaring Brook include editor Emily Feinberg, designer Monique Sterling, production editor Mandy Veloso, and copyeditor Chandra Wohleber. I am also grateful to former Macmillan executive Simon Boughton, whose enthusiasm for Apollo launched me on this project. This book is dedicated to my delightful daughters-in-law, Jessamyn and Hannah. My wife, Susie, whom I met in the publishing business some four decades ago, has been my guiding star.

NOTES

Abbreviations

JSC = NASA Johnson Space Center Oral History Project

LBJ = Lyndon Baines Johnson Library Oral History Collection

NASM = Smithsonian National Air and Space Museum Oral History Project

Statistics for Saturn and Apollo flights are from Orloff and Harland, *Apollo: The Definitive Sourcebook*. Nautical miles have been converted to statute miles.

PART 1: War

3 *"The war made us"*: Renehan, *The Kennedys at War*, p. 2.

Chapter 1: Ensign Faget's Close Call

6 *It was February 20, 1945*: The depth-charging ordeal is recounted most fully by Faget's fellow crewman Marion L. Shinn in Chap. 18 of his memoir, *Pacific Patrol*. See also "Report of Fifth War Patrol" in "History of U.S.S. *Guavina*"; as well as Hargis, "Boats on Patrol" in *U.S. Submarine Crewman*; and Faget, JSC, June 18, 1997.

9 *"We experienced hell"*: "Report of Fifth War Patrol," p. 12, in "History of U.S.S. *Guavina*."

9 *"Words cannot express"*: From Chap. 18 in Shinn, *Pacific Patrol*.

11 *"A submarine is a very high-tech ship"*: Cooper, "Annals of Space," *New Yorker*, September 2, 1991, p. 57.

Chapter 2: Pirates of the Western Pacific

14 *"We were the last of the corsairs"*: Buckley, "NASA's Tom Paine," *New York Times*, June 8, 1969, magazine section, p. 36.

14–16 U.S.S. *Pompon*: Details of *Pompon*'s patrols are in "History of U.S.S. *Pompon*," a day-by-day log of the submarine's activities. Paine's first war patrol was *Pompon*'s third, his second was *Pompon*'s fourth, etc.

15 *"a mere ensign do"*: Calvert, *Silent Running*, p. 9.

15 *Seawater immediately cascaded into the control room*: The official report on the flooding incident is in "Report of War Patrol No. Seven," pp. 7–8, in "History of U.S.S. *Pompon*." The incident is also recounted by Stanley J. Nicholls in Roberts, *Sub*, pp. 34–35; and by Bailey in "The 7th Patrol of the U.S.S. *Pompon*."

17 *By the end of the war, nearly one-fifth of America's fighting subs*: cited in *United States Submarine Losses, World War II*, p. 1.

17 *"I saw many strange and wonderful things"*: Buckley, "NASA's Tom Paine," *New York Times*, June 8, 1969, magazine section, p. 36.

17 *"Youth and the sea"*: Conrad, "Youth," fourth-to-last paragraph. See Paine's "The Transpacific Voyage," where he says, "In his sea classic 'Youth' Joseph Conrad captures my feelings perfectly."

Chapter 3: Lieutenant Slayton Flies Another Mission
20 *the British intensified their own bombing campaign against Germany*: Background on the bomber offensive in Europe is from Overy, *The Bombing War*. U.S. sortie statistics in this chapter are from *Army Air Forces Statistical Digest: World War II*.

20 *Second Lieutenant Donald K. Slayton*: Slayton's service with the 486th Squadron, 340th Bomb Group, is covered in Chap. 3 of Slayton and Cassutt, *Deke!* Reminiscences by other airmen with the group are in Satterthwaite, *Truth Flies with Fiction*; and Meder, *The True Story of Catch-22*, which covers the experiences of novelist Joseph Heller, who also flew with the 340th.

21 *Working with target orders from headquarters*: The duties of operations staff are described in the chapter "Operations" in Casper, *History and Personnel, 489th, 340th Bomb Group*.

21 *usual mission was a formation of eighteen planes*: Satterthwaite, *Truth Flies with Fiction*, pp. 44–45.

22 *headquarters set a limit on how many missions an airman had to fly*: Changing mission limits are described in Meder, *The True Story of Catch-22*, p. 17.

22 *fifty missions gave flyers about a 30 percent chance of getting shot down*: Data is in Satterthwaite, *Truth Flies with Fiction*, p. 254.

22 *"Fly 'til I die"*: Howard, *Whistle While You Wait*, p. 165.

22 *"Same time, same place, same direction!"*: Slayton and Cassutt, *Deke!*, p. 27. Additional quotes and details on the Athens raid are in "November 17, 1943 Mission to Kalamaki Aerodrome, Greece."

25 *The following day the men learned that the fifty-mission limit was being raised*: Under the entries for November 18 in "History: November 1943."

Chapter 4: Captain Phillips Bombs Major von Braun
27 *"Surviving"*: Phillips, NASM (February 23, 1988).

27 *364th Fighter Group*: For the history of Phillips's unit, see Joiner, *The History of the 364th Fighter Group*.

28 *One of the Mustang's most advanced features was its wing*: For NACA research on laminar-flow airfoils, see Hansen, *Engineer in Charge*, pp. 111–118.

29 *"The greatest surprise of the war to us"*: Irving, *Göring*, p. 469.

29 *On August 25, 1944*: For Phillips's participation, see Stuhlinger and Ordway, *Wernher von Braun: A Biographical Memoir*, p. 201; and *The History of the 364th Fighter Group*, p. 45, where Mission No. 187 is the only raid to the Peenemünde area recorded by the 364th. The raid is broken down in "USAAF Chronology," 25 August 1944, Mission 570, No. 3.

32 *"It could have very easily led me to the firing squad"*: Ward, *Dr. Space*, p. 40.

32 *von Braun's rockets began falling on London*: V-2 launch statistics are from Ordway and Sharpe, *The Rocket Team*, pp. 243 and 251.

33 *responsible for some 5,000 deaths—not including the estimated 10,000*: Neufeld, *The Rocket and the Reich*, p. 264.

33 *It took as much labor to build one*: O'Brien, *How the War Was Won*, pp. 28–29.

33 *"Once they felt they could do without you"*: Ward, *Dr. Space*, p. 39.

Chapter 5: Major Webb Faces the Big One

36 *Major James E. Webb*: Webb's reminiscences of the U.S. Marine Corps and the Sperry Gyroscope Company are in Webb, NASM: February 22, 1985; March 8, 1985; and March 29, 1985. For more details on his life, see Lambright, *Powering Apollo*, and Bizony, *The Man Who Ran the Moon*.

38 *"My forte was putting things together"*: Webb, NASM, February 22, 1985.

38 *"War is a hurly-burly kind of thing"*: Webb, NASM, February 22, 1985.

40 *More than 85,000 were built*: Mindell, *Between Human and Machine*, p. 221.

41 *"The contractors said it would take us six, maybe eight months"*: Webb, NASM, February 22, 1985.

Chapter 6: "We Need It Yesterday!"

44 *"We didn't think that much about it"*: Slayton and Cassutt, *Deke!*, p. 35.

45 *the B-29 Superfortress, came out of a more expensive program*: O'Brien, *How the War Was Won*, pp. 47–48.

46 *A famous story*: Recounted in Ricks, "Whatever Happened to Accountability?"; also in Perret, *There's a War to Be Won*, p. 27.

47 *In 1939, he had asked Boeing Company executives*: Geer, *Boeing's Ed Wells*, pp. 93–94; more B-29 specifications are in Vander Meulen, *Building the B-29*, pp. 12–17.

47 *by attacking all of the airplane's intricate systems at the same time*: Johnson, *The Secret of Apollo*, p. 26.

47 *thousands of engineers*: Vander Meulen, *Building the B-29*, p. 15.

47 *thousands of suppliers*: Bilstein, "Aviation Industry," *The Oxford Encyclopedia of American Business, Labor, and Economic History*, Vol. 1, p. 69.

47 *"depends upon everything working as planned"*: Vander Meulen, *Building the B-29*, p. 86.

47 *The worst day was February 18, 1943*: The accident is recounted in Robbins, "Eddie Allen and the B-29." Also see Herman, *Freedom's Forge*, pp. 301–302 (for the accident) and p. 303 (for the political fallout).

48 *A review board ordered changes in the engines*: For engineering changes and production problems, see Vander Meulen, *Building the B-29*, pp. 32–35 and 90.

48 *within fourteen months the B-29 was flying in combat*: Herman, *Freedom's Forge*, p. 320.

PART 2: Dreams
53 *"To place a man in a multi-stage rocket"*: "Space Travel Impossible, States Dr. Lee De Forest," *Boston Globe*, February 25, 1957, p. 11.

Chapter 7: America Lands on Its Feet
56 *life expectancy was just forty-seven years*: The Berkeley Mortality Database.

57 *In 1900, only a third of homes had running water*: Statistics for modern conveniences are in Gordon, *The Rise and Fall of American Growth*, pp. 114–115.

57 *At the end of 1949, a random sample of Americans*: *The Gallup Poll Public Opinion, 1935–1971*. Vol. 2: *1949–1958*, p. 875.

Chapter 8: Von Braun Lands in America
61 *"That guy upstairs wants to go to the Moon"*: Lang, *From Hiroshima to the Moon*, p. 180.

62 *"America is the place for you to build your Moon rockets"*: Neufeld, *Von Braun*, p. 190.

63 *"If Germany had won the war"*: Lang, *From Hiroshima to the Moon*, pp. 185–186.

64 *"At Peenemünde, we'd been coddled"*: Lang, *From Hiroshima to the Moon*, p. 189.

65 *"former pets of Hitler"*: Graham, "Nazi Scientists Aid Army on Research," *New York Times*, December 4, 1946, p. 35. For more on this controversy, see Laney, *German Rocketeers in the Heart of Dixie*, Chap. 1.

65 *"We hold these individuals"*: "Opposes Citizenship for Reich Scientists," *The Spokesman-Review*, December 30, 1946, p. 2.

65 *a majority of Americans agreed*: Gallup, *The Gallup Poll Public Opinion, 1935–1971*. Vol. 1: *1935–1948*, p. 618.

Chapter 9: The Cold War
69 *"We have emerged from this war"*: McMahon, *The Cold War*, p. 6.

70 *twenty years was a good estimate*: Rhodes, *The Making of the Atomic Bomb*, p. 633.

71 *"The calmer the American people take this, the better"*: "Red Alert," *Time*, October 3, 1949, p. 10.

71 *"Better get out your old uniform"*: "The Thunderclap," *Time*, October 3, 1949, p. 10.

72 *he had a remarkably calm discussion*: Sears, *Such Men as These*, p. 175.

Chapter 10: Disney to the Rescue

78 *"With the Redstone, we could do it!"*: Stuhlinger and Ordway, *Wernher von Braun: A Biographical Memoir*, p. 122.

80 *arrived like a trumpet blast from the future*: The making of the *Collier's* and Disney series is told in Liebermann, "The *Collier's* and Disney Series"; and in Smith, "They're Following Our Script."

81 *"What you will read here is not science fiction"*: "What Are We Waiting For?" *Collier's*, March 22, 1952, p. 23.

82 *"Disney's immediate achievement"*: Smith, "They're Following Our Script," *Future*, May 1978, p. 59.

83 *"made all the generals sit down"*: Kimball in Ghez, *Walt's People*, Vol. 3, p. 52.

Chapter 11: The Empire Strikes Back

85 *"a lot of hooey!"*: Bracker, "Truman Varies—Airy to Mundane," *New York Times*, February 5, 1956, p. 56.

86 *By mid-1955, development work on the Redstone was nearly complete*: Bulkeley, *The Sputniks Crisis*, p. 158. For von Braun's souped-up Redstone, see Ward, *Dr. Space*, pp. 97–98.

86 *"I want you to tell him"*: Gray, *Angle of Attack*, pp. 15–16.

87 *"I'll be damned!"*: Ward, *Dr. Space*, p. 99.

87 *"a disaster . . . comparable to Pearl Harbor"*: Divine, "Lyndon B. Johnson and the Politics of Space," p. 223.

87 *"a devastating blow to the prestige of the United States"*: Callahan and Greenstein, "The Reluctant Racer," p. 26.

89 "like sausages": McDougall, *The Heavens and the Earth*, p. 240.

90 *a large audience from all walks of life*: "The Death of TV-3," *Time*, December 16, 1957, National Affairs section.

90 *Reporting to his boss in Washington over a long-distance phone line*: Bracker, "Vanguard Rocket Burns on Beach," *New York Times*, December 7, 1957, p. 8.

90 *"bore a remarkable resemblance to atomic-bomb detonations"*: Talbert, "U.S. Moon Rocket Blows Up," *New York Herald Tribune*, December 7, 1957, p. 1.

90 *a Russian short animated film*: "Soviet Movie Shows Reach for the Moon," *Time*, October 28, 1957, p. 26. The film, *After Sputnik—the Moon?*, is posted on YouTube at youtube.com/watch?v=yl5d2EVPMXY (published August 3, 2015).

Chapter 12: Explorer

93 *Redstone was called Juno I*: The rocket was also called Jupiter-C. The Juno designation was to distinguish it from the Redstone and Jupiter programs, which were both military.

93 *Mary Sherman Morgan:* For her life story, see Morgan, *Rocket Girl*.

94 *In late January*: Details of the Juno launch are in Medaris, *Countdown for Decision*, pp. 200–226.

95 *"tremendous jet burst from the base of the rocket"*: Bracker, "Jupiter-C Is Used," *New York Times*, February 1, 1958, p. 7.

95 *"a flame-footed monster"*: "Voyage of the Explorer," *Time*, February 10, 1958, p. 17.

95 *"terrific"*: "U.S. Fires 'Moon'!" *Chicago Daily Tribune*, February 1, 1958, p. 2.

95 *"Slow rise, faster, faster!"*: Neufeld, *Von Braun*, p. 321.

96 *seven minutes after launch*: "U.S. Fires 'Moon'!" *Chicago Daily Tribune*, February 1, 1958, p. 1.

96 *"with 95 percent confidence"*: Bille and Lishock, *The First Space Race*, pp. 131–132.

97 *"Those moments were the most exciting eight minutes of my life!"*: Ward, *Dr. Space*, p. 116.

97 *"Once the first satellite is in orbit"*: Stuhlinger and Ordway, *Wernher von Braun: A Biographical Memoir*, p. 109.

Briefing: Russia's Rocket
99 *"Do you realize the tremendous strategic importance"*: Holloway, *Stalin and the Bomb*, p. 247.

PART 3: Spacemen
101 *"Your plan will provide"*: von Ehrenfried, *The Birth of NASA*, p. 95. See also Gilruth, NASM, February 27, 1987, where Gilruth recounts the July 2, 1958, meeting at which Kistiakowsky made this remark.

Chapter 13: Max Makes His Pitch
103 *"If voyages were to be made from the Earth"*: Sloane, "Acceleration in Interplanetary Travel."

104 *"it will take iron nerves waiting for the impact that never comes"*: "Man in Space," *Disneyland*.

104 *weightlessness would drive people crazy*: Leonard, *Flight into Space*, p. 94.

105 *"I refuse to recognize that there are impossibilities"*: Ford and Crowther, "My Life and Work," p. 14.

105 *secret conference*: Gray, *Angle of Attack*, p. 45.

106 *Most of the engineers at the conference*: For an account of the high-speed-flight conference, known as the Round Three Conference, see Chaikin, "How the Spaceship Got Its Shape."

108 *Working with two other colleagues, Faget fleshed out the details*: See the very readable short paper by Faget, Garland, and Buglia, "Preliminary Studies of Manned Satellites—Wingless Configuration: Nonlifting."

109 *"Max made his pitch"*: Chaikin, "How the Spaceship Got Its Shape."

109 *Faget was determined to move ahead*: Swenson et al., *This New Ocean*, p. 532, n. 54.

Chapter 14: "Let's Get On with It"

111 *under questioning by a congressional committee*: Dryden's tribulations and the birth of NASA are described in Roland, *Model Research*, Chap. 12.

111 *"Tossing a man up in the air"*: Swenson et al., *This New Ocean*, p. 100.

112 *much to von Braun's dismay*: Neufeld, *Von Braun*, p. 330.

112 *NA¢A had become NA$A*: Roland, *Model Research*, p. 300.

113 *stubborn*: See Faget's comments on von Braun in Faget, JSC, June 18, 1997.

113 *who had little taste for stunts or crash programs*: Glennan's attitudes are covered in Glennan, *The Birth of NASA*, pp. 5, 67.

113 *"All right. Let's get on with it."*: Glennan's order to Gilruth is recounted in Hansen, *Spaceflight Revolution*, p. 55; and Detholff, *Suddenly, Tomorrow Came . . .* , p. 20.

115 *"Okay, we'll go"*: Rives, "'OK, We'll Go,'" *Prologue*, Spring 2014.

115 *"It was one of the best decisions he ever made"*: Cortright, *Apollo Expeditions to the Moon*, p. 146.

Chapter 15: The Original Seven

119 *dead test pilots*: Fredrickson, *Warbird Factory*, p. 141.

119 *sixty-two fighter pilots had died during thirty-six weeks of training*: Wolfe, *The Right Stuff*, p. 15.

120 *"one tragedy would not stop this project"*: "Astronaut's Death Will Not Halt Program," *Los Angeles Times*, April 11, 1960.

121 *"We have gone about as far as we can"*: "The Seven Chosen," *Time*, April 20, 1959, National Affairs section.

121 *"Given the state of NASA and Project Mercury"*: Slayton and Cassutt, *Deke!*, p. 70.

121 *"I don't know"*: Faget in Davis-Floyd et al., *Space Stories*, Chap. 2.

122 *up to twenty g's*: Barratt, "Physical and Bioenvironmental Aspects of Human Space Flight," p. 14.

122 *thinner than a dime*: The thickness of Atlas varied from 0.01 to 0.04 inches (Jenkins, "Stage-and-a-Half," p. 76). A U.S. dime is 0.05 inches thick.

122 *very much like an egg*: Logsdon, *Orbital Mechanics*, p. 122.

123 *"like a hydrogen bomb going off"*: Glenn and Taylor, *John Glenn*, p. 207.

123 *"I sure hope they fix that"*: Wendt and Still, *The Unbroken Chain*, p. 14.

123 *"I spent most of my time that year at the Cape"*: Slayton and Cassutt, *Deke!*, p. 87.

Chapter 16: The Vice President Finds a Space Chief

126 *"Control of space means control of the world"*: Divine, "Lyndon B. Johnson and the Politics of Space," p. 224.

126 *"I don't think I'm the right person for this job"*: Quotes and incidents linked to Webb's appointment as NASA administrator are from Webb, NASM, March 15, 1985; and Webb, LBJ, April 29, 1969. Additional details are in Bizony, *The Man Who Ran the Moon*, pp. 16–17; Lambright, *Powering Apollo*, p. 84; and Logsdon, *John F. Kennedy and the Race to the Moon*, pp. 41–42.

127 *"the greatest . . . capacity"*: Holmes, *America on the Moon*, p. 190.

128 *"marginal"*: Logsdon, *Exploring the Unknown*, Vol. 1, pp. 408–409.

128 *"We mean it's a sick program"*: Garwood, "JFK Gets Report," *Austin Statesman*, January 12, 1961, p. A3.

128 *"a failure in our first attempt to place a man into orbit"*: Logsdon, *Exploring the Unknown*, Vol. 1, p. 422.

129 *Fretting about the reputation of their Atlas missile*: Lambright, *Powering Apollo*, pp. 89–90.

129 *"My philosophy has always been"*: Webb, NASM, November 4, 1985; quoted in Lambright, *Powering Apollo*, p. 90.

129 *Max Faget had already sketched out a more advanced spacecraft*: Gray, *Angle of Attack*, p. 166.

130 *"I feel splendid, very well"*: Grahn, "An Analysis of the Flight of *Vostok*."

130 *"The world's first satellite-ship"*: Siddiqi, *Challenge to Apollo*, p. 278.

131 *"Let the capitalist countries catch up with our country"*: Carruthers, "Russian Orbited the Earth Once," *New York Times*, April 13, 1961, p. 14.

Chapter 17: "Light This Candle"

133 *"Those who say they will stand up to Mr. Khrushchev"*: Rasenberger, *The Brilliant Disaster*, p. 90.

133 *"The communists have been moving with vigor"*: The Fourth Kennedy-Nixon *Presidential Debate*, October 21, 1960.

134 *"Rescue units on the scene"*: Thompson, *Light This Candle*, p. 249.

135 *"Why postpone a success?"*: Swenson et al., *This New Ocean*, p. 350.

135 *"All right, I'm cooler than you are"*: Wolfe, *The Right Stuff*, p. 200.

135 *"a subtle, gentle, gradual rise off the ground"*: The Astronauts (Carpenter et al.), *We Seven*, p. 189.

136 *One oddity*: Scott Carpenter, who made the fourth Mercury flight, describes this experience in his memoir, *For Spacious Skies*, p. 256.

136 *About two minutes into the flight*: Technical details of Shepard's flight are from Swenson et al., *This New Ocean*, Chap. 11; also *Post Launch Report for Mercury-Redstone No. 3*; and "Freedom 7 Mercury-Redstone 3."

Chapter 18: Go to the Moon

139 *"The blaze of Alan Shepard's Redstone"*: "It's a Success," *Time*, May 5, 1961, p. 14.

140 *"Is there any . . . space program which promises dramatic results in which we could win?"*: Kennedy's memorandum to Johnson and the reply are in Logsdon, *Exploring the Unknown*, Vol. 1, pp. 423–424, 427–429.

140 *"tremendous jet burst from the base of the rocket"*: Bracker, "Jupiter-C Is Used," *New York Times*, February 1, 1958, p. 7.

140 *"thunder of the rocket engine"*: "U.S. Fires 'Moon'!" *Chicago Daily Tribune*, February 1, 1958, p. 2.

140 *"When you decide you're going to do something"*: Murray and Cox, *Apollo*, p. 81.

140 *40 billion dollars*: Sidey, *John F. Kennedy*, p. 117.

140 *four times the combined cost of the B-29 and atomic bomb projects*: O'Brien, *How the War Was Won*, pp. 47–48. O'Brien gives a combined cost of $5.7 billion for the two programs, or $9.5 billion in 1961 dollars. Inflation calculated with the Bureau of Labor Statistics tool at data.bls.gov/cgi-bin/cpicalc.pl (accessed September 1, 2017).

143 *His speech*: For the entire speech, see Kennedy, "President Kennedy's Special Message to the Congress on Urgent National Needs, May 25, 1961."

143 *a startling challenge*: "Hopes & Misgivings," *Time*, June 2, 1961, p. 13.

144 *the audience's stunned reaction*: The speechwriter was Theodore Sorenson. See Vine, "Walking on the Moon."

144 *When they tuned in to the speech*: Gilruth's reaction is described in Gilruth, NASM February 27, 1987.

144 *the original deadline had been 1967*: Seamans, *Aiming at Targets*, pp. 85, 90–91.

145 *"I was always a guy"*: Gilruth, NASM, February 27, 1987.

PART 4: The Plan
149 *"So much happened and it happened so fast"*: Murray and Cox, *Apollo*, p. 87.

Chapter 19: Pieces of the Puzzle
151 *"if we were all crazy"*: Seamans, *Aiming at Targets*, p. 91.

151 *Seamans and his colleagues came up with a plan*: Apollo plans as of 1962 are covered in Sullivan, *America's Race for the Moon*, based on a series of articles that appeared in the *New York Times* that summer.

154 *In 1961, NASA had 18,000 employees*: Statistics on NASA employment are from *NASA Historical Data Book: 1958–1968*, Vol. 1, p. 106.

155 *ready for its first Earth orbital missions until 1965*: Miles, "Moon Spacecraft Project Speeded," *Los Angeles Times*, April 1, 1962, p. F6.

157 *Webb and others at NASA pressed Draper*: Brooks et al., *Chariots for Apollo*, p. 41.

Chapter 20: How to Get to the Moon, and Back
159 *"Your figures lie!"*: The quotes are from Sheridan, "How an Idea No One Wanted Grew Up to Be the LM," *Life*, March 14, 1969, p. 22. A full account of Houbolt's crusade is in Murray and Cox, *Apollo*, Chaps. 8 and 9.

164 *"Houbolt has a scheme"*: Logsdon, *Exploring the Unknown*, Vol. 7, p. 524.

164 *"offered a chain reaction"*: Sheridan, "How an Idea No One Wanted Grew Up to Be the LM," *Life*, March 14, 1969, p. 22.

Chapter 21: The Race Heats Up
167 *about every two weeks*: Details of Slayton's heart problem are from Slayton and Cassutt, *Deke!*, pp. 85–86, 110–113.

168 *Newspapers treated it almost like a death*: For the typical newspaper reaction to Slayton's grounding, see the wire service story "Heart Forces Slayton Out of Astronaut Role," *Boston Globe*, July 12, 1962, p. 8.

168 *"Red Spaceman Lands!"*: "Red Spaceman Lands!" *New York Journal-American*, August 7, 1961, p. 1.

168 *A British expert on spaceflight didn't think so*: The expert was Kenneth Gatland. See "Russ Cosmonaut Titov Safely Down on Land," *Austin Statesman*, August 7, 1961, p. 1.

168 *canceling the remaining suborbital flights*: Slayton and Cassutt, *Deke!*, p. 104.

170 *"Bourgeois society always underlines that woman is the weaker sex"*: Topping, "Khrushchev Hails Astronauts," *New York Times*, June 23, 1963, p. 11.

170 *an editorial for* Life *magazine*: Luce's comment and the quotes in the paragraph that follows are from Luce, "But Some People Simply Never Get the Message," *Life*, June 28, 1963, p. 31.

171 *"We will train some women astronauts for sure"*: "U.S. Women Still Grounded by NASA," *Chicago Tribune*, June 17, 1963, p. 2.

Chapter 22: The Great Escape
174 *"Anybody who would spend 40 billion dollars"*: Benson and Faherty, *Moonport*, p. 170.

174 *8 to 12 billion*: Lambright, *Powering Apollo*, p. 101. For a condensed version of Webb's budget and political strategy, see Lambright's article "Leading NASA in Space Exploration."

174 *"If we had an insuperable obstacle"*: Trento, *Prescription for Disaster*, p. 52; quoted in Lambright, *Powering Apollo*, p. 110.

175 *"We walked into the firing room"*: Details are from "Apollo 15 Remembered 40 Years Later," starting at 1:07:00. See also Ward, *Rocket Ranch*, p. 129.

176 *"There are two problems which greatly concern them"*: "Reds Not Sold on Trip to Moon," *Washington Post*, July 17, 1963, p. A3.

176 *The Central Intelligence Agency (CIA) had advised him*: David, *Spies and Shuttles*, p. 38.

176 *ambitious launch site construction*: Day, "From the Shadows to the Stars."

176 *Webb was also starting to have trouble*: Lambright, *Powering Apollo*, pp. 114–116.

177 *"Look, if you want someone else to run the program"*: Webb, NASM, October 15, 1985.

177 *"a candid assessment of the real status"*: The assessment and Mueller's meeting with Seamans are recounted in Slotkin, *Doing the Impossible*, pp. 17–18. See also Seamans, *Project Apollo*, pp. 49, 51.

177 *Mueller had the chance to brief President Kennedy*: See the account in Seamans, *Project Apollo*, pp. 51–53.

178 *"This is fantastic"*: Hunter, "President, Touring Canaveral, Sees a Polaris Fired," *New York Times*, November 17, 1963, p. 44. Additional details are in "JFK Sees Polaris Fired," *Boston Globe*, November 17, 1963, p. 16; and "Sub Fires Missile as JFK Watches," *Hartford Courant*, November 17, 1963, p. 1A.

Chapter 23: General Phillips Joins the Team
181 *"Results are what count"*: Neal, *Ace in the Hole*, p. 16.

184 *No one had ever done an "all-up" launch on the initial outing*: Abramson, "Laconic General," *Los Angeles Times*, October 6, 1968, p. F1.

184 *"crazy" and likely to "blow up on the pad"*: Neal, *Ace in the Hole*, p. 12.

184 *"if you do your piece right"*: Guy, JSC (October 30, 2006).

185 *impossible, reckless, incredulous, harebrained, and nonsense*: Seamans, *Project Apollo*, p. 51.

185 *"The thing that really kills programs"*: Slotkin, *Doing the Impossible*, p. 39.

186 *"Today's work must be done today"*: Mueller's words of inspiration in this paragraph are quoted in Slotkin, *Doing the Impossible*, pp. xxiii, 68–69.

186 *"George was a double whirlwind"*: Seamans, JSC, November 20, 1998. See also Seamans, *Aiming at Targets*, p. 110.

186 *A diary entry from his Apollo years*: Bateman, "The Ultimate Program Manager," p. 37.

186 *"You could stand across the street"*: Armstrong, JSC, September 19, 2001.

Chapter 24: "Do Good Work!"
189 *"Like so many things for my generation"*: Seamans, *Aiming at Targets*, pp. 99–100.

190 *a young engineer named Harrison Storms*: Storms's background is covered in Gray, *Angle of Attack*, Chap. 1.

190 *Alfred Munier came to work at Grumman Aircraft on Long Island in 1943*: Saxon, "Alfred Munier, 78," *New York Times*, December 23, 1993, p. B6.

191 *Stoner had been a test supervisor for the dauntingly complex B-29 bomber*: "G. H. Stoner of Boeing Co.," *Washington Post*, March 3, 1971, p. B3.

191 *"Do good work!"*: This anecdote is told in Wolfe, *The Right Stuff*, p. 116. See also Leopold, *Calculated Risk*, pp. 212–213.

192 *"Do good work" signs spread to contractors all over the country*: Tapper, "Throwback Thursday—'Do Good Work,'" May 8, 2014.

192 *Most were in their twenties*: "Is NASA's workforce too old?" *Space*, April 11, 2008, *New Scientist Blogs*.

192 *"We carried responsibilities for very major aspects of the Mercury program"*: Fries, *NASA Engineers and the Age of Apollo*, p. 68.

Briefing: The Women of Apollo
195 *Patricia Bridges*: See Kopal and Carder, *Mapping the Moon*, Chap. 7.

PART 5: Crews

197 *"Any crew can fly any mission"*: Cernan and Davis, *The Last Man on the Moon*, p. 239.

Chapter 25: Squadron Commander

199 *discussed the situation with the other astronauts*: Wolfe, *The Right Stuff*, p. 300.

204 *"Work your tail off"*: Chaikin, *A Man on the Moon*, p. 45.

205 *Like a good squadron operations officer*: Slayton's approach to crew selection is covered in Slayton and Cassutt, *Deke!*, Chap. 14, especially pp. 136–138.

206 *"Going to the Moon is going from point A to point B"*: Trafford, "Apollos and Oranges," *Washington Post*, July 19, 1994, p. 6.

206 *Oriana Fallaci*: Fallaci's interview with Slayton is in Fallaci, *If the Sun Dies*, Chap. 8.

Chapter 26: The Moon Comes into Focus

209 *"Oh, I am heartily tired of hearing about what Lee is going to do"*: Porter, *Campaigning with Grant*, p. 70.

210 *"The Russians upstage us every time"* . . . *"The target now before us is the Moon"*: Sullivan, "The Week in Science," *New York Times*, March 21, 1965, p. E3.

212 *a thousand times better than those from the largest telescopes*: Hall, *Lunar Impact*, p. 273.

212 *Urey suggested the Sea of Tranquility for Ranger's next target*: Hall, *Lunar Impact*, p. 282.

213 *"one of the dramatic moments in television history"*: "Live from the Moon," *Hartford Courant*, March 25, 1965, p. 14.

213 *"The time is not distant"*: "Moonstruck," *Washington Post*, March 25, 1965, p. A24.

214 *"In a very real sense"*: Kennedy, "President Kennedy's Special Message to the Congress on Urgent National Needs, May 25, 1961."

Chapter 27: Neil Armstrong's Wild Ride

219 *"We are docked!"*: "Gemini VIII Voice Communications," p. 71.

220 *"We have serious problems here"*: "Gemini VIII Voice Communications," p. 75.

220 *"like being on a theme-park ride"*: Scott, Leonov, and Toom, *Two Sides of the Moon*, p. 168.

220 *"I thought they were gone"*: Houston and Heflin, *Go, Flight!*, pp. 82–83.

221 *Deke Slayton had assembled six crews*: Slayton and Cassutt, *Deke!*, p. 184.

221 *projected for 1967*: For the original Apollo mission schedule, see Shayler, *Apollo*, pp. 112–113. The original Apollo 2 was canceled. Thus Apollo 3 became 2, Apollo 4 became 3, etc. The crews here represent the revised plan.

Chapter 28: "Fire in the Cockpit"

226 *the pressure was set a bit higher than sea-pressure level to reveal any leaks in the spacecraft*: Caldwell Johnson in Davis-Floyd et al., *Space Stories*, Chap. 3. The cabin pressure was set at 16.7 pounds per square inch (*Apollo Accident: Hearing*, p. 156).

227 *Apollo's thirty miles of wire*: Apollo Accident: Hearing, p. 222.

227 *"the cockpit of an aircraft in World War II that took a direct hit"*: "Very Little Left in Cabin of Burned-out Spacecraft," *Baltimore Sun*, January 30, 1967, p. A5.

228 *"We should abandon the idea of landing a man on the Moon"*: Lippmann,

"The Race to the Moon," *Newsweek*, February 13, 1967; quoted in White's dissertation, *The Establishment of Blame*, p. 90.

228 *"the inflexible, but meaningless, goal"*: Benson and Faherty, *Moonport*, p. 394.

229 *at a diplomatic event in Washington*: Accounts of the gathering and its immediate aftermath are in Lambright, *Powering Apollo*, pp. 143–147; Hansen, *First Man*, pp. 304–310; and Slotkin, *Doing the Impossible*, pp. 142–147.

229 *"This is the dreadful price you have to pay"*: Collins, "Celebration Ends Instead as a Eulogy," *Newsday*, January 28, 1967, p. 2.

229 *That evening, Webb held a press conference*: French and Burgess, *In the Shadow of the Moon*, p. 166.

229 *"We've always known something like this would happen sooner or later"*: Collins, "Celebration Ends Instead as a Eulogy," *Newsday*, January 28, 1967, p. 2.

229 *"Three superbly trained pilots had died"*: This quote and the drinking incident that follows are from Borman and Serling, *Countdown*, p. 173.

230 *"a labyrinth of systems more complicated than an aircraft carrier"*: Gray, *Angle of Attack*, p. 255.

230 *At Faget's suggestion*: Collins, *Liftoff*, p. 137.

231 *"Spaceflight will never tolerate carelessness, incapacity, and neglect"*: Kranz, *Failure Is Not an Option*, p. 204.

Chapter 29: "Go, Baby, Go!"
233 *"The guys who are going to fly the first lunar missions"*: Slayton's announcement and Cernan's reaction are in Cernan and Davis, *The Last Man on the Moon*, p. 165. The date of the meeting is deduced from Hansen, *First Man*, p. 310.

233 *"the climax of a grand competition"*: Cunningham and Herskowitz, *The All-American Boys*, p. 202.

233 *Both John Young and Neil Armstrong*: Young's thoughts are in Young and Hansen, *Forever Young*, p. 116. Armstrong's are recorded in Hansen, *First Man*, p. 311.

234 *"Be flexible"*: Stafford and Cassutt, *We Have Capture*, p. 109.

235 *Webb and Mueller pressed for a test flight*: Brooks et al., *Chariots for Apollo*, p. 229.

236 *"the longest ten seconds of my life"*: Von Braun's quotes are from Zinman, "Saturn Success Lifts Moon Hopes," *Newsday*, November 10, 1967, p. 2.

236 *"a continuous, pulsating clap of deep thunder"*: Farrar, "U.S. Scores 2 Space Triumphs," *Chicago Tribune*, November 10, 1967, p. 5.

236 *"My God, our building's shaking!"*: "Launch of Apollo 4" on YouTube, starting at 1:50.

236 *As ceiling tiles rained down*: Cronkite, *A Reporter's Life*, pp. 278–279.

239 *"Had the critical test failed"*: Miles, "U.S. Scores Space Triumph," *Los Angeles Times*, November 10, 1967, p. 1.

239 *"Apollo is on the way to the Moon"*: Zinman, "Saturn Success Lifts Moon Hopes," *Newsday*, November 10, 1967, p. 2.

239 *could hardly stop smiling*: McElheny, "A Double Jump on Road to Moon," *Boston Globe*, November 10, 1967, p. 2.

Chapter 30: The Submariner Takes Charge
241 *"If you can visualize a molten streetcar"*: Mann, "Letters Provide Up-close Descriptions of Nuke Blasts," *Laredo Morning Times*, August 5, 2005, p. 8A.

242 *"carrying out a classic naval 'boarders, away!' operation"*: Paine recounts his exploits in his article "The Transpacific Voyage of HIJMS *I-400*."

243 *he headed its innovative think tank, TEMPO*: Buckley, "NASA's Tom Paine," *New York Times*, June 8, 1969, magazine section, pp. 37–38.

244 *"These are the RAF types"*: Paine in Swanson, *Before This Decade Is Out*, pp. 28–29.

244 *President Johnson had told him*: Levine, *The Future of the U.S. Space Program*, p. 101.

245 *"I can give you a very straightforward, simple answer"*: Seamans, *Aiming at Targets*, pp. 148–149.

Briefing: Lunar Reconnaissance
247 *For a variety of reasons*: For the story of lunar reconnaissance and the rationale for landing in the Sea of Tranquility, see Wilhelms, *To a Rocky Moon*, especially pp. 188–191.

PART 6: The Moon
249 *"12 02 alarm! 12 02, what's that?"*: Flight and guidance communications loops for the Apollo 11 landing, "The Eagle Has Landed," CosmoQuest Forum.

Chapter 31: A New Mission Takes Shape
251 *"Are you out of your mind?"*: Chaikin, *A Man on the Moon*, p. 59.

251 *"If a person's shock could be transmitted"*: Murray and Cox, *Apollo*, p. 322.

255 *"After a careful and thorough examination"*: "News Briefing on Apollo 8 Moon Orbital Flight," p. 2.

255 *"This will be within the normal hazards"*: "News Briefing on Apollo 8 Moon Orbital Flight," p. 44.

256 *he would have been too cautious to authorize such a plan*: Murray and Cox, *Apollo*, p. 323.

Chapter 32: "In the Beginning"

260 *a British ground station picked up a voice*: Siddiqi, *Challenge to Apollo*, p. 655.

260 *"a photo finish"*: Turnill, *The Moonlandings*, p. 134.

261 *opened on the 8th of the month*: Russia's launch window was December 8–12. See "Kamanin Diaries," November 26, 1968.

261 *For the United States, it didn't open until the 20th*: Orloff and Harland, *Apollo: The Definitive Sourcebook*, p. 197.

261 *ran the headline*: "Moon Shot for Soviets Sunday?" *Florida Today*, December 7, 1968, p. 1A.

261 *"It is not important to mankind"*: Siddiqi, *Challenge to Apollo*, p. 667.

261 *"a rat in the jaws of a big terrier"*: "Apollo 8 Reunion," YouTube, starting at 25:01.

262 *"a runaway freight train"*: Woods, *How Apollo Flew to the Moon*, p. 83.

262 *"train wreck"*: Woods, *How Apollo Flew to the Moon*, p. 95.

262 *four g's*: Four g's is a velocity increase of 88 miles per hour for every second.

262 *"I suddenly felt like I'd been sitting on a catapult and somebody cut the rope"*: Chaikin and Kohl, *Voices from the Moon*, p. 23.

265 *"We see the Earth now"*: Apollo 8 voice transcripts are from Woods and O'Brien, "The Apollo 8 Flight Journal."

266 *"like a war zone"*: Chaikin and Kohl, *Voices from the Moon*, p. 45.

267 *"Let me tell you"*: "Apollo 8 Reunion," YouTube, starting at 1:04:18.

Chapter 33: Earthrise

271 *"Oh, my God!"*: Apollo 8 voice transcripts are from Woods and O'Brien, "The Apollo 8 Flight Journal."

271 *"It was the most beautiful, heart-catching sight of my life"*: Borman and Serling, *Countdown*, p. 212.

272 *"Here we came all this way to the Moon"*: Wolfinger, "To the Moon," quoted in Poole, *Earthrise*, p. 2.

272 *"For all its upheavals and frustrations"*: "Men of the Year," *Time*, January 3, 1969, p. 13.

273 *Had Gus Grissom been alive*: Slayton and Cassutt, *Deke!*, p. 191.

273 *Frank Borman and Jim McDivitt*: Slayton and Cassutt, *Deke!*, p. 223. See also Michael Cassutt's post on CollectSpace, March 5, 2005.

273 *he sensibly pointed out*: Borman and Serling, *Countdown*, p. 222.

274 *"This is like handling a squadron of fighter pilots"*: Armstrong et al., *First on the Moon*, p. 105.

274 *Slayton gave Armstrong the option to switch Aldrin for Jim Lovell*: Hansen, *First Man*, p. 338.

275 *"You're it"*: Slayton and Cassutt, *Deke!*, p. 224.

Chapter 34: Go Fever

277 *"I do not submit"*: "Worth the Price," *Time*, January 17, 1969, p. 49.

277 *NASA had tightened contractor management and set up new safety procedures*: Levine, *The Future of the U.S. Space Program*, p. 97.

277 *there were roughly 6 million parts in a typical Apollo mission*: Dick, "The Voyages of Apollo."

278 *"an almost religious vigilance"*: Sato, "Reliability in the Apollo Program," p. 23.

278 *"If you don't like the way things look"*: Collins, *Liftoff*, p. 260. See also Paine in Swanson, *Before This Decade Is Out . . .* , pp. 20–22.

278 *"the ability to go up in a hurtling piece of machinery"*: Wolfe, *The Right Stuff*, p. 148.

279 *"rolling them around on his tongue"*: Collins, *Carrying the Fire*, p. 58.

279 *"Neil held on as long as he could"*: Aldrin and McConnell, *Men from Earth*, p. 187.

279 *"Do you know that Neil bailed out of the LLRV"*: Sington, *In the Shadow of the Moon*, 30:16. In the film, Bean mistakenly says "LLTV," which was a later version of the vehicle.

281 *"Neil and Buzz had been descending in the LM"*: Collins, *Carrying the Fire*, pp. 351–352.

281 *Armstrong later claimed that he had been testing the limits*: Hansen, *First Man*, p. 380.

281 *questioned Armstrong's commitment*: Kraft and Schefter, *Flight*, p. 314.

282 *"had set his own rules for the landing"*: Kranz, *Failure Is Not an Option*, p. 262.

282 *returned with some 150 failures*: Nelson, *Rocket Men*, p. 15.

282 *"pretty smooth"*: Woods, Wheeler, and Roberts, "The Apollo 10 Flight Journal."

283 *"To watch a flight is not that big a deal"*: Oberg, "Max Faget," *Omni*, April 1995, p. 62.

285 *Warned about the possibility of delay or worse*: Logsdon, *After Apollo?*, pp. 11–12.

Chapter 35: Tranquility Base

287 *The press went wild with other theories*: Harvey, *Soviet and Russian Lunar Exploration*, p. 211.

287 *"This is undoubtedly quite a challenging mission"*: Turnill, *The Moonlandings*, p. 227.

289 *"Eagle, Houston"*: Air-to-ground and onboard transcripts for the Apollo 11 landing, along with interviews and other background material, can be found at "The First Lunar Landing" in Jones and Glover, "The Apollo 11 Lunar Surface Journal."

292 *the LM had only about a minute of hover time*: Mindell, *Digital Apollo*, p. 203.

293 *which Tom Stafford had warned*: Harland, *The First Men on the Moon*, p. 233.

294 *Duke had a sinking feeling*: Duke, JSC, March 12, 1999.

294 *"12 02 alarm!"*: Selected flight controller audio for the Apollo 11 landing is linked at "Apollo 11 Lunar Landing Audio—Flight and Guidance Loops," NASA Spaceflight.com Forum, July 20, 2014. See also "The Apollo 11 Descent and Landing," Honeysuckle Creek Tracking Station.

295 *"were creating doubt"*: Cunningham and Herskowitz, *The All-American Boys*, p. 217.

295 *"impending disaster"*: Turnill, *The Moonlandings*, pp. 249, 252.

295 *"If it were in my hands, I would call an abort"*: Eyles, *Sunburst and Luminary*, p. 151.

296 *"There wasn't anything obviously wrong"*: Armstrong, JSC, September 19, 2001.

296 *"I licked my dry lips"*: Aldrin, "Lunar Module *Eagle*," *The Bent* of Tau Beta Pi, Fall 1994, p. 15.

296 *"It is as though a terrible screech"*: Eyles, *Sunburst and Luminary*, p. 153.

296 *"Charlie, shut up and let them land!"*: Duke and Duke, *Moonwalker.*

297 *A mile ahead*: Distances during the final approach are based on "Apollo 11 Ground Track Mapped onto LROC Overlay in Google Moon," GoneToPlaid's Apollo website.

297 *"Neil was flying a trajectory"*: Duke, JSC, March 12, 1999.

297 *"We could see on our displays"*: Kraft and Schefter, *Flight*, p. 321.

298 *"I wonder if he's going to make it"*: Sington, *In the Shadow of the Moon*, 59:37.

298 *"If they keep doing this"*: Faget, JSC, June 18, 1997.

298 *"If I'd run out of fuel"*: Armstrong, JSC, September 19, 2001.

298 *with just fifteen seconds of gas left. "It would have been nice"*: Hansen, *First Man*, pp. 471–472.

298 *"Without wanting to say anything to Neil"*: Aldrin and Abraham, *Magnificent Desolation*, pp. 20–21.

299 *150 beats per minute*: Apollo 11 Mission Report, p. 158.

299 *had given up hope they would land*: Carlton told an interviewer, "I didn't think there was a chance in the world of us landing." Carlton, JSC, April 10, 2001.

300 *"It was like watching a man, some snake trainer"*: Easter, JSC, May 3, 2000.

300 *felt like he was levitating off his chair*: Fendell, JSC, October 19, 2000.

300 *"My God, this is the real thing"*: Garman, JSC, March 27, 2001.

300 *"landing an airplane when there's a real thin layer of ground fog"*: "The First Lunar Landing" in Jones and Glover, "The Apollo 11 Lunar Surface Journal."

300 *"He's using a lot of RCS"*: Carlton, JSC, April 10, 2001.

Chapter 36: One Small Step

303 *"not something that I thought was really very important"*: Hansen, *First Man*, p. 367.

303 *Armstrong ranked walking on the Moon as a one*: Armstrong, JSC, September 19, 2001.

304 *it made sense for the copilot*: For example, lunar module pilot Rusty Schweickart made the space walk (in Earth orbit) on Apollo 9.

304 *General Phillips felt strongly that a single, brief outing by a single explorer*: Brooks et al., *Chariots for Apollo*, p. 320.

305 *Frank Borman described his fellow astronauts this way*: Logsdon, *After Apollo?*, p. 17.

305 *top managers thought he was the wrong individual to wear the hero's mantle*: The account of this behind-the-scenes drama is in Hansen, *First Man*, pp. 370–372. NASA's official reason for choosing Armstrong to go first was that it was easier for the astronaut at the commander's station to get out the door. Lunar module pilots privately objected that it was a relatively simple matter for the two astronauts to switch places.

305 *"That's one small step"*: The actual first words spoken from the surface of the Moon were when Aldrin said, "Okay, engine stop," just after Armstrong landed.

306 *his statement became even more meaningful*: I owe this insight to poet James Nicola (personal communication).

308 *"I never expected to hear that word 'pretty'"*: "Apollo 11 Moon Walk CBS News Coverage" on YouTube, starting at 4:11:17.

308 *black you felt you could touch*: Chaikin and Kohl, *Voices from the Moon*, p. 68.

310 *Armstrong and Aldrin were instructed to move with great care to avoid falling*: "Apollo 11 Moon Walk CBS News Coverage" on YouTube, starting at 4:10:34.

310 *"When you move"*: Chaikin and Kohl, *Voices from the Moon*, p. 72.

310 *"Exploring this place"*: Aldrin and Abraham, *Magnificent Desolation*, p. 37.

310 *Frank Borman talked him out of it*: Borman and Serling, *Countdown*, p. 238.

311 *"our marble-sized planet"*: Aldrin and Abraham, *Magnificent Desolation*, p. 34.

313 *"Two guys walk in and sit down"*: Fendell, JSC, October 19, 2000.

Epilogue: "We Must Stop"
315 *The astronauts used to joke*: Chaikin and Kohl, *Voices from the Moon*, p. 114.

316 *"achieved the Moon's surface in the preselected area"*: Harland, *The First Men on the Moon*, p. 293.

317 *researchers in the West*: See Oberg, "Russia Meant to Win the Moon Race," *Spaceflight*, May 1975, pp. 163–164.

318 *"We must stop"*: Gilruth, NASM, March 2, 1987.

318 *just over 25 billion dollars*: $25.4 billion according to Logsdon, *John F. Kennedy and the Race to the Moon*, p. 2.

318 *that was just for a single Moon landing*: See Diamond, *The Rise and Fall of the Space Age*, p. 40: "In March 1963, D. Brainerd Holmes . . . testified . . . that the cost of all activities directly related to fulfilling the President's goal would be $20 billion . . . Holmes' figure also made no provision for more than one lunar trip . . ."

319 *"Wernher is like a great conductor"*: Stuhlinger and Ordway, *Wernher von Braun: A Biographical Memoir*, p. 302.

319 *"I was impressed"*: Abramson, "Laconic General," *Los Angeles Times*, October 6, 1968, p. F1.

320 *seventy-seventh and seventy-eighth persons in space*: Counted as those who have flown above the generally accepted boundary of space at 100 kilometers (62 miles).

321 *He chose the gold dolphin pin*: Paine, "The Transpacific Voyage of HIJMS *I-400*."

322 *"We weren't going to fight a war on the lake"*: Faget, JSC, June 19, 1997.

322 *"You know, Max"*: Chaikin, "Management Lessons of the Moon Program," on YouTube, starting at 55:35.

Briefing: Six Landing Sites
325 *"It's absolutely mind-boggling"*: Chaikin and Kohl, *Voices from the Moon*, p. 66.

REFERENCES

Interviews and Oral Histories

Armstrong, Neil A., Jr. NASA Johnson Space Center Oral History Project, interviewed by Stephen E. Ambrose and Douglas Brinkley. www.jsc.nasa.gov/history/oral_histories/ArmstrongNA/armstrongna.htm (updated July 16, 2010).

Carlton, Robert L. NASA Johnson Space Center Oral History Project, interviewed by Kevin M. Rusnak. www.jsc.nasa.gov/history/oral_histories/CarltonRL/carltonrl.htm (updated July 16, 2010).

Duke, Charles. M., Jr. NASA Johnson Space Center Oral History Project, interviewed by Doug Ward. www.jsc.nasa.gov/history/oral_histories/DukeCM/dukecm.htm (updated July 16, 2010).

Easter, William B. NASA Johnson Space Center Oral History Project, interviewed by Kevin M. Rusnak. www.jsc.nasa.gov/history/oral_histories/EasterWB/EasterWB_5-3-00.htm (updated July 16, 2010).

Faget, Maxime A. Robbie Davis-Floyd, Kenneth J. Cox, and Frank White, eds., *Space Stories: Oral Histories from the Pioneers of America's Space Program*, interviewed by Davis-Floyd and Cox. Amazon Digital Services, 2012. Kindle edition.

Faget, Maxime A. NASA Johnson Space Center Oral History Project, interviewed by Carol Butler and Jim Slade. www.jsc.nasa.gov/history/oral_histories/FagetMA/fagetma.htm (updated July 16, 2010).

Fendell, Edward I. NASA Johnson Space Center Oral History Project, interviewed by Kevin M. Rusnak. www.jsc.nasa.gov/history/oral_histories/FendellEI/FendellEI_10-19-00.htm (updated July 16, 2010).

Garman, John R. NASA Johnson Space Center Oral History Project, interviewed by Kevin M. Rusnak. www.jsc.nasa.gov/history/oral_histories/GarmanJR/garmanjr.htm (updated July 16, 2010).

Gilruth, Robert R. Smithsonian National Air and Space Museum Oral History Project, interviewed by David DeVorkin, Martin Collins, John Mauer, Linda Ezell, and Howard Wolko. airandspace.si.edu/research/projects/oral-histories/gwspi-p1.html#GILRUTH (revised September 6, 1996).

Guy, Walter W. NASA Johnson Space Center Oral History Project, interviewed by Rebecca Wright. www.jsc.nasa.gov/history/oral_histories/GuyWW /guyww.htm (updated July 16, 2010).

Johnson, Caldwell. Robbie Davis-Floyd, Kenneth J. Cox, and Frank White, eds., *Space Stories: Oral Histories from the Pioneers of America's Space Program*, interviewed by Davis-Floyd and Cox. Amazon Digital Services, 2012. Kindle edition.

Kimball, Ward. Didier Ghez, ed., *Walt's People*. Vol. 3; interviewed by Klaus Strzyz. Theme Park Press, 2015.

Paine, Thomas O. Glen E. Swanson, ed., *Before This Decade Is Out . . . : Personal Reflections on the Apollo Program*, interviewed by Robert Sherrod. Washington, D.C.: NASA, 1999.

Phillips, Samuel C. Smithsonian National Air and Space Museum Oral History Project, interviewed by Martin Collins. airandspace.si.edu/research/projects /oral-histories/gwspi-p2.html#PHILLIPS (revised September 6, 1996).

Seamans, Robert C., Jr. NASA Johnson Space Center Oral History Project, interviewed by Michelle Kelly and Carol Butler. www.jsc.nasa.gov/history/oral _histories/SeamansRC/seamansrc.htm (updated July 16, 2010).

Webb, James E. Lyndon Baines Johnson Library Oral History Collection, interviewed by T. H. Baker. lbjlibrary.net/collections/oral-histories/webb-e. -james.html (accessed September 1, 2017).

Webb, James E. Smithsonian National Air and Space Museum Oral History Project, interviewed by Martin Collins, David DeVorkin, Joseph Tatarewicz, Allen Needell, Linda Ezell, and Michael Dennis. airandspace.si.edu /research/projects/oral-histories/gwspi-p3.html#WEBB (revised September 6, 1996).

Documents and Statistics

"Apollo 11 Ground Track Mapped onto LROC Overlay in Google Moon." GoneTo-Plaid's Apollo Web Site. Linked at history.nasa.gov/alsj/a11/images11.html (revised February 18, 2018).

Apollo 11 Mission Report. Washington, D.C.: NASA, 1971. www.hq.nasa.gov/alsj /a11/a11MIssionReport_1971015566_Sec12BiomedEvaluation.pdf.

Apollo Accident: Hearing on a Review of Background Information and Systems Decisions Preceding the Apollo Accident of January 27, 1967. Part 1. Senate

Committee on Aeronautical and Space Sciences. Ninetieth Congress, First Session, February 7, 1967. U.S. Government Printing Office: Washington, D.C., 1967. spaceflight.nasa.gov/outreach/SignificantIncidents/assets/apollo-1-hearing.pdf.

Army Air Forces Statistical Digest: World War II, U.S. Army Air Forces, Office of Statistical Control, December 1945. dtic.mil/dtic/tr/fulltext/u2/a542518.pdf.

The Berkeley Mortality Database. u.demog.berkeley.edu/~andrew/1918/figure2.html (accessed September 1, 2017).

Casper, Jack A. *History and Personnel, 489th, 340th Bomb Group: Combat Campaigns Participated in by the 489th Bomb Squadron*, 1947. warwingsart.com/12thAirForce/squadbook.html.

Ellis, John. *World War II: A Statistical Survey: The Essential Facts and Figures for All the Combatants*. New York: Facts on File, 1993.

Faget, Maxime A., Benjamine J. Garland, and James J. Buglia. "Preliminary Studies of Manned Satellites—Wingless Configuration: Nonlifting," *NACA Research Memorandum*, August 11, 1958. ntrs.nasa.gov/archive/nasa/casi.ntrs.nasa.gov/19930090134.pdf.

The Fourth Kennedy-Nixon Presidential Debate, October 21, 1960. Commission on Presidential Debates. debates.org/index.php?page=october-21-1960-debate-transcript (accessed September 1, 2017).

Gallup, George H. *The Gallup Poll Public Opinion, 1935–1971*. 2 vols. New York: Random House, 1972.

"Gemini VIII Voice Communications (Air-to-Ground, Ground-to-Air, and Onboard Transcription)." NASA Johnson Space Center History Portal. www.jsc.nasa.gov/history/mission_trans/GT08_TEC.PDF (accessed September 1, 2017).

"History: November 1943," 12th Air Force, 57th Bombardment Wing, 321st Bombardment Group. warwingsart.com/12thAirForce/3211143.html (accessed September 1, 2017).

"History of U.S.S. *Guavina* (SS-362)." U.S. Navy Department, Division of Naval History, (October 1953). maritime.org/doc/subreports.htm (accessed September 1, 2017).

"History of U.S.S. *Pompon* (SS-267)." U.S. Navy Department, Division of Naval History, (November 30, 1953). maritime.org/doc/subreports.htm (accessed September 1, 2017).

Joiner, Oliver W. *The History of the 364th Fighter Group*. Marceline, Mo.: Walsworth, 1991.

Jones, Eric M, and Ken Glover. "The Apollo 11 Lunar Surface Journal." NASA History Division. www.hq.nasa.gov/alsj/a11/a11.html (revised December 17, 2015).

Kennedy, John F. "President Kennedy's Special Message to the Congress on Urgent National Needs, May 25, 1961." John F. Kennedy Speeches. John F. Kennedy Presidential Library and Museum. jfklibrary.org/Research/Research-Aids/JFK-Speeches/United-States-Congress-Special-Message_19610525.aspx (accessed September 1, 2017).

Logsdon, John M., ed., with Linda J. Lear, Jannelle Warren-Findley, Ray A. Williamson, and Dwayne A. Day. *Exploring the Unknown: Selected Documents in the History of the U.S. Civil Space Program*. Vol. 1: *Organizing for Exploration*. Washington, D.C.: NASA, 1995.

Logsdon, John M., ed., with Roger D. Launius. *Exploring the Unknown: Selected Documents in the History of the U.S. Civil Space Program*. Vol. 7: *Human Spaceflight: Projects Mercury, Gemini, and Apollo*. Washington, D.C.: NASA, 2008.

NASA Historical Data Book: 1958–1968. Vol. 1: *NASA Resources*. Washington, D.C.: NASA, 1976.

"News Briefing on Apollo 8 Moon Orbital Flight." NASA News, Washington, D.C. (November 12, 1968).

"November 17, 1943 Mission to Kalamaki Aerodrome, Greece," 340th Bombardment Group History, War Diary. 57thbombwing.com/340th_History/487th_History/missions/111743_Kalamaki.htm (accessed September 1, 2017).

Orloff, Richard W., and David M. Harland. *Apollo: The Definitive Sourcebook*. Chichester, U.K.: Springer-Praxis, 2006.

Post Launch Report for Mercury-Redstone No. 3 (MR-3). Langley Field, Va.: NASA Space Task Group, June 16, 1961.

United States Submarine Losses, World War II. Washington, D.C.: Naval History Division, 1963.

"USAAF Chronology: Combat Chronology of the U.S. Army Air Forces, August 1944." paul.rutgers.edu/~mcgrew/wwii/usaf/html/Aug.44.html (accessed September 1, 2017).

Woods, W. David, Ken MacTaggart, and Frank O'Brien. "The Apollo 11 Flight Journal." NASA History Division. history.nasa.gov/afj/ap11fj/index.html (updated March 23, 2018).

Woods, W. David, and Frank O'Brien. "The Apollo 8 Flight Journal." NASA History Division. history.nasa.gov/afj/ap08fj/index.html (updated April 10, 2017).

Woods, W. David, Robin Wheeler, and Ian Roberts. "The Apollo 10 Flight Journal." NASA History Division. history.nasa.gov/afj/ap10fj/index.html (updated January 15, 2018).

Books

Aldrin, Buzz, and Ken Abraham. *Magnificent Desolation: The Long Journey Home from the Moon*. New York: Harmony Books, 2009.

Aldrin, Buzz, and Malcolm McConnell. *Men from Earth*. New York: Bantam Books, 1989.

Armstrong, Neil, Michael Collins, and Edwin E. Aldrin Jr., written with Gene Farmer and Dora Jane Hamblin. *First Men on the Moon*. Boston: Little, Brown and Company, 1970.

The Astronauts (Carpenter, M. Scott, et al.). *We Seven*. New York: Simon & Schuster, 1962.

Benson, Charles D., and William Barnaby Faherty. *Moonport: A History of Apollo Launch Facilities and Operations*. Washington, D.C.: NASA, 1978.

Bille, Matt, and Erika Lishock. *The First Space Race: Launching the World's First Satellites*. College Station: Texas A&M Press, 2004.

Bizony, Piers. *The Man Who Ran the Moon: James E. Webb and the Secret History of Project Apollo*. New York: Thunder's Mouth Press, 2006.

Blair-Smith, Hugh. *Left Brains for the Right Stuff: Computers, Space, and History*. East Bridgewater, Ma.: SDP Publishing, 2015. Kindle edition.

Borman, Frank, and Robert J. Serling. *Countdown: An Autobiography*. New York: William Morrow, 1988.

Brooks, Courtney G., James M. Grimwood, and Lloyd S. Swenson Jr. *Chariots for Apollo: The NASA History of Manned Lunar Spacecraft to 1969*. Mineola, N.Y.: Dover, 2009.

Bulkeley, Rip. *The Sputniks Crisis and Early United States Space Policy*. Bloomington: Indiana University Press, 1991.

Calvert, James F. *Silent Running: My Years on a World War II Attack Submarine.* New York: Wiley, 1995.

Carpenter, M. Scott, and Kris Stoever. *For Spacious Skies: The Uncommon Journey of a Mercury Astronaut.* Orlando, Fla.: Harcourt, 2002.

Cernan, Eugene, and Don Davis. *The Last Man on the Moon: Astronaut Eugene Cernan and America's Race in Space.* New York: St. Martin's, 1999.

Chaikin, Andrew. *A Man on the Moon: The Voyages of the Apollo Astronauts.* New York: Viking, 1994.

Chaikin, Andrew, and Victoria Kohl. *Voices from the Moon: Apollo Astronauts Describe Their Lunar Experiences.* New York: Viking Studio, 2009.

Collins, Michael. *Carrying the Fire: An Astronaut's Journey.* New York: Bantam, 1983.

Collins, Michael. *Liftoff: The Story of America's Adventure in Space.* New York: Grove Press, 1988.

Cortright, Edgar M., ed. *Apollo Expeditions to the Moon: The NASA History.* Washington, D.C.: NASA, 1975.

Cronkite, Walter. *A Reporter's Life.* New York: Knopf, 1996.

Cunningham, Walt, and Mickey Herskowitz. *The All-American Boys.* New York: Macmillan, 1977.

David, James E. *Spies and Shuttles: NASA's Secret Relationships with the DoD and CIA.* Gainesville, Fla.: University Press of Florida, 2015.

Dethloff, Henry C. *Suddenly, Tomorrow Came . . . : A History of the Johnson Space Center.* Houston: NASA, 1993.

Diamond, Edwin. *The Rise and Fall of the Space Age.* Garden City, N.Y.: Doubleday, 1964.

Duke, Charlie (Charles. M., Jr.); and Dotty Duke. *Moonwalker*, 2nd ed. Rose Petal Press, 2011. Kindle edition.

Eyles, Don. *Sunburst and Luminary: An Apollo Memoir.* Boston: Fort Point Press, 2018.

Fallaci, Oriana. *If the Sun Dies.* New York: Atheneum, 1966.

Fredrickson, John M. *Warbird Factory: North American Aviation in World War II.* Minneapolis, Minn.: Zenith, 2015.

French, Francis, and Colin Burgess. *In the Shadow of the Moon: A Challenging Journey to Tranquility, 1965–1969.* Lincoln, Nebr.: University of Nebraska Press, 2007.

Fries, Sylvia Doughty. *NASA Engineers and the Age of Apollo*. Washington, D.C.: NASA, 1992.

Geer, Mary Wells, *Boeing's Ed Wells*. Seattle: University of Washington Press, 1992.

Glenn, John, and Nick Taylor. *John Glenn: A Memoir*. New York: Bantam, 1999.

Glennan, T. Keith. *The Birth of NASA: The Diary of T. Keith Glennan*, Washington, D.C.: NASA, 1993.

Gordon, Robert J. *The Rise and Fall of American Growth: The U.S. Standard of Living Since the Civil War*. Princeton: Princeton University Press, 2016.

Gray, Mike. *Angle of Attack: Harrison Storms and the Race to the Moon*. New York: Penguin, 1994.

Green, Constance M., and Milton Lomask, *Vanguard: A History*. Washington, D.C.: NASA, 1970.

Hall, R. Cargill. *Lunar Impact: A History of Project Ranger*. Washington, D.C.: NASA, 1977.

Hansen, James R. *Engineer in Charge: A History of the Langley Aeronautical Laboratory, 1917–1958*. Washington, D.C.: NASA, 1987.

Hansen, James R. *First Man: The Life of Neil A. Armstrong*. New York: Simon & Schuster, 2005.

Hansen, James R. *Spaceflight Revolution: NASA Langley Research Center from Sputnik to Apollo*. Washington, D.C.: NASA, 1995.

Hanson, Victor Davis. *The Second World Wars: How the First Global Conflict Was Fought and Won*. New York: Basic Books, 2017.

Hargis, Robert. *U.S. Submarine Crewman 1941–45*. Oxford, U.K.: Osprey, 2003. Kindle edition.

Harland, David. M. *The First Men on the Moon: The Story of Apollo 11*. Chichester, U.K.: Springer-Praxis, 2007.

Harvey, Brian. *Soviet and Russian Lunar Exploration*. Chichester, U.K.: Springer–Praxis, 2007.

Herman, Arthur. *Freedom's Forge*. New York: Random House, 2012.

Holloway, David. *Stalin and the Bomb: The Soviet Union and Atomic Energy, 1939–1956*. New Haven, Conn.: Yale University Press, 1994.

Holmes, Jay. *America on the Moon: The Enterprise of the Sixties*. Philadelphia: Lippincott, 1962.

Houston, Rick, and Milt Heflin. *Go, Flight!: The Unsung Heroes of Mission Control, 1965–1992*. Lincoln: University of Nebraska Press, 2015.

Howard, Fred. *Whistle While You Wait*. New York: Duell, Sloan, & Pearce, 1945.

Irving, David. *Göring: A Biography*. New York: Morrow, 1989.

Johnson, Stephen B. *The Secret of Apollo: Systems Management in American and European Space Programs*. Baltimore: Johns Hopkins University Press, 2002.

Kopal, Zdenek, and Robert W. Carder. *Mapping the Moon: Past and Present*. Boston: D. Reidel, 1974.

Kraft, Christopher C., and James L. Schefter. *Flight: My Life in Mission Control*. New York: Dutton, 2001.

Kranz, Gene. *Failure Is Not an Option: Mission Control from Mercury to Apollo 13 and Beyond*. New York: Simon & Schuster, 2000.

Lambright, W. Henry. *Powering Apollo: James E. Webb of NASA*. Baltimore: Johns Hopkins University Press, 1995.

Laney, Monique. *German Rocketeers in the Heart of Dixie: Making Sense of the Nazi Past during the Civil Rights Era*. New Haven: Yale University Press, 2015.

Lang, Daniel. *From Hiroshima to the Moon: Chronicles of Life in the Atomic Age*. New York: Simon & Schuster, 1959.

Leonard, Jonathan Norton. *Flight into Space: The Facts, Fancies, and Philosophy*. New York: Signet, 1954.

Leopold, George. *Calculated Risk: The Supersonic Life and Times of Gus Grissom*. West Lafayette: Perdue University Press, 2016.

Levine, Arthur L. *The Future of the U.S. Space Program*. New York: Praeger, 1975.

Logsdon, John M. *After Apollo?: Richard Nixon and the American Space Program*. New York: Palgrave Macmillan, 2015.

Logsdon, John M. *John F. Kennedy and the Race to the Moon*. New York: Palgrave Macmillan, 2010.

Logsdon, Tom. *Orbital Mechanics: Theory and Applications*. New York: Wiley, 1998.

McDougall, Walter A. *The Heavens and the Earth: A Political History of the Space Age*. New York: Basic Books, 1985.

McMahon, Robert. *The Cold War: A Very Short Introduction*. New York: Oxford University Press, 2003.

Medaris, John B., with Arthur Gordon. *Countdown for Decision*. New York: Putnam, 1960.

Meder, Patricia Chapman. *The True Story of Catch-22: The Real Men and Missions of Joseph Heller's 340th Bomb Group in World War II*. Havertown, Pa.: Casemate, 2012.

Mindell, David A. *Between Human and Machine: Feedback, Control, and Computing before Cybernetics*. Baltimore: Johns Hopkins University Press, 2002.

Mindell, David A. *Digital Apollo: Human and Machine in Spaceflight*. Cambridge, Mass.: MIT Press, 2008.

Morgan, George D. *Rocket Girl: The Story of Mary Sherman Morgan, America's First Female Rocket Scientist*. Amherst, N.Y.: Prometheus Books, 2013.

Murray, Charles, and Catherine Bly Cox. *Apollo: The Race to the Moon*. New York: Simon & Schuster, 1989.

Neal, Roy. *Ace in the Hole: The Story of the Minuteman Missile*. Garden City, N.Y.: Doubleday, 1962.

Nelson, Craig. *Rocket Men: The Epic Story of the First Men on the Moon*. New York: Penguin Books, 2009.

Neufeld, Michael J. *The Rocket and the Reich: Peenemünde and the Coming of the Ballistic Missile Era*. New York: Free Press, 1995.

Neufeld, Michael J. *Von Braun: Dreamer of Space, Engineer of War*. New York: Knopf, 2007.

O'Brien, Phillips Payson. *How the War Was Won*. Cambridge: Cambridge University Press, 2015.

Ordway, Frederick I., III, and Mitchell R. Sharpe. *The Rocket Team*. New York: Crowell, 1979.

Overy, Richard. *The Bombing War: Europe 1939–1945*. London: Allen Lane, 2013.

Perret, Geoffrey. *There's a War to Be Won*. New York: Ballantine, 1991.

Poole, Robert. *Earthrise: How Man First Saw the Earth*. New Haven: Yale University Press, 2008.

Porter, Horace. *Campaigning with Grant*. New York: Century, 1906.

Rasenberger, Jim. *The Brilliant Disaster*. New York: Scribner, 2011.

Renehan, Edward J., Jr. *The Kennedys at War: 1937–1945*. New York: Doubleday, 2002.

Rhodes, Richard. *The Making of the Atomic Bomb*. New York: Simon & Schuster, 1986.

Roberts, Mark. *Sub: An Oral History of U.S. Navy Submarines*. New York: Berkley, 2007.

Roland, Alex. *Model Research: A History of the National Advisory Committee for Aeronautics, 1915–1958*. Vol. 1. Washington, D.C.: NASA, 1985.

Satterthwaite, Dale J. *Truth Flies with Fiction: Flying B-25 Bombers into Battle during 1944*. Bloomington: Archway, 2014.

Scott, David, Alexei Leonov, and Christine Toom. *Two Sides of the Moon: Our Story of the Cold War Space Race*. New York: Dunne, 2004.

Seamans, Robert C., Jr. *Aiming at Targets: The Autobiography of Robert C. Seamans, Jr.* Washington, D.C.: NASA, 1996.

Seamans, Robert C., Jr. *Project Apollo: The Tough Decisions*. Washington, D.C.: NASA, 2005.

Sears, David. *Such Men as These: The Story of the Navy Pilots Who Flew the Deadly Skies over Korea*. Cambridge, Mass.: Da Capo Press, 2010.

Shayler, David J. *Apollo: The Lost and Forgotten Missions*. Chichester, U.K.: Springer, 2002.

Shinn, Marion L. *Pacific Patrol: A WWII Submarine Saga*. Lewiston, Idaho.: Triad, 1993. Kindle edition.

Siddiqi, Asif A. *Challenge to Apollo: The Soviet Union and the Space Race, 1945–1974*. Washington, D.C.: NASA, 2000.

Sidey, Hugh. *John F. Kennedy, President*. New York: Atheneum, 1964.

Slayton, Donald K., and Michael Cassutt. *Deke! U.S. Manned Space: From Mercury to the Shuttle*. New York: Doherty, 1994.

Slotkin, Arthur L. *Doing the Impossible: George E. Mueller and the Management of NASA's Human Spaceflight Program*. Chichester, U.K.: Springer, 2012.

Stafford, Tom, and Michael Cassutt. *We Have Capture: Tom Stafford and the Space Race*. Washington, D.C.: Smithsonian Institution Press, 2002.

Stuhlinger, Ernst, and Frederick I. Ordway III. *Wernher von Braun: Crusader for Space*. 2 vols.: *A Biographical Memoir* and *A Pictorial Memoir*. Malabar, Fla.: Krieger, 1994.

Sullivan, Walter, ed. *America's Race for the Moon:* The New York Times *Story of Project Apollo*. New York: Random House, 1962.

Swanson, Glen E., ed., *Before This Decade Is Out . . . : Personal Reflections on the Apollo Program*. Washington, D.C.: NASA, 1999.

Swenson, Lloyd S., Jr., James M. Grimwood, and Charles C. Alexander. *This New Ocean: A History of Project Mercury.* Washington, D.C.: NASA, 1966.

Thompson, Neal. *Light This Candle: The Life and Times of Alan Shepard—-America's First Spaceman.* New York: Crown, 2004.

Trento, John J. *Prescription for Disaster: From the Glory of Apollo to the Betrayal of the Shuttle.* New York: Crown, 1987.

Turnill, Reginald. *The Moonlandings: An Eyewitness Account.* Cambridge, U.K.: Cambridge University Press, 2003.

Vander Meulen, Jacob. *Building the B-29.* Washington, D.C.: Smithsonian Institution Press, 1995.

von Ehrenfried, Manfred "Dutch." *The Birth of NASA: The Work of the Space Task Group, America's First True Space Pioneers.* Chichester, U.K.: Springer-Praxis, 2016.

Ward, Bob. *Dr. Space: The Life of Wernher von Braun.* Annapolis: Naval Institute Press, 2005.

Ward, Jonathan H. *Rocket Ranch: The Nuts and Bolts of the Apollo Moon Program at Kennedy Space Center.* Cham, Switzerland: Springer, 2015.

Wendt, Guenter, and Russell Still. *The Unbroken Chain.* Burlington, Ont., Canada: Apogee, 2001.

Wilhelms, Don E. *To a Rocky Moon: A Geologist's History of Lunar Exploration.* Tucson: University of Arizona Press, 1993.

Wolfe, Tom. *The Right Stuff.* New York: Bantam, 1980.

Woods, W. David. *How Apollo Flew to the Moon.* Second ed. Chichester, U.K.: Springer-Praxis, 2011.

Young, John W., and James R. Hansen. *Forever Young: A Life of Adventure in Air and Space.* Gainesville, Fla.: University Press of Florida, 2012.

Articles, Audio, and Video

Abramson, Rudy. "Laconic General—Zero at Small Talk—Is Super Manager of Apollo Project." *Los Angeles Times*, October 6, 1968.

Aldrin, Buzz. "Lunar Module *Eagle*." *The Bent* of Tau Beta Pi, Fall 1994.

"Apollo 8 Reunion." The LBJ Presidential Library (April 23, 2009). youtube.com /watch?v=Wa5x0T-pee0 (published May 15, 2012).

"The Apollo 11 Descent and Landing." Honeysuckle Creek Tracking Station.

honeysucklecreek.net/audio/A11_Network/A11_landing_FD_loop.mp3 (accessed September 1, 2017).

"Apollo 11 Lunar Landing Audio—Flight and Guidance Loops." NASA Spaceflight .com Forum. forum.nasaspaceflight.com/index.php?topic=35230.0 (revised July 21, 2014).

"Apollo 11 Moon Walk CBS News Coverage." YouTube, youtube.com/watch?v =ntyPG1xewJ8 (published January 17, 2017).

"Apollo 15 Remembered 40 Years Later." NASA video. youtube.com/watch?v =zrbS0B3l56A (published July 24, 2011).

"Astronaut's Death Will Not Halt Program," *Los Angeles Times*, via Associated Press, April 11, 1960.

Bailey, Robert G. "The 7th Patrol of the U.S.S. *Pompon* (SS-267)," *Polaris*, August 1994. subvetpaul.com/SAGA_8_94.htm (accessed September 1, 2017).

Barratt, Michael R. "Physical and Bioenvironmental Aspects of Human Space Flight" in *Principles of Clinical Medicine for Space Flight*, edited by Michael R. Barratt and Sam Lee Pool. New York: Springer, 2008.

Bateman, Jeffery S. "The Ultimate Program Manager: General Samuel C. Phillips." *Air Power History*, Winter 2011.

Bilstein, Roger. "Aviation Industry," in Melvyn Dubofsky, ed., *The Oxford Encyclopedia of American Business, Labor, and Economic History*. Vol. 1. New York: Oxford University Press, 2013.

Bracker, Milton. "Army Takes Over Satellite Firing with Jupiter-C." *New York Times*, January 28, 1958.

Bracker, Milton. "Jupiter-C Is Used." *New York Times,* February 1, 1958.

Bracker, Milton. "Truman Varies—Airy to Mundane," *New York Times*, February 5, 1956.

Bracker, Milton. "Vanguard Rocket Burns on Beach," *New York Times*, December 7, 1957.

Buckley, Tom. "NASA's Tom Paine—Is This a Job for a Prudent Man?" *New York Times*, June 8, 1969, magazine section.

Callahan, David, and Fred I. Greenstein. "The Reluctant Racer: Eisenhower and U.S. Space Policy" in *Spaceflight and the Myth of Presidential Leadership*, edited by Roger D. Launius and Howard E. McCurdy. Urbana: University of Illinois Press, 1997.

Carruthers, Osgood. "Russian Orbited the Earth Once, Observing It through Portholes; Spaceflight Lasted 108 Minutes." *New York Times*, April 13, 1961.

Cassutt, Michael. CollectSpace, March 5, 2005. collectspace.com/ubb/Forum38/HTML/000134.html.

Chaikin, Andrew. "How the Spaceship Got Its Shape," *Air & Space,* November 2009.

Chaikin, Andrew. "Management Lessons of the Moon Program." Knowledge Management Workshop, NASA Goddard Space Flight Center, July 31, 2012. YouTube. youtube.com/watch?v=RaskWhy5pYE (published November 30, 2012).

Collins, Thomas. "Celebration Ends Instead as a Eulogy." *Newsday*, January 28, 1967.

Conrad, Joseph. "Youth, a Narrative," Project Gutenberg, 2012. gutenberg.org/files/525/525-h/525-h.htm (updated September 9, 2016).

Cooper, Henry S. F., Jr. "Annals of Space: We Don't Have to Prove Ourselves," *The New Yorker*, September 2, 1991.

Day, Dwayne A. "From the Shadows to the Stars: James Webb's Use of Intelligence Data in the Race to the Moon." www.thefreelibrary.com/From+the+shadows+to+the+stars%3a+James+Webb%27s+use+of+intelligence+data . . . -a0126317213 (accessed September 1, 2017).

"The Death of TV-3." *Time*, December 16, 1957.

Dick, Steven J. "The Voyages of Apollo." NASA essays in *Why We Explore*, May 30, 2006. nasa.gov/exploration/whyweexplore/Why_We_20.html.

Divine, Robert A. "Lyndon B. Johnson and the Politics of Space," in Robert A. Divine, ed. *The Johnson Years*. Vol. 2: *Vietnam, the Environment, and Science*. Lawrence, Kans.: University Press of Kansas, 1987.

"The Eagle Has Landed." CosmoQuest Forum. forum.cosmoquest.org/archive/index.php/t-152388.html (accessed September 1, 2017).

Farrar, Fred. "U.S. Scores 2 Space Triumphs." *Chicago Tribune*, November 10, 1967.

Ford, Henry, and Samuel Crowther. "My Life and Work," Part III. *McClure's*, July 1922.

"Freedom 7 Mercury-Redstone 3: The Complete Flight of Alan Shepard, First American in Space." Space Opera France, 2010. youtube.com/watch?v=4LziZpAmMy8 (published March 12, 2011).

"G. H. Stoner of Boeing Co.: Honored by NASA." *Washington Post*, via Associated Press, March 3, 1971.

Garwood, Darrell. "JFK Gets Report: Spaceman Try Delay?" *Austin Statesman*, January 12, 1961.

Graham, Frederick. "Nazi Scientists Aid Army on Research." *New York Times*, December 4, 1946.

Grahn, Sven. "An Analysis of the Flight of Vostok." www.svengrahn.pp.se/his tind/Vostok1/Vostok1X.htm#Tape (accessed September 1, 2017).

"Hopes & Misgivings." *Time*, June 2, 1961.

Hunter, Marjorie. "President, Touring Canaveral, Sees a Polaris Fired." *New York Times*, November 17, 1963.

"Is NASA's workforce too old?" *Space*, April 11, 2008. *New Scientist Blogs.* new scientist.com/blog/space/2008/04/is-nasas-workforce-too-old.html (accessed September 1, 2017).

"It's a Success," *Time*, May 5, 1961.

"JFK Sees Polaris Fired." *Boston Globe*, via United Press International, November 17, 1963.

Jenkins, Dennis R. "Stage-and-a-Half: The Atlas Launch Vehicles," *To Reach the High Frontier: A History of U.S. Launch Vehicles*, edited by Roger D. Launius and Dennis R. Jenkins. Lexington, Ky.: The University Press of Kentucky, 2002.

"Kamanin Diaries." Encyclopedia Astronautica. astronautix.com/k/kamanindi aries.html (accessed September 1, 2017).

Lambright, W. Henry. "Leading NASA in Space Exploration: James E. Webb, Apollo, and Today," *Leadership and Discovery*, edited by G. Goethals and J. Wren. New York: Palgrave Macmillan, 2009.

"Launch of Apollo 4 first Saturn V as seen LIVE on CBS w/ Walter Cronkite." YouTube, youtube.com/watch?v=1uoVfZpx5dY (published November 10, 2010).

Liebermann, Randy. "The *Collier's* and Disney Series," *Blueprint for Space: Science Fiction to Science Fact*, edited by Frederick I. Ordway, III, and Randy Liebermann. Washington, D.C.: Smithsonian Institution Press, 1992.

Lippmann, Walter. "The Race to the Moon." *Newsweek*, February 13, 1967.

"Live from the Moon." *Hartford Courant*, March 25, 1965.

Luce, Clare Boothe. "But Some People Simply Never Get the Message." *Life*, June 28, 1963.

"Man in Space." *Disneyland*. ABC, March 9, 1955. Television.

Mann, William C. "Letters Provide Up-close Descriptions of Nuke Blasts." *Laredo Morning Times*, via Associated Press, August 5, 2005.

McElheny, Victor. "A Double Jump on Road to Moon." *Boston Globe*, November 10, 1967.

"Men of the Year," *Time*, January 3, 1969.

Miles, Marvin. "Moon Spacecraft Project Speeded," *Los Angeles Times*, April 1, 1962.

Miles, Marvin. "U.S. Scores Space Triumph." *Los Angeles Times*, November 10, 1967.

"Moon Shot for Soviets Sunday?" *Florida Today* (Cocoa, Fla.), December 7, 1968.

"Moonstruck." *Washington Post*, March 25, 1965.

Norman, Lloyd. "Army to Try Soon to Send Up Satellite." *Chicago Daily Tribune*, January 28, 1958.

Oberg, James. "Max Faget: Master Builder," *Omni*, April 1995.

Oberg, James. "Russia Meant to Win the Moon Race," *Spaceflight*, May 1975.

"Opposes Citizenship for Reich Scientists." *The Spokesman-Review* (Spokane, Wa.), via Associated Press, December 30, 1946.

O'Toole, Thomas. "Honesty, Distaste for Fanfare Make Apollo Program Chief." *Washington Post*, July 18, 1969.

Paine, Thomas O. "I Was a Yank on a Japanese Sub." U.S. Naval Institute, *Proceedings* 112, September 1986.

Paine, Thomas O. "The Transpacific Voyage of HIJMS *I-400*: Tom Paine's Journal: July 1945–January 1946." Self-published, 1984. Available at freerepublic .com/focus/f-news/1367585/replies?c=6 (revised February 1991).

"Red Alert." *Time*, October 3, 1949.

"Red Spaceman Lands!" *New York Journal-American*, August 7, 1961.

"Reds Not Sold on Trip to Moon, Lovell Says." *Washington Post*, via Associated Press, July 17, 1963.

Ricks, Thomas E. "Whatever Happened to Accountability?" *Harvard Business Review*, October 2012.

Rives, Tim. "'OK, We'll Go': Just What Did Ike Say When He Launched The D-day Invasion 70 Years Ago?" *Prologue*, Spring 2014.

Robbins, Bob. "Eddie Allen and the B-29," November, 29, 2000. avweb.com
/news/profiles/182933-1.html.

"Russ Cosmonaut Titov Safely Down on Land: Next Red Target Is Moon?" *Austin Statesman*, via Associated Press, August 7, 1961.

Sato, Yasushi. "Reliability in the Apollo Program: A Balanced Program Behind the Success." *Quest*. Vol. 13, No. 1, 2006.

Saxon, Wolfgang. "Alfred Munier, 78; Worked on Design for Lunar Module." *New York Times*, December 23, 1993.

Setzer, Daniel. "Historical Sources for the Events in Joseph Heller's Novel, *Catch-22*" (2008). dansetzer.us/heller/JHeller.pdf (accessed September 1, 2017).

"The Seven Chosen," *Time*. April 20, 1959.

Sheridan, David. "How an Idea No One Wanted Grew Up to Be the LM," *Life*, March 14, 1969.

Sington, David (director). *In the Shadow of the Moon*. DOX, 2007.

Sloane, T. O'Conor. "Acceleration in Interplanetary Travel." *Amazing Stories*, November 1929.

Smith, David R. "They're Following Our Script: Walt Disney's Trip to Tomorrowland," *Future*, May 1978.

"Soviet Movie Shows Reach for the Moon," *Time*, October 28, 1957.

"Space Travel Impossible, States Dr. Lee De Forest." *Boston Globe*, via Associated Press, February 25, 1957.

Sullivan, Walter. "The Week in Science: A Russian Steps into Space." *New York Times,* March 21, 1965.

Talbert, Ansel E. "U.S. Moon Rocket Blows Up at Start." *New York Herald Tribune*, December 7, 1957.

Tapper, Dan. "Throwback Thursday—'Do Good Work,'" May 8, 2014. Sullivan & LeShane Public Relations. ctpr.com/throwback-thursday-do-good-work/.

"Thomas Otten Paine," *Current Biography Yearbook* 31. New York: Wilson, 1970.

"The Thunderclap." *Time*, October 3, 1949.

Topping, Seymour. "Khrushchev Hails Astronauts, Asks Peace in Space." *New York Times*, June 23, 1963.

Toth, Robert C. "It's Official: Astronaut Grounded for Bad Heart." *New York Herald Tribune*, July 12, 1962.

Trafford, Abigail. "Apollos and Oranges." *Washington Post*, July 19, 1994.

"U.S. Fires 'Moon'!" *Chicago Daily Tribune*, February 1, 1958.

"U.S. Women Still Grounded by NASA." *Chicago Tribune*, June 17, 1963.

"Very Little Left in Cabin of Burned-out Spacecraft." *Baltimore Sun*, via Associated Press, January 30, 1967.

Vine, Katy. "Walking on the Moon." *Texas Monthly*, July 2009. texasmonthly.com /articles/walking-on-the-moon/.

"Voyage of the Explorer." *Time*, February 10, 1958.

"What Are We Waiting For?" *Collier's*, March 22, 1952.

White, Thomas Gordon, Jr. *The Establishment of Blame as a Framework for Sensemaking in the Space Policy Subsystem: A Study of the Apollo 1 and Challenger Accidents* (doctoral dissertation). Blacksburg, Va.: Virginia Polytechnic Institute and State University, 2000. vtechworks.lib.vt.edu/handle/10919 /27037.

Wolfinger, Kirk (director). "To the Moon." PBS *Nova* TV documentary, 1999. Transcript at pbs.org/wgbh/nova/transcripts/2610tothemoon.html (accessed September 1, 2017).

"Worth the Price." *Time*, January 17, 1969.

Zinman, David. "Saturn Success Lifts Moon Hopes." *Newsday*, November 10, 1967.

PHOTO CREDITS

INDEX

Haber, Heinz, 104
Haise, Fred, 273
Hamilton, Margaret, *194*, 195
Hammill, James P., 61, 62
heat shields, 160–61, 169, 253
Himmler, Heinrich, 31
Hitler, Adolf, 6–7, 29–30, 32, 33, 61, 62–63, 65
Holmes, Brainerd, x, 176–77, 183
Houbolt, John, x, 159, 161, 164, 315
Humphrey, Hubert H., 245

I-400 submarine, 241–42, *242*
Irwin, Jim, 325
Italy, 206–7

Jackson, Henry M., 87, 89
Japan, 8, 22, 44
Japanese destroyer, *14*
Japanese Zero aircraft, *50*, 51
Jet Propulsion Laboratory, 112
Jews, Nazis and, 63
Johnson, Lyndon B., xi, 87, 89, 126, *132*, 154, 229, 244, *285*
Juno, 93–95, *96*, *123*

Kelly, Thomas, 190
Kennedy, Jackie O., *132*
Kennedy, John F., xi, 3, 125, 127, *128*, *132*, 133–34, 136, *141*, 143–44, *146*, 147, 154, *172*, 176–77, *178*, 179, *179*, 214, 229
Kennedy, Robert F., 272
Kepler Crater, *196–97*
Kerr, Robert, 127
Khrushchev, Nikita, xi, 69, 89, 99, 130–31, 133, *166*, 170, 210, 212
King, Martin Luther, Jr., 272
Kistiakowsky, George, 101
Komarov, Vladimir, 259
Korean War, 71–72, *73*, 75
Kraft, Christopher C., x, 281
Kranz, Eugene, xi, 282, 296

Laird, Melvin, 245
landing, *76*, 290–301, *299*, *301*
launch acceleration, 103–5
Leonov, Alexi, *208*
life-support system, 104
Lippmann, Walter, 228

LLRV. *See* Lunar Landing Research Vehicle
LM. *See* lunar module
Lockwood, Ralph, 9
Loewy, Raymond, *54*
London bombing, 32–33
Lovell, James, x, 176, *201*, 233, 234, *250*, *256*, 261, 265, 275, *286*, 318
Low, George, x, 252, *253*, 254, *314*
Lucchitta, Baerbel, *194*, 195
Luce, Clare Boothe, 170–71
Luna, 287–88, 316
Lunar Landing Research Vehicle (LLRV), 279, *280*, *281*
lunar module (LM), 162–65, 183, 185, *240*, 252, 274, 281–82, *288*, 290–301, *294*, *301*, 305, 317
Lunar Orbiter, 156, *196–97*, 214, *215*, *246*, 247
lunar rover trainer, *194*

Mach, *106*, 106–7
Manhattan Project, 44, 46, 70
Manned Spacecraft Center, 154, 184, 186–87
Marshall, George C., 46, 56
Marshall Plan, 56
Mattingly, Tom, 325
McQueen, Steve, 173
Medaris, John, 93, 94, 96
medical advances, *58*
Mercury spacecraft, *114*, *116*, 117, *118*, 120, 122, 128, 129, 134, 135, 155, 170, 191–92, 326
military, 73, 115, 120
missile gap, 125
Mission Control, 231, 296, *314*
Mitchell, Ed, 325
Moltke crater, *291*
moon, *2*
    Apollo 8, *266*
    Apollo steps to, *162–63*
    bootprint on, *302*
    color of, 266
    Copernicus map of, *194*, 195
    craters, *196–97*, 212, *291*, 310
    distance to, 140, *142–43*
    earth and, 77–78, *312*
    eclipse, 183
    far side of, *213*, *215*, 266
    figure-eight trajectory to, *254*
    flag in, 310